In memory of Michael George Barratt
(1927-2015)

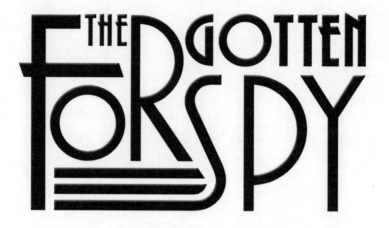

THE FORGOTTEN SPY

NICK BARRATT

BLINK
bringing you closer

Published by Blink Publishing
107–109 The Plaza,
535 King's Road,
Chelsea Harbour,
London, SW10 0SZ

www.blinkpublishing.co.uk

facebook.com/blinkpublishing
twitter.com/blinkpublishing

978-1-910536-68-1

Design by Blink Publishing
Cover design by Steve Leard – Leard.co.uk
Printed and bound by Clays Ltd, St Ives Plc

1 3 5 7 9 10 8 6 4 2

Blink Publishing is an imprint of the Bonnier Publishing Group
www.bonnierpublishing.co.uk

CONTENTS

DRAMATIS PERSONAE

This is a complex story with many different characters. To help keep track of the key players, here is a summary of their names and positions (code names given in brackets).

British security services

SURNAME	FIRST NAME	POSITION
Archer née Sissmore	Jane	MI5 agent
Argyll Robertson	Thomas	MI5 agent
Boddington	Herbert 'Con'	MI5 agent
Canning	Albert	Head of Special Branch, Metropolitan Police
Harker	Charles 'Jasper'	MI5 agent
Hunter	Herbert	MI5 agent
Kell	Sir Vernon	Head of MI5, 1909–1940
Liddell	Guy	Special Branch, Metropolitan Police then MI5 agent
Miller	Hugh	Special Branch, Metropolitan Police
Sinclair	Sir Hugh	Head of SIS, 1923–1939
Smith-Cumming	Sir Mansfield	Head of SIS, 1909–1923
Thomson	Sir Basil	Head of CID, Metropolitan Police
Vivian	Major Valentine	SIS agent
Watson	Nigel	MI5 agent
Ottaway	John	MI5 agent

Soviet agents and officials

SURNAME	FIRST NAME	POSITION
Agabekov	Georges	Soviet OGPU agent
Bazarov aka Da Vinci	Boris	Soviet 'Great Illegal' (KIN)
Bazhanov	Boris	Personal Assistant, Stalin
Bessedovsky	Gregori	Soviet chargé d'affaires, Paris embassy
Bystrolyotov aka Gallas aka Perelly aka Galleni	Dimitri Alexander Joseph Hans	Soviet 'Great Illegal' (ANDREI or HANS)
Deutsch	Arnold	Soviet agent
Helfand	Leon	Soviet secretary, Paris embassy
Ianovitch	Vladimir	Soviet OGPU agent
Krivitsky	Walter	Soviet intelligence officer
Leppin	Dr Joseph	Soviet agent (PEEP)
Mally	Theodor	Soviet 'Great Illegal'
Orlov	Aleksander	Soviet 'Great Illegal'
Pieck	Henri Christian	Soviet agent (COOPER)
Weinstein	Erica	Soviet agent (ERIKA)

Oldham's family and friends

SURNAME	FIRST NAME	POSITION
De la Chapelle	Count Victor	International lawyer, friend of the Oldhams
De la Chapelle	Rachel	Count Victor's 'wife'
Holloway	Alfred Ernest	Oldham's uncle
Holloway	Henry George	Oldham's uncle
Hoover	Herbert Clark	President of USA, friend of Lucy Oldham
Oldham née Holloway	Carrie	Oldham's mother
Oldham	Ernest Holloway	Foreign Office, staff officer (ARNO)
Oldham	Frank	Oldham's father
Oldham née Kayser formerly Wellsted	Lucy	Oldham's wife (MADAM)
Wellsted	James Raymond	Oldham's step-son
Wellsted	Thomas Arthur	Oldham's step-son
Everett	William Bostock	Royal Naval Reserve, friend of the Oldhams

Foreign Office staff and associated officials

SURNAME	FIRST NAME	POSITION
Antrobus	George	Foreign Office, King's Messenger
Balfour	Arthur	Foreign Secretary, 1916–1919
Binden	Herbert James	Foreign Office, assistant clerk
Chamberlain	Sir Austin	Foreign Secretary, 1924–1929
Crowe	Sir Eyre	Head of Foreign Office, 1920–1925
Curzon	Lord George	Foreign Secretary, 1919–1924
Grey	Lord Edward	Foreign Secretary, 1905–1916
Harvey	Captain John	Principal Passport Control Officer, Geneva
Henderson	Arthur	Foreign Secretary, 1929–1931
Hilbery	Clarence Anderson	Foreign Office, clerk
Jesser-Davies	Charles	Foreign Office, King's Messenger
Kemp	Thomas Eldred	Foreign Office, clerk (ROLAND)
King	John Herbert	Foreign Office, temporary clerk (MAG)
Macdonald	Ramsay	Prime Minister and Foreign Secretary, 1924
Mason	Enid	Step-daughter of Captain John Harvey (NORA)
Montgomery	Sir Charles 'Hubert'	Foreign Office, Chief Clerk 1919–1933
Nicolson	Sir Arthur	Head of Foreign Office, 1910–1916
Norton	Clifford John	Secretary to Head of Foreign Office
Oake	Raymond Charles	Foreign Office, temporary clerk (SHELLEY)
Quarry	Major Francis	Foreign Office, temporary clerk
Roberts	Charles	Foreign Office, temporary clerk
Simon	Sir John	Foreign Secretary, 1931–1935
Smith	Howard	Foreign Office, Chief Clerk, 1933–1939
Tilley	Sir John	Foreign Office, Chief Clerk 1913–1919
Vansittart	Sir Robert	Head of Foreign Office, 1930–1938
Wheeler-Holohan	Victor	Foreign Office, King's Messenger
		Foreign Office clerk, (unknown ID) (BOY)
		Foreign Office clerk, (unknown ID) (TED)
		Foreign Office clerk, (unknown ID) (TOMMY)

INTRODUCTION

The Kensington police are trying to discover the identity of a man, aged about 35, who was found dead in a gas-filled kitchen at a house in Pembroke Gardens, Kensington.

Apart from a table, there was no furniture in the house, but in a cupboard were a number of suits of clothes, including evening dress.

The man was 5-feet 6-inches in height, well-built, clean-shaven and had dark brown hair and eyes. He was wearing a brown mixture suit and a brown striped shirt with collar and tie to match.

THE STAR, 30 SEPTEMBER 1933

History is at its most compelling when a gripping story provides insight about the past. Most historians focus upon dramas played out on national or international stages, featuring politicians, aristocrats, royalty, criminal masterminds, military heroes, state scandals and secrets. However in recent years, a new area of interest has opened up with the rise of genealogy. For the first time, stories within families have started to emerge that are equally fascinating – although they rarely make the pages of history textbooks, and are treasured within a small circle who have traditionally passed them word of mouth from one generation to the next. The internet has changed things slightly, with easier access to research materials, instant means of communication via social media and a vast array of self-publication tools. Even so, it is unusual that our family stories make headline news or do anything other than provide case studies for professional historians to include in their own account of the past.

I've spent a decade researching other people's backgrounds, both on television as part of shows such as *Who Do You Think You Are?* and for newspapers, books and magazines. However, it's been difficult finding the time or (let's be honest about it) the motivation to investigate my own family history. We all love a mystery, especially one that can't be solved, but the best that I could come up with relates to my uncle Michael and a story from his childhood that he used to puzzle over, the sort of event that stuck in his mind as the moment when he became aware of a wider world outside his front door. He recalled that he was six years old when a curious incident took place, in October 1933. His brother David – my father – was seriously ill in the Southgate isolation hospital, north London, with scarlet fever, a 'notifiable disease' that was considered potentially life-threatening at the time. His parents would make the short walk each morning from their home in Berkshire Gardens, Wood Green, crossing the busy Wolves Lane to the hospital gates to check the danger lists posted outside daily at noon. This became a ritual, with anxiety building until they were certain David had made it through the night; a rush of relief, only for concern to grow steadily throughout the day in preparation for another night of worry.

Michael takes up the story.

> Later that week it seemed that there was a domestic crisis: my mother had to go to something and earnestly wished for her husband's support, but also wished for the latest news of David's health – it was not dying that was feared but a relapse.[1]

It was decided that Michael, who had been kept off school all week having been in contact with his brother, should go instead; the 1930s really was a different age in every sense.

> The only snag at that time was the crossing of Wolves Lane, though the light traffic consisted only of bicycles and horse-drawn carts...
> They drilled me in crossing-the-road procedures, with the special-care-in-crossing-Wolves-Lane subroutine; they made sure that

I could tell when it was noon and knew where to look for the danger list and could recognise David's handwritten or printed name.

However they omitted to warn me that my brother's name might not be on the danger list. When I failed to find it, no matter where I looked near the isolation hospital, at first I was cheered, but on the way home began to deal with a most unpalatable idea, that there were two ways for a patient to be out of danger... Did this mean he was dead? I wished there was a way of making the notice speak.[2]

At some point later that afternoon, Michael's parents finally returned home without a single word of explanation. Michael was bursting to tell them about his adventure, but having imparted his news that David was still alive and expecting lavish praise for his successful lone mission, he was somewhat disappointed with their response – 'they seemed gladdened by my news, but not outstandingly happy'. He never found out what had caused his parents to leave in such a terrible hurry. David made a full recovery and the incident was never spoken about again.

This is hardly a mystery worthy of the detective powers of Sherlock Holmes or Hercule Poirot, but nevertheless the sudden disappearance of his parents haunted Michael from that day on. Equally, he was vaguely puzzled by the fact that around this time his grandparents decided to move to Shanklin, on the Isle of Wight, leaving their home of 20-plus years in Edmonton.

Michael's mystery was dramatically solved in 2002 with the release of an MI5 file at The National Archives into a man called Ernest Holloway Oldham, who was his maternal uncle – and therefore my great-uncle. It contained some shocking revelations about Oldham's life, including the newspaper clipping at the start of this introduction. The file also revealed that the date that Michael went on his 'grand adventure' to the hospital was the same one as the inquest into Oldham's death, 2 October 1933. My grandmother Marjorie Holloway Oldham had decided to attend, but only if her husband, George Bernard Barratt came too – hence the decision to leave their six-year-old son at home.

Thus with one mystery solved, an even greater one was posed: who really was Ernest Holloway Oldham? For the first time, this book tells the remarkable tale of a seemingly unremarkable man who became the forgotten spy of the Cold War.

In the 1920s, communist Russia had supplanted Germany as the nation most feared by British intelligence services, until the rise of Hitler, fascism and the Nazis in the 1930s shifted attention westwards once more. The secrets of Britain's communication network lay in Room 22 at the heart of the Foreign Office in London, where a man in a brown suit plotted to betray his colleagues and countrymen as stock markets tumbled, the League of Nations failed and the storm clouds of war gathered over Europe once more.

It is a story of weakness, greed and a tragic descent into treachery, deception and desperation played out in the shadowy world of inter-war espionage. It is the story of my great-uncle.

Chapter one

AN ORDINARY LIFE (1894–1914)

I think it is not untrue to say that in these years we are passing through
a decisive period in the history of our country. The wonderful century
which followed the battle of Waterloo and the downfall of Napoleonic
domination, which secured to this small island so long and so resplendent
a reign, has come to an end. We have arrived at a new time. Let us
realise it. And with that new time strange methods, huge forces, larger
combinations – a Titanic world – have sprung up around us.

THE TIMES, 24 MAY 1909

Many dramatic stories have a humble beginning and this one is no exception. On 10 September 1894, a boy was born at 6 Sunningdale Cottages, a
small property on Bury Street in the recently developed London suburb of
Lower Edmonton. The boy's parents, Frank Oldham and Carrie Holloway,
were talented and hard-working teachers who had married in Christ Church,
Ramsgate, on the first day of the year; rather endearingly, Carrie firmly believed that she had conceived on her wedding night.

A few weeks after her son's birth, she set out to formally register his appearance in the world, walking the short distance from her cottage past rows
of recently built terraced houses, towards the Green – nothing more than a
small triangle of grass in the centre of Edmonton that was a reminder of the
rural village that had been slowly transformed into a built-up residential area,
a haven for families drawn to the outskirts of London by the promise of work
who now formed part of a new class of suburban commuters.

Crossing the Green, Carrie bought a ticket at Lower Edmonton station and, after a short wait, joined the north-bound train. Two stops later she alighted at Enfield Town, where she trudged with babe in arms to the registry office. She named him Ernest Holloway Oldham, probably in honour of her half-brother Alfred Ernest Holloway, who was affectionately known to his friends and family as 'Ern'.

Carrie had met her husband, Frank Oldham, while they were both teachers. Frank was much younger than his wife, born on 3 June 1867 in Station Road, Hadfield, a small village in Derbyshire's Peak District that today is perhaps best known as the setting for the fictional town of Royston Vasey in the BBC's quirky dark comedy *The League of Gentlemen*. Hadfield formed part of the manor of Glossop, long the possession of the dukes of Norfolk, who spotted an opportunity to capitalise on the growing movement towards mechanised factories in the early 19th century and decided to transform Glossop into an industrial town.

Neighbouring Hadfield was developed along similar lines by the Sidebottom family, who purchased the Waterside and Bridge Mill complex from John Turner and John Thornley in 1820 and spent the remainder of the 19th century developing the site as a large spinning and weaving combine. For example, they funded and built their own branch railway to the mill so that raw materials could be brought in and finished goods transported around the country or to the ports for export. This was a thriving business – in 1880, the mills ran 293,000 spindles at 4,800 looms and Frank's father had a key position as loom manager, sufficiently well paid to enable him to purchase and convert six stone cottages in Post Street, Padfield, which were rented out, apart from the one that the family lived in. This was a typical story of working-class man turned middle manager, rising through the factory ranks to obtain a better station in life.

However, young Frank decided the world beyond Hadfield and Padfield had other attractions, possibly as a result of an unhappy apprenticeship as a grocer when he was 12, and maybe due to lingering trauma caused by the 1874 death of his only sibling, five-year-old Lowe Oldham, of scarlet fever – a known killer before the discovery of antibiotics which would affect one of Frank's grandsons many years later in 1933. Frank left home to attend the Westminster Training College on Horseferry Road, London, which specialised in training teachers for Methodist schools. Formal training to qualify as a certified teacher had become more widespread after the 1870 Elementary Education Act, with the provision of education still seen as a vocation akin to that of a missionary 'bringing enlightenment to the uneducated masses',[3] but it was still quite a journey and even steeper learning curve for a young man with an industrial background from a small village in the Peak District. Frank had to adapt to the discipline of a formal training course in the bustling metropolis that London had become.

After graduation, Frank Oldham returned north to take a position as first assistant master at Wellington Street board school in Oldham between 1889 and 1891. He lodged with the Lee family in Churchill Street, a school placement that was probably secured through connections within the Methodist movement via the training college. In 1892, Frank moved south from Lancashire to Cheshire to become the headmaster at the Tarporley British school. It is said that his hair was completely white by the time he reached the age of 25, so perhaps his employment in Tarporley was not entirely to his liking or the children in his care were somewhat of a more disruptive nature than he had been used to. Either way, he left the same year and headed back to London for a new challenge, securing promotion as assistant master at Croyland Road board school in Edmonton – the equivalent to a deputy headship today.

Carrie's journey to the north was more challenging. She was born on 27 January 1859, the last of four daughters, to Henry George Holloway senior and Caroline Wood. The couple had met while employed as the school master and mistress of the Minster workhouse on the Isle of Thanet, Kent, and married on 7 July 1851. Shortly after their wedding, the couple became master and matron of the workhouse – a big change in status that was accompanied by a pay rise (£60 per year between them as opposed to £20 each as teachers) and a house of their own within the grounds of the workhouse, complete with the provision of meals, coals and washing facilities.

Tragically, Caroline died of apoplexy on 19 October 1864 when Carrie was only five years old, leaving Henry without a wife, the children without a mother – and the workhouse without a matron. These were expedient times and within a year Henry remarried. His bride, 13 years his junior, was Rosina Wood, who appears to have been Caroline's half-sister. To avoid a scandal and awkward questions about the legality of the relationship under the terms of the 1835 Lyndhurst Act (which equated the status of sister-in-law with sister in issues of consanguinity), Henry and Rosina took a train to Margate and married in the Zion Chapel of a rare non-conformist sect, the Countess of Huntingdon's Confession. They were in the presence of an assistant registrar whose wife, alongside an official from the chapel, acted as the witnesses.

Within a year of her own mother's death, Carrie had a stepmother to deal with, followed swiftly by five half-siblings. It was not an easy situation for the feisty Carrie and in 1875, aged 16, she quarrelled with her stepmother and ran away from home. She ended up in Higher Booths, Rawtenstall, in Lancashire – a small hamlet whose residents were economically dependent like so many others on the cotton factories for employment.

Following in her parents' footsteps, Carrie at first found work teaching day-release pupils – children aged 12 who attended half of each school day, as long as they had employment for the rest of the time, and who left school at 13 to take up full-time work. Barely older than the children in her care, Carrie probably started out as a pupil teacher – a system whereby elementary school pupils aged over 13 would act as teachers throughout the day and then themselves receive tuition from the head teacher after school hours. Hers was a paid position, with boys receiving considerably more than girls, and the head teacher securing an emolument for the education of their charges.

Life in the classroom of a northern industrial town was not easy. This was an era when you grew up fast and most of the half-day students resented being treated like children when they were considered adult enough to work for the remainder of the day, often alongside their parents and older siblings. Discipline was a common problem in the village classroom, particularly for a young southern girl who was only a few years older than her charges and – unlike Frank – had not undergone any formal training to become a certified teacher.

In the 1870s, children normally wrote on slates with slate pencils – grey sticks of rock that squeakily left a whitish grey trace on a heavy slice of shale that would be fitted into a wooden frame for ease of handling. Once, a rebellious boy, on being rebuked by Carrie for failing to pay attention to his work, waved his slate at Carrie with the words 'I'll buzz t'slate at t'head'.[4] Unfazed by this threat, Carrie reached up to the boy's ear – she was much shorter than most of her pupils, never reaching five feet in height as an adult – and dragged him off to the head teacher's office to receive corporal punishment, then deemed acceptable to dispense at that time.

When she first started work she lodged with Jane Rushton, a widow who let rooms in her property in Rock Terrace, but by 1891 she was living as a boarder at 3 Mount Terrace, Higher Booths, Rawtenstall, with George Littlewood, the school master and his wife Maud and their son Harry Beaumont Littlewood who was a 13-year-old pupil teacher in Carrie's school.

Quite how and when Frank and Carrie met is a matter of conjecture, but they decided to tie the knot and married on the first day of 1894 at Christ Church, Ramsgate. Carrie moved back temporarily into her father's house in St Lawrence, Thanet, safe in the knowledge that her stepmother Rosina had passed away ten years previously, in 1884. The newlyweds set up home in 6 Sunningdale Cottages, Lower Edmonton, Frank having found work as a teacher in the local elementary school.

Croyland Road board school catered for the educational needs of the local community. It was opened in 1884 with the capacity for 200 boys, 100 girls and 261 infants and it had been necessary to enlarge the school in 1889 and 1891 to cater for the growing population as Edmonton continued its expansion as a commuter suburb. In the Bury Street district alone, the population grew from a shade under 23,500 people in 1891, just prior to Frank's move into the area, to around 62,000 in 1911. Despite Frank's position in the school, he was still teaching in the lower echelons of the education hierarchy. Certified teachers – let alone uncertified ones such as Carrie – were still seen as second class, mainly drawn from working-class roots and somewhat unfairly categorised as 'struggling to move out of their class on the basis of limited academic and social aptitude and training'.[5] This was in comparison to secondary school teachers, who tended to find employment in grammar or private schools. They often came from a similar background to their middle or upper-class pupils and usually held a university degree in their chosen subject.

Carrie's firm hand and strong character were probably essential qualities in the Oldham household. The family expanded over the next six years with the arrival of Marjorie Holloway Oldham on 26 December 1896 and Kathleen Helen Oldham on 22 June 1900. By 1911 the cottage was no longer large enough and they had moved to a new house on the same road, 135 Bury Street, which would remain the family home throughout Ernest's childhood and indeed for much of his adult life as well. It was a cramped space by modern standards, built out of brick and slate but comfortable for the time. Upstairs were three rooms – Marjorie and Kathleen were forced to share – with two rooms and a scullery downstairs and a further room at the rear. Their small garden backed onto glass houses associated with the long-standing nurseries in the area and a brick works. Beyond that lay a few open fields.

The house was uncluttered by the range of domestic technology that we'd take for granted today – there was no radio or television to provide household entertainment, unlikely to be a telephone given the annual cost of a line and no electrical appliances to help with the daily chores or indeed heat the property – a real concern when trying to look after a new baby, especially during the harsh winter of 1894–95 when temperatures in mid-February never crept above freezing. Hand-powered washing machines had been in use from Victorian times but refrigerators for food storage were not invented until the 1910s and remained unwieldy, unaffordable and often unsafe until the 1920s' introduction of Freon. This was an early CFC which was far less dangerous to people in terms of domestic leaks but, as we now know, incredibly damaging to the ozone layer.

When the Oldham children were growing up at the start of the 20th century, people used outdoor pantries to keep food chilled but mostly bought daily produce from local shops, farms or dairies. Electric street lighting had started to appear in the area from the early 1900s, although it wasn't until 1913 that Edmonton fully abandoned gas lamps. The supply of domestic electricity from 1907 brought the enticing prospect of modern conveniences, although on the grounds of cost most appliances would remain a dream for many of the residents of Bury Street. Into the first decades of the 20th century and beyond, women like Carrie would still beat carpets and rugs in the street and scrub their doorsteps while her children played in the car-free roads outside.

Frank embraced his new life in the community. He already had a talent for music and was asked by the vicar of St Michael's to become the organist for the congregation. His position secured his family their seats in the vicar's pew at the front of the church for every service and his children a first-hand view of the sermons that were preached. Frank also found time to train local choirs, reputedly to competition-winning standard, and spent the remainder of his spare time involved in study, acquiring a range of certificates and diplomas to prove his academic merit.

Despite never breaking through the class divide to teach at Latymer school, Edmonton's nearby grammar school, in 1903 he was selected to serve as first assistant master of Houndsfield Road council school before eventually being made headmaster in 1916, a position he retained until his retirement in 1930. The council school was a much larger establishment than its older and more refined neighbour; in contrast with the 24 pupils taught at Latymer's new buildings which opened in 1910, the staff at Houndsfield had over a thousand students in their care. As such, it is fair to assign to Frank the rather hackneyed but well-merited description of pillar of the community, for which he was formally recognised by the Anglican Consultative Council with the award of the Distinguished Service Medal in 1928. A clasp was granted for it five years later, when he and Carrie made the somewhat sudden and unexpected decision in 1933 to leave their home of 40 years and retire to Shanklin on the Isle of Wight.

Ernest Oldham, however, attended Tottenham County School, one of the first co-educational secondary schools in the county that had been established by Middlesex County Council in 1901, pre-empting Balfour's Education Act passed the following year which gave more power to local councils to create state schools. Then, instead of following in his parents' footsteps and pursuing a career in community-based education – and perhaps reinforcing the aspirational nature of Frank's rise through the elementary school ranks – a decision was taken to send Ernest to Muncaster House school, often rather confusingly called Muncaster College, a small sixth-form boarding school situated in the small village of Laleham on Ferry Lane by the banks of the River Thames.

This was the sort of school usually reserved for the sons of senior army officers or even the offspring of members of Parliament – by no means an elite public school such as Eton, but nonetheless a step up from Ernest's social background and a world away from the working-class terraces of Edmonton. Behind the scenes, one detects the influence of Carrie's family, who were continuing to move up in the world – her brother, Henry George Holloway junior, was building a commercial empire in Thanet whilst performing civic tasks as a registrar and collector of local taxes. Another brother, William, was despatched at the earliest possible opportunity into the Royal Marines where he eventually attained the rank of lieutenant. Meanwhile, Ern Holloway had chosen a career overseas in the Diplomatic Service and rose through the echelons of the postal service in Southern Rhodesia, to the point where he was listed in the Colonial Office lists as a key civil servant in the administration. By coincidence, he returned to England on 6 August 1909, having sailed first-class on the *Imanda* from Durban and it may well have been his encouragement – and possibly funding as well – that enabled his nephew to attend Muncaster House. This was the sort of schooling that would prepare a young man for a white collar professional career or a commission in the army.

Whatever the motivation for the later part of his schooling, the experience had the desired effect. Rather than train as a teacher, Ernest Oldham decided to apply to join the civil service, which at the time was only accessible via competitive examination. Later documents, based on information provided by Oldham himself, stated that he successfully sat and passed the test for the position of second division clerk in the civil service on 13 November 1913. This is untrue. There was no examination for second division clerk held on that date and the surviving papers kept by the Civil Service Commission for the examination held on 22 September 1913 fail to reveal Oldham's name amongst the candidates. Earlier records show that he actually sat the exam on 7 October 1912, just after his 18th birthday, having left Muncaster House in the summer. The reason for this deception is clear when the results are examined more closely; candidate no 721, EH Oldham, came a disappointing 702nd out of a field of over 1,500 candidates – only the top 150 were offered jobs, which meant that he was unsuccessful in securing work.

His English and handwriting weren't too bad – 380 and 360 marks out of a possible 400 respectively – but manuscript-copying, an important skill for a clerk, only earned him 136 marks out of 200, while he was weak in languages (Latin 195 out of 400, French much better with 307, but no attempt made to take German) and he hardly covered himself in glory with his mathematical abilities (elementary maths and arithmetic 230 and 290 out of 400). In fact, his strongest subject aside from English was science (360 marks).[6]

At the tender age of 18, this setback should have marked the end of Oldham's aspirations for a civil service career before it had even got off the ground, but there was still a glimmer of hope. Many of the unsuccessful candidates ended up being selected over the course of the year as those above them failed to take up their posts and replacements were summoned further down the list. Even so, it would have been an awfully long time before Oldham could have expected to be called up, given his lowly position. Once again the influence of his uncle can be discerned behind the scenes.

Ern Holloway returned to England from East London, South Africa, on the *Galician*, docking at Southampton on 23 July 1913 – once again travelling first-class but this time accompanied by his young wife who was 18 years his junior. Holloway was described as a civil servant on the passenger list and one suspects that during his stay in England he caught up with his London chums in the service and put in a good word for his nephew, as one did in those days, before he returned to South Africa on 15 November. It is perhaps no coincidence that Ernest Oldham was called up for the civil service the same month and on 11 December 1913 was formally appointed to the Board of Education.

It is fair to say that he did not hang around – certainly not long enough to leave any trace in the official records – as 20 days later he was transferred to the Board of Trade where he commenced his new duties on New Year's Day 1914. His employment there was of only slightly longer duration, as he moved to the Foreign Office on 1 April 1914 as a second division clerk in the Chief Clerk's Department. The institution was steeped in history, there being an unspoken assumption that to succeed one needed to have schooled in Eton. Nevertheless, despite these obstacles that would have blocked most other men, Oldham's career at the heart of Britain's global diplomatic network had begun.

Chapter two

INSIDE THE FOREIGN OFFICE (APRIL–AUGUST 1914)

No one knows so well as the politician whose privilege it is for the time being to represent the Foreign Office in Cabinet and in Parliament, how impossible his task would be if it were not for the devoted and disinterested labour of the men whose life-work lies within the walls of the Department.

SIR JOHN SIMON, FOREIGN SECRETARY (1931–1935)

Ernest Holloway Oldham had joined one of the most venerable institutions in Britain, if not the world, at a time when the global reach of the Foreign Office was never wider or its role in international politics more challenging. Indeed, challenging described the environment in which the 19-year-old Ernest Oldham found himself working – especially when you consider that he was state-school educated in an age when most of his new colleagues had attended one or other of the finest private schools in the land and he was still living in his parent's working-class terraced cottage in Edmonton.

The Foreign Office was a highly structured world, a hierarchical mix of politicians, permanent civil servants and temporary staff, despite changes which had seen attempts at modernisation over the previous decade. At the very top was the Secretary of State for Foreign Affairs (or Foreign Secretary), Sir Edward Grey. He was assisted by an Under-Secretary of State the Liberal MP for Camborne, Sir Francis Dyke Acland. However, politicians came and went on the shifting tides of public opinion expressed at the ballot box, so a body of professional civil servants undertook the bulk of the work as well as provided necessary continuity. In charge was the Permanent Under-Secretary – not to be confused with Acland's role – who was by this stage the real Head of the Foreign Service and the main advisor to the Secretary of State. The role frequently required him to receive foreign ambassadors, oversee the general running of the office, and act as the point of liaison with other government departments, especially with the armed services and rudimentary intelligence services. In 1914, this important position was held by Sir Arthur Nicolson, who had entered the service of the Foreign Office in 1870 and was coming to the end of his career; it was his misfortune to be overshadowed by his dynamic Assistant Under-Secretary of State, Sir Eyre Crowe, who oversaw widespread changes to the way the office was run after 1905 in response to new technology such as the telegram and later the telephone, which generated a vast increase in the volume and speed of communication.

Crowe's fellow Assistant Under-Secretary was Sir John Tilley, and he described the main points of the reforms – in particular the creation of a General Registry to log the influx of correspondence and papers, with subsidiary registries which would be maintained by second division clerks such as Oldham:

> They were to take complete charge of the archives, and deal with all such matters as docketing, registration, finding and putting away papers, and with the distribution and management of the print.[7]

Thus all correspondence and official material – much of it highly sensitive – passed through the hands of fairly junior staff. However, there was a problem, as Tilley identified:.

> [They] soon acquired much the same familiarity with their subjects as we had previously had. They saw all the papers, read them carefully in order to give a correct description of them on the dockets and in the registers and, if they wished to be efficient, learned the subjects in such a way as to be able to produce the

correct papers at the correct moment, but they did not express opinions, except perhaps an occasional verbal one. After a few years of this work, their occupation naturally tended to become monotonous and they were bound to wish for release in favour of the higher class of work for which they considered that their training had made them competent.[8]

Tilley also revealed his disdain for the means of examination that was used to recruit new staff, an attitude from the 'old days' of the Foreign Office – goodness knows what he made of Oldham's performance:

I have already pointed out that they were recruited by means of a competitive examination of relatively great simplicity and it would have stultified our system of recruiting to say that their training in routine matters placed them on an equality with the new recruit who was the finished product of university. Moreover, if the Office wishes to attract that finished product it must maintain an adequate number of annual vacancies and a reasonable rapidity of promotion. In so small a Service every vacancy that is filled otherwise than from the normal source has a discouraging effect. At the same time, there were obviously good brains among the second division clerks and their disposal was a serious problem.[9]

In total, there were usually three or four assistant under-secretaries, one of whom was Oldham's superior, the Chief Clerk – the post that Tilley had held since October 1913. His job was one of utmost importance – the pivot around which most of the daily routine within the Foreign Office turned, covering the general establishment of the office, and all its finances:

[The Chief Clerk's] department pays the salaries, records the promotions, receives the medical certificates, lists the misdeeds, notes the qualifications, in short, supervises the activities generally of the entire staff of the office. He it is who makes the principal contacts with the Treasury, who holds the purse strings and without whose approval no appointment can be made and no additional personnel engaged... He must have not only ability and force of character; he must have tact, vision, and a sound psychological instinct.[10]

In terms of the other departments in existence when Oldham joined, a quick summary of the key areas will suffice, as he had little connection with them during his early days in the Foreign Office. The routine management of the Registry fell within the remit of the Librarian, whose department managed the internal archives of the Foreign Office. The Parliamentary Department, originally set up to prepare materials should questions for the Secretary of State arise in the House of Commons, mainly dealt with the ciphering and deciphering of communications and housed the King's Messengers. This was the body of staff who had traditionally delivered diplomatic messages at home and abroad and whose work was somewhat diminished by the rise of telegraphy but was still nonetheless important in ensuring the secrecy and security of Britain's communications. One of their number, Victor Wheeler-Holohan described the two categories of messenger that operated in Oldham's time:

> The Home Service Messengers are appointed by the Secretary of State for Foreign Affairs, and are carefully picked men of the warrant officer type. They carry secret papers from Whitehall to persons in London and the same country and are a fine body of men. At one time they wore the badge, but this practice has now ceased. They need no passports for their work, and have other means of identification.
>
> The Foreign Service Messengers are also appointed by the Secretary of State for Foreign Affairs, after they have passed the necessary Civil Service examination and have also been recommended by a selection board. They are given the Silver Greyhound badge, their passports are printed in red (describing the holders as being 'charged with despatches') and are also bound in red cloth stamped in gold with the legend 'King's Messenger's Passport'.[11]

These were so-called Red Passports and were a much prized possession, along with the Silver Greyhound badge, as it provided a form of diplomatic immunity when on one's travels.

The remaining staff of the Parliamentary Department numbered no more than four or five secretaries and a Staff Clerk who would deal with the administration of the department plus the care of the records, archives and – most importantly – the cipher books and codes. This was Mr John Gritton who was, in the inimitable view of another of the King's Messengers, George Antrobus:

> One of the most loyal and devoted public servants I have ever known. He seemed to work 12 to 15 hours a day and I do not remember his taking a holiday in the 20 years I knew him. He was never ill and never tired and his work, which involved a vast and intricate mass of detail, was always up to date. How he did it I never knew; if you asked him he would just smile and murmur: 'Nothing, my dear fellow, it's nothing at all when you're used to it.'[12]

The main diplomatic work of the Foreign Office was dealt with by various political departments which were arranged geographically; a separate Consular Department handled correspondence to the various consulates around the world; and the Treaty and Royal Letter Department prepared formal documents of diplomatic representation, including matters of protocol, rather than the actual negotiation of treaties. The Passport Office issued passports, as its name suggests.

Aside from introducing the Registry and implementing changes to the internal administrative machinery within the Foreign Office, Sir Eyre Crowe also attempted to bring in young men such as Oldham from a wider range of backgrounds, and therefore develop a new class of civil servant. According to Antrobus, 'his contempt of the public school system led him to distrust and therefore not to make the best use of, its products'.[13] This was an oblique reference to the fact that many people working in both the Foreign Office itself, as well as the diplomatic and consular service around the world in embassies and consulates, were the product of the public school system, with a perception held widely throughout society (as well as by men within the Foreign Office such as Tilley) that scholars from Eton generally received the top jobs.

Furthermore, there had been a property qualification of £400 in place – an independent income was considered important to maintain a suitable standard of living overseas, as well as possibly remove the risk of any temptation from corrupt local officials – with the result that the diplomatic corps before 1914 was largely staffed by those from a more aristocratic background. There was still a clear class divide in operation, according to Antrobus:

> Life in 1915 was still much as it had been a generation earlier. Society in England still lay in well-defined strata of two main orders. You belonged either to what were known as the Upper Classes or you did not and there, so far as 'Society' with a capital S was concerned, was an end of it. But the great point about these two divisions – a point which is now usually forgotten – is that they had nothing to do with wealth or position or occupation. They were concerned solely with birth, breeding and (in a less degree) education.[14]

Oldham had joined the Foreign Office when many of these restrictions were being swept away, but these reforms would only fully take hold in the decades after World War I, when the Foreign Office was merged with the Diplomatic Service and the property qualification was finally removed. However in 1914, some traditions remained. In keeping with the fashion of the day, Oldham would have conformed to the smart dress code expected of a civil servant described by Antrobus:

> The man about town of the early years of the century never walked abroad without three essential articles of adornment – the morning coat, the top hat – or, as hatters would say, the silk hat – and the walking stick.[15]

This was the world that Oldham had joined from his more humble roots – hierarchical, with strict codes of dress and professional conduct that reflected the legacy of an 'old boy' network that was still largely in place. He travelled to work from his parents' house in Edmonton by public transport, catching the train to Liverpool Street station and then commuting across town to Whitehall. His working hours were predominantly 10.00 am till 5.00 pm, with an hour for lunch, working on files in the Chief Clerk's Department and drawing an initial annual salary of £100.

The nature of work was routine and, dare one suggest even slightly dull, throughout the spring and early summer of 1914, until the morning of Sunday 28 June. Just after 10.45 am Archduke Franz Ferdinand, the heir presumptive to the Austro-Hungarian Empire, and his wife Sophie were shot dead in Sarajevo by Gavrilo Princip, a Serb belonging to a group that supported the formation of a separate Yugoslavian state. Although the assassination took place at a weekend, everyone associated with the Foreign Office who heard the news would have known that the delicate balance of alliances and treaties that maintained an uneasy peace within Europe had just been shattered. They would have waited in trepidation for the return to work the next day. Meanwhile, those officers who remained on duty over the weekend, such as the cipher clerks and King's Messengers, were faced with a growing flood of telegrams and correspondence from around the world as consular staff and diplomats tried to contact the politicians and senior civil servants who would frame Britain's reaction to the shocking news.

The atmosphere on Monday was tense but there was no great sense of panic; these were, after all, seasoned professionals. Nevertheless, the following days must have been deeply unnerving for the young Ernest Oldham, still a novice within the corridors of the Foreign Office, watching his elders and superiors involved in constant discussions about what responses to send out. The bigwigs at the top were summoned for crisis meetings with the Prime Minister and his Cabinet while messages flowed thick and fast via the King's Messengers, all ciphered or deciphered with the help of the clerks before the urgent correspondence was typed up and despatched.

Sir John Tilley recalled the unfolding drama from the perspective of one of the senior – and therefore calmer – heads in the department, and naturally emphasised how well the Foreign Office coped with the sudden increase in business:

The first difficulty in any great crisis in the Office is to deal with the flood of telegrams which have to be ciphered and deciphered; this is work which must be done and must be done at once; moreover, at such moments, telegrams are not only much more numerous but much longer than usual; communications to be made to this or that government, lengthy arguments by this or that government in favour of some particular course of action, mean a tremendous burden of work for the Office and the embassies.[16]

The standard answer was to throw resource at the problem – not all of it willing, by the sound of it. Many staff found themselves co-opted into working longer hours or switching to new duties dealing with the influx of correspondence. Even this was not sufficient to cope with demand. For perhaps the first time in its long history, the Foreign Office worked around the clock:

In normal times the telegrams which arrived after office hours were dealt with by the Resident Clerk on duty. At an ordinary time of crisis the Resident Clerks were helped by benevolent juniors… In July and August 1914, it soon became evident that no arrangement of this sort would suffice and the department responsible for ciphering and deciphering was largely augmented and divided into three shifts so that the work could be carried out continuously. Juniors, diplomatic or consular, returning from enemy countries, provided an immediate increase of staff.[17]

From then on, events moved quickly, with the Foreign Office staff at the heart of the unfolding diplomatic drama. Relations between Serbia and Austria-Hungary had remained strained ever since the controversial annexation of Bosnia and Herzegovina by the Austrians in 1908 and the assassination provoked anti-Serbian riots in Sarajevo over the next few days, raising the political temperature in the Balkans.

On 5 July, German Kaiser Wilhelm II promised to support any Austrian reprisals taken against Serbia, whose government was blamed for the atrocity

– though this was largely political expediency on behalf of the Austrians who wished to further exert their influence over Serbia. Primarily, the German position was an attempt to block any Russian military response, whose own interests in the area were tied to an agreement to aid Serbia if it was threatened; but in effect it widened the crisis by drawing in the other Great Powers, in particular France and Britain, who were bound by the Triple Entente to support Russia.

After a meeting of the Austro-Hungarian Ministerial Council on 7 July and discussions lasting a further two weeks, an ultimatum was issued to the Serbian government in Belgrade on Thursday 23 July. It demanded ten points of action, mainly linked to the suppression of separatist movements opposed to the Austro-Hungarian monarchy. The action points would also include Austro-Hungarian officials acting on Serbian sovereign territory and the Serbian response was required by 5.00 pm the following Saturday – 25 July.

Sir Edward Grey noted at the time that he had 'never before seen one state address to another independent state a document of so formidable a character'[18] – indeed, it is said that the Austro-Hungarian emperor, Franz Joseph, was himself taken aback with the strength of demands when he saw a draft on 21 July – but along with France and Russia, Britain urged the Serbians to comply – despite recognising that the deadline was far too tight for meaningful consideration of the terms.

The day before the deadline, frantic diplomatic initiatives took place across the courts of Europe. The French ambassador tried desperately to impress upon Grey that, should Austro-Hungary invade Serbia, then mediation would be useless. It was now or never. In turn, Grey attempted to persuade the German ambassador to take part in a four-power summit in Vienna with the aim of securing an extension to the Austro-Hungarian ultimatum, urging that Britain, France, Italy and Germany 'who had no direct interests in Serbia, should act together for the sake of peace simultaneously'.[19]

There comes a point in every international crisis when the spectre of war becomes more of a probability than a possibility. The tipping point arrived on that Saturday 25 July, when Serbia delivered its response. The Serbian government went further than many had expected in meeting Austro-Hungarian demands, conceding virtually all of the major points in the ultimatum – bar one or two clauses which threatened to compromise its status as an independent nation. But the Austro-Hungarian government still rejected the terms – including international mediation for any outstanding issues – and promptly broke off diplomatic relations. Both sides began mobilising for war.

Levels of diplomatic activity within the Foreign Office were elevated and took on a new gravity. In what can only be described as frantic shuttle diplomacy, Grey desperately tried to persuade the Russians to negotiate with Austria-Hungary while attempts were made on 26 July to convene the international summit proposed two days previously. Russia had already started to mobilise its troops in readiness for any aggression towards Serbia but agreed to halt until mediation had taken place. However, although Italy and France agreed to attend the summit, Germany refused.

In a last ditch effort to prevent what looked like inevitable military conflict in the Balkans, Sir Edward Grey met with the German ambassador to Britain, Prince Karl Max Lichnowsky, whose own diary records how close Grey came to averting disaster between 24 and 27 July.

> Sir E Grey went through the Serbian reply with me and pointed out the conciliatory attitude of the government of Belgrade. Thereupon we discussed his proposal of mediation, which was to include a formula acceptable to both parties for clearing up the two points.
>
> Given goodwill, everything could have been settled at one or two sittings, and the mere acceptance of the British proposal would have brought about a relaxation of the tension, and would have further improved our relations with England. I therefore strongly backed the proposal, on the ground that otherwise there was danger of the world war, through which we stood to gain nothing and lose all; but in vain. It was derogatory to the dignity of Austria – we did not intend to interfere in Serbian matters – we left these to our ally. I was to work for 'the localisation of the conflict.'[20]

Berlin was in no mood to urge restraint upon its ally and the following day Austria-Hungary declared war on Serbia. Belgrade was bombarded, provoking the Russians into a full mobilisation of their forces. In turn, Germany issued its own ultimatum on 31 July to demand that the Russians stand down their troops while at the same time requesting that France remain neutral in event of war with Russia. The Russians refused while the French coldly replied that they would act in accordance with their own interests. In consequence Germany prepared to march its troops through neutral Belgium against France.

Britain insisted that the neutrality of Belgium, framed in 1839 by the Treaty of London, should be respected by all sides and once again Grey summoned Lichnowsky in a futile attempt to limit the scale of a conflict that neither man wanted but seemed unable to prevent. Diplomatic correspondence between London and Berlin continued throughout the day, with last-ditch attempts made by the Russian Tsar himself to prevent hostilities – but to no avail.

Late on 1 August, Germany declared war on Russia and, when French forces started to mobilise in response, invaded Luxembourg and prepared to invade Belgium. Although a formal request was made to the Belgians on 2 August to allow German troops free passage towards France, this was rejected. Germany declared war on France on 3 August and began the full-scale invasion of Belgium, with troops pouring over the border.

The final diplomatic attempts to avoid conflict had been overtaken by military events on the ground as the first shots were fired on what would become the Western Front, and the mood in Whitehall was that of resignation towards the inevitability of war. The staff in the Foreign Office had literally worked around the clock during the crisis and, caught in the eye of the storm, men like Oldham would have felt the failure to broker a solution more keenly than most. These were employees rendered increasingly helpless to prevent the conflict and fearful of the days ahead.

Grey certainly suspected the full horror of what was to come, no doubt mindful of the words of Sir Eyre Crowe, who had advocated an anti-German stance for a decade. Stood at the window of his room in the Foreign Office alongside John Alfred Spender, editor of the *Westminster Gazette*, Grey gazed out across St James's Park as the sun set. As the first lights appeared along the Mall, he murmured 'The lamps are going out all over Europe and we shall not see them lit again in our lifetime.'[21]

The following day, the Cabinet voted to issue a final ultimatum to Germany: if its troops did not withdraw from Belgium then a state of war would exist between the two countries. At 7.00 pm that evening, the ambassador to Berlin, Sir Edward Goschen, delivered the message to the German Secretary of State to the Ministry for Foreign Affairs, Gottlieb von Jagow, leaving five hours for the Germans to comply. The terms were rejected. Goschen sent a telegram to Sir Edward Grey, informing him of the refusal, but Grey never received it. Thus there was uncertainty over the exact diplomatic status between Germany and Britain within the Foreign Office until the deadline expired. This led to mistakes being made by the harassed staff of the Foreign Office as the enormous strain of the previous few days finally showed. As the clock ticked down, Sir John Tilley recalled.

> The first piece of duty that was thrown upon us mingled comedy with tragedy. Owing to some mistake which arose because someone had forgotten the difference between Berlin and London time, a certain proclamation had at the last moment to be altered by hand in time for issue as soon as war was declared. Accordingly a large party of us were gathered on the ground floor and told, like naughty schoolboys, to write out a thousand times the words 'His Majesty, mindful that a state of war now exists between this country and Germany'...[22]

Furthermore, the terms of the earlier ultimatum had mistakenly suggested that Germany had declared war on Britain, not the other way around. Henry Nicolson, the son of the Permanent Under-Secretary, was hastily despatched just after 11.00 pm to the German embassy in Carlton House to retrieve the earlier version, in an attempt to clarify the diplomatic situation.

> At length the butler appeared and led Nicolson up to the private apartments, where the ambassador, Karl Max Fürst (Prince) von Lichnowsky, lay on a brass bed in his pyjamas. Nicolson told him there had been a slight error in the document sent previously

and he had come to substitute for it the correct version. Prince Lichnowsky pointed to the table, where an envelope was lying unattended: 'You will find it there,' he said, as if in a daze. It seemed he had not read it, but guessed its significance since the passports of the embassy staff were enclosed. Nicolson had been told to get a receipt, so he took the blotting pad, pen and inkbottle across to the bed. While the ambassador was signing, shouting came from The Mall, and then singing – the 'Marseillaise' – as crowds streamed back from Buckingham Palace. Earlier in the day they had broken the embassy windows. Lichnowsky took no notice. Without a word, having signed the receipt he turned out the pink lamp beside the bed – but then, perhaps feeling that he had been uncivil, turned it on again. 'Give my best regards to your father,' he said, sadly, with the pronounced 'r' and short 'a' of the accent of Silesia, his birthplace: 'I shall not in all probability see him before my departure'.[23]

On this farcical note, the Great War had begun.

Chapter three

IN THE FIRING LINE (1914–1918)

You have fought valiantly and never lost a trench, or failed to do what was required of you. You have often been hungry and thirsty, had to endure intense cold and rain, mud and discomfort, had to work and march in the course of your duty, till you had hardly strength to stand. You have done all this without a murmur, and with a cheerfulness which has been beyond all praise.

UNIT WAR DIARY, 5TH BATTALION KING'S OWN SHROPSHIRE LIGHT INFANTRY, 2
FEBRUARY 1918

Before the retirement to the Haig Line, those of the battalion... seeing themselves surrounded, determined to fight to the last. Owing to the fact that very few got away from this melee very little is known of the actual details of this fight.

UNIT WAR DIARY, 1ST BATTALION KING'S OWN SHROPSHIRE LIGHT INFANTRY, 21 MARCH
1918

On 4 August, the knowledge that Britain had issued an ultimatum to Germany brought crowds onto the streets of London, congregating outside Downing Street, considered the most likely place where a formal response from the German ambassador would be announced.

The Times described the scene in its edition published the next day:

As the evening wore on, the crowd became denser and excitement grew. The German reply was not expected before 11.00 pm.

Towards 11, a number of visitors and members of the permanent staff of the Foreign Office gathered in the corridors, which were brilliantly lighted. But the expected dispatch from Sir Edward Goschen was unaccountably delayed. For reasons which can only be surmised, the German Government appears to have delayed it.

Information from a reliable quarter nevertheless reached His Majesty's Ministers, shortly before 11, that the British demand for assurances in regard to the neutrality of Belgium had been summarily rejected. The necessary decisions were therefore taken and an official statement was issued to the effect that, in consequence of this rejection, His Majesty's Ambassador at Berlin had received his passports and that his Majesty's Government had declared to the German Government that a state of war existed between Great Britain and Germany as from 11.00pm.

Notwithstanding the lateness of the hour, several members of the Diplomatic Corps called at the Foreign Office to ask for information. The scene was one of extraordinary animation, though a sense of the extreme gravity of the moment was everywhere noticeable.

As the news of the declaration of war reached the street, the crowd expressed its feelings in loud cheering. It left the precincts of Downing Street and gathered in front of the War Office, where patriotic demonstrations continued until an early hour this morning.[24]

Although adverts and messages occupied the first two pages as always, there was extensive coverage in the rest of the paper, including a large notice at the heart of page three, the first news page, which left the public in no doubt as to the seriousness of the unfolding events – a pre-prepared recruitment advert:

Your King and Country Needs You!
Will you answer your country's call? Each day is fraught with the gravest possibilities and at this very moment the empire is on the brink of the greatest war in the history of the world.

> In this crisis your country calls on all young unmarried men to rally round the flag and enlist in the ranks of her army.
>
> If every patriotic young man answers her call, England and her empire will emerge stronger and more united than ever.
>
> If you are unmarried between 18 and 30 years old will you answer your country's call? And go to the nearest recruiter – whose address you can get from any post office – and
>
> JOIN THE ARMY TODAY![25]

Swept up in the patriotic fervour, people from all walks of life responded to the impassioned call to arms, with 750,000 recruited by September and over a million by January 1915. Many men joined together from the same town, workplace or sports club, encouraged by figures such as General Sir Henry Rawlinson to enlist; his direct appeal to financiers in the City of London led to 1,600 stockbrokers signing up to the 10th (Service) Battalion of the Royal Fusiliers within days of the outbreak of war. General Rawlinson would oversee the British assault on the first day of the Battle of the Somme on 1 July 1916, during which many of the Pals battalions would receive horrific casualties that left entire communities bereft of their menfolk.

Another leading figure to inspire mass recruitment was Edward Stanley, the 17th Earl of Derby, who captured the spirit of the time when he announced his aim of raising troops from Liverpool: 'This should be a battalion of pals, a battalion in which friends from the same office will fight shoulder to shoulder for the honour of Britain and the credit of Liverpool.'[26] Local pride and national duty combined with sufficient fervour that four battalions were raised within days.

Inside the Foreign Office there had been a similar eagerness to sign up, particularly amongst the King's Messengers, who had traditionally come from a military background. At the outbreak of war there were four majors on the army reserve list who were keen to re-enlist so that they could 'do their bit'. According to their colleague, Victor Wheeler-Holohan, the senior staff at the Foreign Office had other ideas:

They were all liable to be called up, but the Foreign Office had the prior claim on their services, and at once communicated with the War Office with regard to securing their exemption from mobilisation.[27]

It was not just prior experience of active military duty that made the King's Messengers such a valuable commodity – their familiarity with Europe and the various diplomatic networks around the world made them prime candidates for other work:

Custance promptly reported to the War Office for duty, and was sent down to Falmouth for Military Intelligence duties... However, the Foreign Office was soon after him and on 10 August he was ordered back. His request to serve on with the army was refused, for in view of the fact that in addition to the usual languages he spoke Spanish and Portuguese fluently, he was too valuable and he was sent out to South America for intelligence work. At the same time he was laden with over 50 new and secret ciphers which had to be distributed all over the place.[28]

King's Messengers were not the only personnel that the Foreign Office hierarchy were keen to retain, given the anticipated volume of work that the outbreak of war was likely to cause. As Chief Clerk and therefore holding responsibility for personnel, Tilley recalled:

There was some divergence of opinion as to releasing any of our own men for military service. Crowe, for whom the office came very much first, would have liked to keep everyone. Others were inclined to think that we should let the younger men go but there was a special difficulty in this because the second division clerks had come in at about the age of 18 whereas the diplomatic clerks had come in at 22 to 25, so that to take all the youngest men first meant to take all second and no first division men.[29]

This meant that there was no immediate pressure on men like Ernest Oldham to enlist – although the perception that they were essential to the continued running of the Foreign Office was soon dispelled:

> On the other hand, the second division men were more easily replaced by women. It was a considerable time before it was arranged to let anyone go, but in the end a certain number of both categories were released, though many more second division than first. Of the second division clerks several died gallantly.[30]

Underpinning the initial public enthusiasm for war was a belief (if not actual downright confidence) that the stalwarts of the British Army – the Old Contemptibles – would prevail, sweeping the Hun aside and delivering a quick success within months. At the time of mobilisation, the strength of the army stood at 710,000, of which there were only 80,000 trained regulars, with the remainder in the Territorial forces – many of whom were simply not ready for front line action. Nevertheless, the British Expeditionary Force was sent to France on 7 August to halt the German advance.

One person who did not share the public confidence was the new Secretary of State for War, Lord Kitchener, who on the eve of the conflict thought that it would last for at least two or three years – hence the need to recruit more men, provided they were properly trained. Unfortunately, Kitchener was proved right. Both French and British forces were surprised by the sheer number of German troops massing in front of them. The various assaults over the first six weeks of the war, known collectively as the Battle of the Frontiers, failed to repel the German invasion and resulted in a general retreat. The British Expeditionary Force fought its first major engagement at the Battle of Mons on 23 August, suffering over 1,600 casualties and was similarly forced to retreat beyond their defensive lines even though they inflicted far greater damage on the enemy.

An offensive campaign quickly turned into a rearguard action. By October, remaining British units were involved in a frantic race to halt the German advances to the coast which would have cut off British supply lines and effectively curtailed their involvement on the Western Front, possibly ending the war as quickly as some had predicted. With the line stabilised, thanks to little known but crucial actions such as the defence of Gheluvelt, a new pattern of war developed around defensive trenches and artillery bombardment. Although they were not to realise it at the time, the troops on the Western Front had dug in for the long haul.

Increasingly bad news from the front, coupled with growing casualty numbers and a realisation that the war would not end quickly, punctured public optimism. As a result, the number of volunteers gradually tailed off so that by the middle of 1915 there was a crisis in recruitment. On 11 October, the Prime Minister appointed the aforementioned Earl of Derby as the Director General of Recruitment and five days later he unveiled a new scheme to enforce a form of moral conscription, encouraging men to voluntarily register their name. They were then placed into a group according to their age and marital status with the promise that this group would only be formally enlisted to a service battalion when needed. Perhaps it was the stipulation that bachelors would be called up before married men that made Oldham rather reluctant to come forward.

A poster issued in November 1915 made it clear that time was running out. Voluntary attestation into one of the groups had to be made by 11 December, with rumours that conscription was on its way. While Ernest Oldham doubtless wished to play his part for King and country, he left it very late to do so. On 10 December 1915, aged 21 years and 2 months, he walked out of the Foreign Office building to enlist at the Whitehall recruitment centre. He signed a short service attestation form, agreeing to serve 'for the duration of the war' after which he would be 'discharged with all convenient speed'.[31]

Oldham had elected for deferred recruitment – class A – whereby he was recruited for a nominal day's active service before being immediately placed with the army reserves and sent back to resume his civilian duties until the time came for his call up to the colours. He was placed in group 4 – single men born in 1894.

Five days later, the Derby scheme was abandoned, deemed to be a failure because only 215,000 men were directly recruited for immediate service as class B – although around 2.75 million were placed on the reserve list as class A. Oldham's group was called up for service between 20 December 1915 and mobilised on 20 January 1916 but under the deferred scheme he was one of the staff for whom Tilley secured an exemption from service. By stepping forward, Oldham had acted in the nick of time; conscription was introduced in January 1916 under the terms of the Military Service Act.

Although initial efforts were made to keep as many staff within the service as possible, by the end of 1915, the need was less intense.

> At a later period of the war the number of telegrams fell off, nego-
> tiations being less necessary as more and more of the neutrals be-
> came allies; two shifts from 8.00 am to 4.00 pm and from 4.00 pm
> to midnight were thus enough. Eight hours was as much as any eyes
> could stand at a time of this sort of work. A minor difficulty was that
> of sending home the typists who worked for the Cipher Depart-
> ment till midnight. Trams and omnibuses had sometimes stopped
> and those who lived in the suburbs had to be sent home by car.[32]

Now that Oldham was on the reserve list and business was less frantic, cou-
pled with the impact of the new intake of staff, his position within the Foreign Office was less secure. As with many other occupations, once the men started to be called to active service it was natural for women to step in to take their place. It must be said that this phenomenon was not wholly appreciated by the powers that be in the Foreign Office, as Tilley reflected afterwards:

> In addition to the men whom we took in from outside, we engaged
> gradually a great number of women. Of these, many were natu-
> rally amateurs; some had difficulty, according to their male col-
> leagues, in acquiring habits of precision and in the registries were
> said to be apt to think one number on a paper as good as another.
> Others were hard to persuade that, once engaged, they could not
> go off at once when their mothers and aunts and children were sick
> or otherwise in need of their help.[33]

With this rapid turnover of staff and the presence of women in the corridors of Whitehall, a major concern was that the Foreign Office would be infiltrated by a spy. Anti-German feeling was running at an all-time high, with German businesses attacked and people forced to flee their homes before mobs. Internment had been introduced shortly after the outbreak of war, given the large number of Germans living in the country, and there was a genuine fear amongst the population at large that enemy agents would try to gather intelligence on British soil. This was fuelled by popular publications such as *The Riddle of the Sands* (1903) and *The Thirty-Nine Steps* (1915) which included lurid – and wholly fictional – accounts of German espionage. Yet men from Oldham's section of the Foreign Office had been directly involved in spy-catching, such as honorary King's Messenger, Sir Park Goff:

> During the war he was closely associated with the Intelligence Service and made his reports to the responsible authority after each journey and was responsible for at least two spies being shot in the Tower.[34]

The phrase 'intelligence services' masked a rather nebulous collection of agencies, including naval and military intelligence departments, separate units in the War Office, and the Metropolitan Police Special Branch. In 1909, an attempt was made to bring some clarity to operations and a decision was taken to create the Secret Service Bureau, which would give rise to both MI5 (the home Security Service) and MI6 (the foreign Secret Intelligence Service).

The Secret Service Bureau initially comprised only two officers, Commander Mansfield Smith-Cumming (Royal Navy) and Captain Vernon Kell (Army). Its founding was a response to growing hysteria that a well-developed German spy network was operating in places such as Essex, planning for an invasion that never materialised mainly because no such network ever existed. Nevertheless, a number of suspected German agents were arrested in the years prior to 1914 and a further 21 people were seized as spies in the hours following the outbreak of war. Further clampdowns on enemy aliens and the possibility of going so far as to impose martial law made people feel a lot more secure. Certainly, Tilley expressed confidence that the Foreign Office was an impregnable fortress and remained safe from espionage throughout the conflict.

> Neither among men or women was there any instance of anybody in the nature of a spy finding his or her way into the office as any novelist would certainly have expected. One woman was found to have doubtful connections and had to leave.[35]

Yet by 1916, Oldham was keen to depart this safe haven for more exotic climes, possibly on account of the exciting tales of derring-do told by the King's Messengers as they returned to the office. A Royal Commission on the Civil Service reported in December 1914 and a key recommendation was the removal of the £400 private means income bar that had prevented candidates like Oldham from entering the Diplomatic Service. Tilley expressed the concern that:

> The feeling persisted among possible candidates that, whatever might be said, private means were almost essential. Possibly also there still remained the old idea that existence in the Diplomatic Service was that of a social butterfly, in which men without a taste for society would be out of place.
>
> At the same time, diplomats ought obviously, if they are to make a success of their profession, to be able to make friends with any sort or kind of people who may be a useful source of knowledge, not by any means necessarily secret, about their country. To many Englishmen even this is difficult when it comes to dealing with foreigners and doubtless life in a big public school, particularly so big a one as Eton, and in a university, makes it seem easier.[36]

Despite his background, Oldham was certainly not deterred – indeed he was probably heartened by his ability to fit in at the Foreign Office. So towards the end of 1916, he sought a place as part of the diplomatic corps. He clearly demonstrated sufficient skills to receive the required recommendation from the Secretary of State to proceed, with the endorsement that 'in view of your knowledge of language and your suitability in other respects for an appointment in HM Consular Service, the Selection Board nominated you to compete for a post in that service.'[37] Clearly, Oldham had been having lessons to brush up on his French and had added other languages too.

It may well have been with his future career as a diplomat in mind that Oldham took the difficult decision to activate his enlistment and join the army. He sought permission for his temporary release for military service, which was granted, and Oldham duly reported for duty at the Old Drill Hall, 17 Duke's Road – the headquarters of the 28th County of London Battalion, also known as the Artists' Rifles, just off Euston Road – on 9 February 1917.[38]

He wanted to train as an officer, although he was initially enlisted as private EH Oldham, No 765905, in the second sub-battalion. He first underwent a medical examination, where his height (5 feet 5 and a quarter inches), weight (126 pounds) and chest measurement (34 and a half inches) were dutifully recorded, along with the fact that he had been vaccinated in 1914. The examination also revealed that Oldham suffered from myopia so he was given prescription glasses from the Royal Army Medical Corps ophthalmic centre to correct his vision.

The regiment was perhaps a natural option for him. It had formerly been the unit of choice for volunteers from the artistic community who wished to join a territorial force – men such as Paul Nash and Wilfred Owen passed through its ranks – but by the time Oldham enlisted it was primarily set up as an officer training corps, attracting professional classes from public school and university backgrounds such as lawyers and architects. This was the sort of social grouping that Oldham now considered himself part of. It was an environment in which a civil servant from the Foreign Office would not feel out of place, even as a humble private.

Oldham was attached to B Company and, like Wilfred Owen before him, was sent to the Hare Hall camp in the grounds of Gidea Park near Romford. His new accommodation was hut 35, which may actually have been slightly more spacious than his small bedroom at home in Edmonton. The building was part of a complex of purpose-built dormitory huts catering for the growing number of cadets.

The camp was close enough to Squirrel Heath and Gidea Park station to catch a train to Romford and back into London for a trip home but many of the young men chose to stay locally, frequenting the Unicorn or Ship pubs in Hare Street, joining the bustling crowds in Romford market or strolling through Raphael Park, where many a dashing young officer cadet caught the eye of one of the local girls who congregated there. Oldham would have been given his cadet's uniform, had his hair cropped short and issued with a swagger cane.

The training regime was tough, especially for those used to the more sedate pace of life in an office environment. Drill and marching would often take place from early in the morning to late at night in order to whip the new recruits into shape. Marches often took place through the local streets, much to the excitement of local school children who never failed to cheer as the cadets went past. Other activities, such as bayonet practice, took place in the grounds. Food and refreshments were issued in the large and spacious refectory hut – a far more civilised place than anywhere they would encounter on the front.

On 24 February, Oldham formally applied to join an officer cadet battalion with a view to a temporary commission in the regular army for the period of the war. He had initially selected the option of joining a territorial force but crossed this through on his application form in favour of ' regular army', knowing full well that this would almost certainly mean a posting abroad. His preferred choice of regiment was the King's Liverpool Regiment, for which there was no obvious family or geographical connection.

As part of the application process he was required to provide evidence of his background, standing and education – as well as confirm that he was 'of pure European descent'. The certificate of his moral character during the previous four years was meant to be provided by the head of his school but was signed on 26 February by Thomas Henry Skinner, 'clerk in Holy Orders' at St Michael's Church, Edmonton – the longstanding family friend who had known Oldham since he was a boy. Skinner also stepped in to sign the

certificate that proved the candidate had attained a standard of education suitable for commissioned rank – a leaving certificate from the Royal Military
College, passing an army entrance examination or passing the matriculation
examination of a university. Oldham had none of these and should at least have
passed the certificate to the headmaster of his secondary school to sign. However, these were desperate times and Skinner's recommendation that 'I certify
from personal knowledge that Ernest Holloway Oldham has attained a standard of education suitable for commissioned rank'[39] was deemed sufficient.

Finally, permission was granted from his employer on 27 February and any
doubts over Oldham's education history were brushed aside when no less a
man than the Chief Clerk himself, Sir John Tilley, stated, 'Mr EH Oldham,
who has been employed in this Office since 1 April 1914, having been passed
for general service, is hereby given permission to make application for admission to an Officer Cadet Unit'.[40]

Next up was Oldham's medical, which took place on 29 March at the camp.
An officer of the Royal Army Medical Corps examined him, taking further mea-
surements of his height, weight and chest – all of which, incidentally, were larger
than in early February and suggested that the physical training had paid off.

Finally, Oldham was assessed by an officer and was found to be suitable
on 9 May. He was instructed to join No 19 Officer Cadet Battalion based at
Pirbright, a small village in Surrey, not far from Guildford, on 5 July 1917.
Here, up to 600 officers at a time were trained on courses lasting between
three and four months. This was nowhere near the recommended full training
offered at facilities such as Sandhurst for cadets who would become regular
commissioned officers, but it was long enough to learn basic officer skills such
as tactics (both Allied and enemy), drilling and training of one's men and, of
course, to undergo plenty of physical exercise.

Given the changing nature of warfare, important briefing sessions were
provided on the latest techniques in trench warfare, sniping and bayonetting,
weapons' maintenance, field engineering, musketry (including the new Lewis
machine guns) and – a topic that would have brought home the grim reality of
the Western Front – how to enable a junior officer to 'come with confidence
through the frequent gas attacks he will meet overseas'.[41] Added to these field

skills were background lectures on the geography of the theatre of war, military law and administration – of which there was also plenty.

At the end of his training, Oldham successfully completed a final examination and attended a passing out inspection. On 30 October 1917, he was granted a temporary commission as a second lieutenant and posted to the 5th Battalion of the King's Shropshire Light Infantry, part of the 42nd Infantry Brigade, 14nd Division – ironically one of Kitchener's 'New Army' divisions, then embroiled in the Third Battle of Ypres. Oldham had a month to say his farewells to friends, colleagues and family.

Oldham set out on 29 November to join his regiment in France, a note being published in the *London Gazette*. He met up with his new charges the following day at Eecke, after they had departed from Ypres, and was assigned to D Company. Once rifles and equipment were inspected, Oldham underwent another medical plus training with the box respirators, serving to remind him of the constant threat of a gas attack.[42]

On 3 December, D Company marched across the border into Belgium, billeting in huts far smaller than Hare Hall, in the small hamlet of Brandhoek. Over the next week or so, Oldham oversaw working parties that repaired roads and transport lines to the front, under the constant menace of hostile aeroplane activity. His first experience of the trenches came on 12 December 1917, when the unit was ordered to relieve the 10th Battalion of the Durham Light Infantry in the front line north of Passchendaele. They took up a position on the left of the line and remained there for three days. Although enemy artillery was fairly quiet during this period, when the time came for the battalion to be relieved the bombardment increased, leading to several casualties. The muddy terrain also added to the difficulty of the relief operation.

A steady routine was set for the remainder of the month. They witnessed occasional aeroplane battles – the first time many of the new men had seen such technology in action. One dogfight led to the crash of a British observer plane near Capricorn camp where they were based. Both pilot and observer were killed – the fate of so many young aviators on the front. Oldham's first encounter with gas shells came on 22 December during a particularly heavy bombardment, but no casualties were incurred. The following night several bombs were dropped by hostile aeroplanes, resulting in repair works on Christmas Eve. Oldham spent Christmas Day 1917 on duty, dodging shells, before his unit was relieved and marched back to St Jean station. The unit boarded a train for Wizernes, where they were given hot cocoa and biscuits. Then, at 9.00 pm, it was time for a one-hour march to cover the 1.8 miles to their new billets at Longuenesse. The rest of the month was spent conducting parades, doing physical training and practising bayonet technique, before the men were moved on New Year's Day 1918 to St Omer station. They caught the 7.20 pm train to Edgehill, arriving at 9.20 am the next morning. Cocoa and biscuits were served once again to bolster strength before a gruelling 18-kilometre march to Suzanne. It was a source of great pride to the commanding officer that no men fell out during the march.

Most of January 1918 was spent training, although on several occasions severe snow interrupted the various drills and practice. The seasoned soldiers would have known what was coming – an imminent spell in the line. Sure enough, a warning order was received on 20 January about a move and, two days later, the battalion covered the 12 miles from Suzanne to Rosières-en-Santerre in five hours, followed by a further 8-mile march the next day to Guerbigny, where they stayed for a couple of days.

On 25 January, they marched out for a couple of miles and were doubtless glad to be met by motorised transport that took them to Berlancourt, at which point they marched to overnight billets at Beine. The next day they tramped to Montescourt, not far from Jussy, near the banks of the Somme, where they were warned to prepare for the trenches. All through 27 January they waited in nervous anticipation before the order came through at 5.20 pm to proceed to the front at St Quentin, relieving the French 413e Infantry Regiment on the left sector. D Company, including Oldham, and C Company were in the trenches, with A and B companies in reserve. It was an uneventful duty and they remained in position until 2 February when the surprise orders were received that the battalion was to be disbanded as part of a reorganisation. Troops would be reallocated to other regiments of the King's Shropshire Light Infantry in order of company. Oldham and his comrades in D Company were sent to join the 1st Battalion and the promise of more front line duty.

Before the men dispersed to their new postings, commanding officer Lieutenant Colonel Smith was moved to say a few words about the farewell order and the gallantry his charges had shown during the previous years:

> You have fought valiantly and never lost a trench or failed to do what was required of you.
>
> You have often been hungry and thirsty, had to endure intense cold and rain, mud and discomfort, had to work and march in the course of your duty, till you had hardly strength to stand. You have done all this without a murmur and with a cheerfulness which has been beyond all praise.
>
> I know full well that you will carry on the same splendid work in the other battalions of the dear old corps that you are going to. No regiment in the British service has a finer record and, remember this, it is each one of you who help to keep that record unsullied and its honour bright. It has been the proudest and happiest time of my life during which I have had the honour of commanding you, and I still hope I may continue to solider with you.[43]

Stirring stuff, and with these words ringing in his ears, Oldham marched off to join the 1st Battalion, part of the 16th Infantry Brigade, 6th Division, stationed in the Lagnicourt sector, where he and 30 other ranks arrived on 12 February.[44] Unfortunately, this was exactly where the Germans had planned to launch Operation Michael as part of the so-called spring offensive, made possible following the withdrawal of the Russians from the war under the terms of the Treaty of Brest-Litovsk on 3 March.

The Russian withdrawal was a direct result of domestic turmoil throughout 1917. Tsar Nicholas II had been forced to abdicate at the end of the February Revolution and was replaced by a provisional government that in turn failed to repress the anti-war, radical Bolsheviks. This ultimately led to the October Revolution that saw Vladimir Lenin sweep to power and establish rule by local soviets – councils run by the workers – in the new Russian Soviet Federative Socialist Republic. Almost immediately, the 'White' Army of monarchists and liberal reformers confronted the Bolshevik 'Red' Army, sparking the Russian civil war that engulfed the country in 1918 and dragged on until 1922.

Recognising the catastrophic effect that the war was having on the Russian economy, the Bolshevik government secured an armistice with the Central Powers in December 1917. However, peace negotiations collapsed and after German forces made rapid gains along the Eastern Front, the Russians were forced to accept considerably less favourable terms and the peace treaty was signed on 3 March. As a result, Russia abandoned the Triple Entente and made large territorial concessions, while Germany was free to move nearly 50 divisions to the Western Front.

For almost a week, since unusual enemy activity was reported on 14 March and Oldham's battalion stood to at battle positions in the early hours, there was an uneasiness amongst the troops holding the line 'as to the enemy's intention to attack', according to the official unit war diary.[45] Then, on 21 March, the German assault began. Operation Michael was the main attack of four planned offensives that day, the plan being to punch through Allied lines with the overwhelming numerical advantage gained by the move of the divisions from the Eastern Front. The first objective would be to pour as many men through a breach as possible and outflank the British troops who held the line that ran along the Somme to the Channel. The aim was to cut off supply lines in a repeat of the original 1914 strategy. In theory this would render the British forces inoperative and hasten the French to the negotiating table.

A summary of the action in the unit war diary records the events as they unfolded from the perspective of Oldham and his men based just outside St Quentin.

> At 5.00 am, the enemy heavily bombarded our trenches in the forward area but did not shell the defended area until 5.45 am. He used gas shells and high explosive mixed, and also shelled our batteries around Vaulx and Bois de Vaulx very heavily with high explosives.[46]

In fact, over 3.5 million shells were fired in five hours, decimating the lines but also cutting off communication lines at around 7.30 am, making it much harder for the British troops to understand what was going on or coordinate a response with the units on either side in the line. An early morning fog added to the growing sense of confusion, making it very hard to see beyond 10 metres in front. However, those in the front line trenches that had held their position during the bombardment were suddenly faced with thousands of Germans appearing, wraith-like, out of the mist, firing as they came:

> At around 8.00 am the barrage lifted from the front line. Battalion HQ then received a message from officer commanding A Company by runner that B Company was falling back onto A company, and that no officer of B Company had been seen; also that the enemy were right through Noreuil and advancing over ridge towards the left flank of the King's Shropshire Light Infantry.[47]

The daily entry from the diary makes for even more dramatic reading as knowledge of the fate of one's comrades was often sketchy or down to guesswork as the battle unfolded, with fractured communication making it hard to piece together what was happening from hour to hour:

> 21 March
> Desperate enemy offensive commences, remnant of battalion mixed with portions of other units, endeavour to hold the enemy in the Haig Line. Inflicted enormous losses on the enemy; before the retirement to the Haig Line those of the battalion (the great majority under Col HM Smith, DSO, seeing themselves surrounded, determined to fight to the last). Owing to the fact that very few got away from this melee very little is known of the actual details of this fight. Sunset found a handful of the battalion under Lieutenant Rogers MC still in the Haig Line.[48]

In fact, all front line units retreated throughout the day under the weight of German firepower, using the communications trenches to fall back to the Haig Line and beyond. They abandoned Noreuil and Lagnicourt – ground held for several years was lost in a matter of hours. Fighting resumed the next day with even greater levels of intensity as officers struggled to prevent the retreat from becoming a rout. Infantry troops desperately sought artillery support, but the guns were taken further back to prevent them falling into German hands. Word came through that German forces had broken through the new defensive positions at Vaulx de Bois, and so the Allied retreat continued – Vaulx itself was lost and under intense fire the British line fell back further.

> 22 March
> The remnant of the battalion wedged between 1st the Buffs and 2nd Yorks and Lancasters put up a desperate fight in the Haig line. About 3.00 pm, unsupported by artillery who were moving back, the enemy having succeeded in outflanking the line in overwhelming numbers, it became necessary to fall back on to Vaulx. The retirement was conducted in good order. At dusk the battalion received orders to withdraw to the G[eneral] H[ead]Q[uarters] line behind Vraucourt.[49]

The battalion sustained heavy losses; although Oldham was in the thick of the fighting, he was extremely lucky not to be injured.

> In this, the heaviest fighting the battalion has ever known, ie 21 – 22 March 1918, the battalion loss was in 'killed, wounded and missing' 21 officers and 492 other ranks and earned for itself the admiration of all who fought with them and added fresh laurels to the history of a gallant regiment. Only 77 other ranks survived on the evening of the 22nd of those who were in the battle.[50]

The shattered remnants of the battalion were relieved the next day, battle-scarred, weary and lucky to be alive. However, they had to march to Achiet-le-Grand, where they collapsed on trains bound for Doullens. Arriving at 8.00 pm, they set up bivouacs in the moat of the citadel and rested. Further marches were required on 25 March before they reached Chauny camp in the early hours of the following morning. At this point, the strength of the battalion was assessed; only 13 officers and 272 other ranks remained.

Fighting continued along the line until early April and the Germans advanced over 40 miles into Allied territory, taking over 75,000 prisoners of war, 1,300 artillery pieces and 200 tanks. However, the orderly retreat meant that the Germans were unable to outflank the British and reach the coast and the advance slowed to a halt. Furthermore, the captured ground was very difficult to defend as it was effectively muddy wasteland created by years of artillery fire. Losses were horrific on both sides – around 178,000 British troops killed, wounded, imprisoned or missing, with a further 75,000 French troops suffering the same fate. Around 250,000 Germans were lost in the slaughter, a large proportion being elite troops who were very hard to replace. This had been the main throw of the German dice and once the attack lost its impetus Allied reinforcements were able to pour into the area.

Oldham's battalion spent early April in training and drills before stepping back into the front line at Ypres towards the end of the month. There they faced further bombardment – including heavy gas attacks during 20 and 21 April which incapacitated 95 men and killed three others. The troops fell into a regular pattern of trench duty followed by defensive works throughout the remainder of the month and May.

Oldham left to join the transport unit on 28 May and, during this time, made discreet inquiries about the possibility of applying for a post on Military Intelligence Staff, before formally submitting an application on 18 June to the division's Intelligence Officer. Given his Foreign Office pedigree and a glowing commendation from his colleagues across the Channel in London – 'his service whilst employed by them gave entire satisfaction'[51] – he would have been confident that his skills would make him a useful asset in the various aspects of work that the Intelligence Corps undertook. This included prisoner debriefing, identification of enemy agents among Allied forces, analysis of aerial photography secured by Royal Flying Corps observers, signals intelligence and even undercover missions behind enemy lines. By mid-1918 the corps was around 1,300 strong and primarily focused on the Western Front, although plans were in place to raise a new company to support the campaign on the Italian front.

By this stage of the war, a more formal process was in place to recruit intelligence officers as third-class agents – the level at which Oldham was aiming, given his rank. Assessment where possible involved the Intelligence Personnel section of the War Office. Candidates were tested on language skills, especially German, and on military knowledge. It is also possible that Oldham underwent some elementary counter-intelligence fieldwork – including a demonstration of his ability to extract information from a stranger and the art of disappearing in crowds.

However, either Oldham's German was not up to scratch or his military knowledge deemed too limited and he was not selected. It did not help that, at the time he was applying, a request to the War Office to expand the Intelligence Corps establishment in the light of increased signals activity was rejected, with the note that any new capacity for wireless and communications work had to be found from existing numbers.[52] Doubtless dejected at this setback, Oldham returned to the front line on 14 July.

By this stage, the Second Battle of the Marne was about to start – a key moment in which French forces first repulsed and then reversed a German assault, resulting in a series of counter-attacks known as the Hundred Days Offensive, as Allied numerical superiority against stretched defences finally punctured the German lines. The Battle of Amiens that started on 8 August and was described as 'the black day of the German Army' created a 15-mile gap, shattering German morale; the Second Battle of the Somme which opened a week later produced similar results. From this point onwards, the German Army was in retreat towards the Hindenburg Line.

During this period, Oldham's battalion was stationed at Dickebusch and in the lines at Ouderdom, and thus escaped most of the fighting. However, towards the end of August, they were on the move – including a 'very trying march' from St Momelin to Quelmes on which one of the soldiers actually died.[53] From there, they moved to Licques on 28 August and were treated to a battalion dinner at the Hôtel des Voyageurs. Thereafter followed several weeks of intensive attack training interspersed with rest, including bathing in the River Ancre at Heilly or baths for those who did not want a dip. There was also a variety of evening performances performed by a local troupe of entertainers called the 'Kancies' in the grounds of Heilly Château.

On 11 September the battalion moved back into action, first marching to Aubigny and then embarking on 14 September onto buses and driving the 30 or so miles to their final destination at Trefcon, arriving at 1.30 pm the same afternoon. Having settled in their billets, they spent the next few days in reconnaissance operations, checking the line were they were to be posted to, ostensibly in case of enemy attack but in reality to put all the recent assault training into practice – 'making preparations for the coming show', as their commanding officer wrote in the war diary.[54] The coming show turned out to be the Battle of Épehy, an attack on German outpost positions that were stationed on high ground in front of the Hindenburg Line – a preliminary attack ordered by Field Marshal Haig before a planned major offensive along the entire line. This was sparked by an earlier success at the Battle of Havrincourt on 12 September that saw Allied troops breach the Hindenburg defensive line for the first time. It was none other than General Sir Harry Rawlinson who oversaw operations.

From their base at Trefcon, the men of the battalion made their final preparations. On the afternoon of 17 September, the troops moved up to the west side of St Quentin wood in readiness for an assault on the German lines the next day. At 8.30 pm, the company commanders met up with the senior officers to receive their instructions for the next morning's action, with all necessary stores moved in readiness for the attack. The officers returned to their men and ordered everyone to don service dress. By 11.00 pm it had started to rain and a torrential thunderstorm thereafter raged constantly from midnight until the early hours, the nervousness of the soldiers compounded by heavy enemy bombardment.

At 3.20 am on the morning of 19 September, with rain still falling heavily, the sodden men under the cover of complete darkness slowly made their way towards their positions and formed up into their attack deployment, as ordered by the officers who were struggling to read their papers in the dark and wet. To maintain the element of surprise, British artillery did not clear the German lines with an advance barrage. Instead, at 5.20 am prompt – zero hour – a creeping barrage was laid down, behind which the first British troops were given the signal to advance, stumbling forward amidst the falling shells and rain.

The King's Shropshire Light Infantry were part of the second wave and received their orders to attack at 7.00 am, but visibility was extremely poor on account of a very heavy mist which obscured Badger Copse, their target landmark. Because the 2nd York and Lancaster Battalion had failed to take their own objectives in the first wave of attacks, the advancing troops encountered heavy German machine-gun fire from Fresnoy le Petit on their right, which pinned them down for most of the morning. The war diary records that 'the fighting grew very bitter'[55] and the operational instructions no longer bore any semblance to the reality of the situation. The composite battalions within the brigade were mixed up and by 10.30 am the battalion HQ was forced to move forward to try to sort out the mess, since orders on the ground were no longer effective.

With no further objectives gained throughout the day, the commanding officers held a conference at 5.00 pm and decided to consolidate their position. The attack had not succeeded so a decision was reached to try again the following morning. The unit war diary hints at the reaction of the field officers when they heard the news, as well as the appalling conditions they were working under.

> Without warning, brigade operation orders were received at 1.30 am at the new battalion HQ at Trout Copse to attack Fresnoy le Petit at 5.30 am. Great difficulty presented itself in writing battalion operation orders owing to no lights being possible, however those were written in the bottom of a trench and despatched about 3.00 am. Casualties to runners prevented them being received by the officer commanding D (support) Company and officers commanding front line companies found great difficulty in reading them before dawn.[56]

Tired officers, with no preparation and only a tentative grasp of what was intended, then issued the orders to assemble once more and face the enemy.

As before, heavy machine-gun fire came from the right flank, but this time the objective was to take those positions.

> B Company fought its way into Fresnoy le Petit, meeting stubborn resistance, including the two remaining officers and entirely losing touch with the remainder of the battalion. Throughout the day the several small parties of which the company was now composed resisted all attempts of the enemy to surround them.[57]

Their gallantry was in vain, however:

> At dusk, being still isolated, these parties withdrew, still fighting, onto our line of posts.[58]

Oldham had been involved in the first stage of the assault. Under the German bombardment that accompanied the British advance, a shell exploded near his position. The blast knocked him unconscious and he was buried under the mud and debris thrown up by the explosion. He was dragged out by his men, still unconscious, and immediately taken to a first-aid post and then transferred to the nearest casualty clearing station for assessment, where he regained consciousness. Despite having no obvious physical injuries, he was clearly concussed and in no fit state to return to his unit, continuing to vomit and suffering from crippling headaches.[59]

He was moved to a field hospital on 20 September and three days later was sent home from Le Havre, arriving in Southampton on the morning of 24 September. While recuperating, he contracted flu on 8 October – possibly a mild strain of the deadly swine or Spanish flu which started to sweep across the globe from August onwards. He survived, though this delayed his recovery for several weeks. For Oldham, the war was over.

A medical board sat in judgment on Oldham's injuries at 3rd London General Hospital, Wandsworth, on 14 November 1918, three days after the Armistice had been signed that ended hostilities. Given the minor nature of his injuries, he was passed fit to return to service. His period of absence was classified as leave and extended to 5 December 1918, at which point he was discharged from active service. He was entitled to wear his uniform for another month – just in case he needed time to buy civilian dress – and on ceremonial occasions thereafter. Although he was placed on the reserve list, where he would remain until December 1921 in case of military emergency, Oldham was instructed to return to civilian duties in the Foreign Office. He retained his Sam Browne belt and bayonet for his Lee-Enfield rifle and reputedly his service revolver – 'just in case'. His experiences in the trenches had changed him forever, and according to his sisters he returned 'shattered and broken' by the Great War.

Chapter four

THE PARIS PEACE CONFERENCE (1918–1919)

No matter how hard you try, you cannot imagine the shambles, the chaos, the incoherence, the ignorance here. Nobody knows anything because everything is happening behind the scenes.

PAUL CAMBON, FRENCH AMBASSADOR TO BRITAIN, 1898 – 1920

With the Armistice signed, thoughts of politicians and diplomats alike turned to the peace process – although the possible shape of the post-war world had been raised as long ago as September 1916, when the Parliamentary Under-Secretary of State for Foreign Affairs, Lord Robert Cecil, first circulated a 'Memorandum on proposals for diminishing the occasion of future wars'. This was seen, albeit primarily by Cecil himself, as the first British articulation of the need for a global organisation that would ensure the maintenance of peace.

In January 1918, US President Woodrow Wilson issued 'Fourteen points' that outlined the American view about how the world would operate after peace had been brokered. These included self-determination for smaller nations, free trade, open diplomatic processes, freedom of navigation on the high seas, disarmament to the lowest possible level, various territorial adjustments including the contentious issue of colonial claims and a general association of nations under specific covenants to safeguard the previous points (the League of Nations).

Wilson's ideas were based on an inquiry led by foreign policy advisor Edward House and a team of around 150 staff. From the British perspective, the Permanent Under-Secretary of State, Lord Hardinge, established the Political Intelligence Department within the Foreign Office in March 1918 to draw together as much information as possible on both Allied and enemy countries. This could be used when peace arrived. Under the direction of men such as William Tyrrell and James Headlam-Morley, 180 country guides were compiled by an army of technical experts and were crammed with every piece of information that was considered of potential use. Inside the Foreign Office, there was a growing confidence that the peace process would mark the moment when diplomacy would finally and rightfully be returned to the hands of the professionals rather than the politicians.

Yet despite these meticulous preparations, the rapidity with which fighting ceased took many officials by surprise. Whilst Oldham was recuperating in hospital and undergoing his final medical examination by the doctors in Wandsworth, plans were hastily assembled by the Allies for a grand conference. Once Paris was confirmed as the venue over Geneva – despite initial opposition from Lloyd George, and US fears that Switzerland was 'saturated with every kind of poisonous element and open to every hostile element in Europe' – attention began to focus on what would actually be discussed. The French, led by Prime Minister Georges Clemenceau, had drafted an outline proposal which was circulated to the Allies on 29 November. With the help of Foreign Office Librarian Alwyn Parker, Hardinge produced his own complicated blueprint for the conference, with various interlinked geographical committees that placed Foreign Office officials at the heart of the process.

However, the politicians had other ideas; Foreign Secretary Arthur Balfour duly presented Hardinge's plan to the War Cabinet in October 1918. Prime Minister Lloyd George, long distrustful of the Foreign Office or indeed any institution comprised of 'experts', simply laughed at it. Instead he asked War Cabinet member General Jan Smuts to come up with an alternative. The result was even more complicated than Hardinge's and required the presence of a range of experts from different government departments. Alongside six groups of territorial experts from the Foreign Office, there were specialists from the Board of Trade for advice about the pros and cons of free trade and the global economy; a delegation from the Treasury to advise on financial issues including the economist John Maynard Keynes; representatives from the branches of the armed forces, including the recently formed Royal Air Force, and a plethora of advisors for discussions about the proposed League of Nations and freedom of the seas. Needless to say, many lawyers were invited. In a further snub to Hardinge, Lloyd George asked the Cabinet Secretary, Maurice Hankey, to head the British secretariat, a move which left Hardinge even more bitter and resentful despite Hankey's best attempts to smooth ruffled feathers. Things had not got off to an auspicious start.

It was apparent from the outset that large numbers of backroom staff were required to support the British delegation at the conference, whatever shape it took. Office space was required to house the clerks, typists, cipher staff, messengers and payroll officers, plus the official delegates and technical experts – all of whom needed accommodation as well as somewhere to work. Around 400 people were required, as well as a separate printing operation with a further 130 staff to ensure that briefing documents and reports were speedily produced for the various meetings. The budget came from the beleaguered Treasury, already shattered by the war effort. Preparations got underway at once. The administrative and logistical burden largely fell upon the Foreign Office, with the long-suffering Alwyn Parker organising the necessary accommodation in Paris within two days of the Armistice – the Hôtel Majestic for personnel, with higher ranking officials taking either secure flats or suites next door in the Villa Majestic and the Hôtel Astoria was set aside for office space. The Foreign Office was initially allocated to the fourth floor.

There was also the issue of security – in terms of protecting British intelligence, given that large numbers of nations would be attending, as well as ensuring the safety of the politicians involved, given continuing fears of revolutionary activity articulated by Wilson in the context of Geneva. Such fears were well-founded; Clemenceau was lucky to survive an assassination attempt on 19 February 1919.

The task of intelligence protection was the responsibility of Sir Henry Penson's intelligence clearing house, also allocated an entire floor, while the

Assistant Commissioner of the Metropolitan Police and Head of the Criminal Investigation Department, Basil Thomson, was assigned the latter task. He took his work very seriously, down to the level of ensuring that the rooms at the hotels were cleaned by British hands brought over especially for the purpose, rather than leave it to chance that a 'native' cleaner might try to secure secrets from the delegates' rooms. His preferred plan was to bring in demobilised Women's Auxiliary Army Corps staff, not simply because they were female, but because many had undertaken signals intelligence work during the war – the 'Hush-WAACs' – and could therefore be trusted on a security detail.

Alongside various plain-clothed police officers from Special Branch, he requested two men for 'subterranean activities' – his own intelligence-gathering operation, which included Major Stewart Menzies, who would rise to lead Britain's Secret Intelligence Service. The entire staff of the hotel were replaced by British workers and even local messenger services were shunned on the grounds of security. A group of ten Girl Guides – the youngest being Jessie Spencer from Richmond, Surrey aged only 13 years and 7 months – were sent over to run messages and undertake light office work. This provoked an outcry from various groups shocked at the exploitation of children – 'prurient little flappers who should be at school and under parental control', according to the chairman of the advisory committee for Eltham schools, Lady Ellen McDougall.[60]

Back in England, the task of assembling the support staff from within the Foreign Office who would work at the Astoria continued through November and December, alongside the job of ensuring that sufficient arrangements were made for those left behind. In effect, there would be two Foreign Offices in place, a shadow one in Paris focusing on conference activity under the control of Balfour and Hardinge and the permanent one in London which was temporarily placed under the command of Lord Curzon, Lord President of the Council.

During this period of frenzied activity and growing excitement, Oldham finally returned to his desk in Whitehall – a war hero, and a wounded one at that, who had served his King and country valiantly with tales to tell worthy of any of the King's Messengers. Coupled with his application to join the diplomatic corps in 1916, which had received strong support from his superiors, it is clear that his star was in the ascendancy. Even so, it is still surprising to find that Oldham was selected as one of the team of six clerks who would travel to Paris for the conference, part of the centralised Establishment Section that would oversee all the day to day administration, filing, correspondence and registry work for all the delegations from different departments. This was a pivotal role – the key bureaucracy not just for the Foreign Office but the entire British presence in Paris.

Correspondence to secure the funds to enable selected staff to go to Paris flowed thick and fast between the Foreign Office and the Treasury as time started to run out. On 12 December, Assistant Under-Secretary Sir Maurice de Bunsen made it clear to Treasury officials that the Foreign Secretary himself had approved their plans to create a fully staffed secretariat in Paris.

> With reference to the semi-official correspondence which has passed between this office and your department on the subject of the arrangements to be made for the control of the expenditure of the British delegation to the peace conference at Paris, I am directed by Mr Secretary Balfour to request that you will lay before the lords commissioners of His Majesty's Treasury the following proposals which have been framed with a view to the setting up of a strong establishment section which shall ensure both economical administration and efficient accountancy.[61]

The post of Establishment Officer was granted to Alexander Allen Paton, a Liverpool-based businessman who had made his name in cotton and was closely associated with Balfour. He had acted as attaché to the British Embassy in Washington in 1915 and organised the arrangements for Balfour's mission to the US to cement American intervention in 1917. He was a trusted advisor with a track record of work within the Contraband Department of the Foreign Office. In a move to secure Treasury support, it was pointed out that:

> Mr Paton is prepared to give his services without a salary but he will, of course, be repaid his out-of-pocket expenses for

> travelling etc and the Secretary of State desires to reserve the right
> to recommend that some suitable recognition of his services shall
> be awarded at the conclusion of the present mission.[62]

Paton would receive the support of William Henry Robinson, the Assistant to the Foreign Office Chief Clerk, to whom was delegated the responsibility for managing the office accommodation set up by poor Parker at the Hôtel Astoria, with oversight for all staff issues once the Establishment Section had been set up. To assist him, Robinson would require a personal staff of not less than six clerks:

> It has not been possible, up to the present, to select them all, but
> two of them will be Mr FO Baron and Mr EH Oldham, both of
> whom have been serving as officers in His Majesty's forces.[63]

To be named as one of the six shows real confidence in Oldham's abilities and doubtless his newly honed language skills helped his cause. Furthermore, it seems that he had come to the attention of some of the bigwigs because a special case was laid before the Treasury about his salary, endorsed by none other than Balfour himself:

> Mr Oldham is a second division clerk of five years seniority, and
> his present salary is £100 a year. Mr Balfour feels it would not be
> fair to expect an officer to accept employment in Paris on a salary
> of less than £150 and he proposes that Mr Oldham's salary shall be
> made up to that amount for the time being. The other members
> of staff will probably be either junior second division clerks, who
> should receive treatment similar to that proposed for Mr Oldham,
> or women, for whom salaries of £2 10s or £3 a week, according to
> their experience and capacity, should be provided, together with
> the same terms in regard to lodging and maintenance as to other
> members of the staff of the delegation.[64]

This was quite a pay rise, along with free board and lodging. A £30 uniform allowance was thrown in as well, as even junior officials such as Oldham were considered likely to have to wear diplomatic uniform should the situation arise. The Treasury replied on 20 December with grudging acceptance of de Bunsen's request, though they were not happy about the special provisions made for Oldham:

> While, in view of the provision of free board and lodging in Paris, as well as outfit allowances, My Lords cannot but regard as somewhat illogical the proposal to fix an overriding minimum salary of £150 for male clerks and £130 per annum for certain women clerks employed there and while they would have preferred the simple principle of arranging that all officers should draw their London salaries, they are willing in the exceptional circumstances to sanction its adoption on the understanding that the salaries fixed are in all cases inclusive of all overtime worked.[65]

Also approved were payments for Mr Bebb from the Exchequer and Audit Department, who would be the Accounting Officer for the Establishment – supported by Miss Cullis and her team of clerks responsible for payroll – and for Captain Butler-Stoney, formerly of the Coldstream Guards, to act as Secretary to the Establishment Committee.

However, given the relentless time pressure to have everything in readiness for the politicians and experts at the end of December, the Treasury endorsement was provided retrospectively. The Establishment Section was required immediately so that they could assist with the preparations. An advance party was originally scheduled to leave England on 11 December but due to various delays finally departed three days later. Oldham found himself part of a group consisting of his five clerical colleagues, 70 lady clerks, ten girl guides, two nurses, a doctor, a representative from the Ministry of Food and Alwyn Parker. All waited at Charing Cross station for their Pullman car to leave at 11.00 am, destined for Folkestone Harbour station.

Once they had disembarked from the train and ferried their luggage to the

harbour, they caught the 2.15 pm boat to Boulogne. They docked at 4.00 pm
– arrangements having been made in advance to ensure the minimum delay at
customs, with everyone vouched for by Thomson – before catching another
train, complete with dining car, at 5.30 pm, to arrive in Paris four hours later.
Parker, reliable as always, had sent a telegram the night before to ensure that
they were met by cars at Gare du Nord, the Paris station, to escort them to the
Majestic, along with two motor lorries for their bags.

Someone who accompanied Oldham to Paris in December was George
Antrobus, who provided his own take on proceedings:

> This preliminary party consisted, if I remember right, of some two
> dozen men and 96 women... The Government had taken over the
> palatial Hotel Majestic in the Avenue Kleber to house the person-
> nel and had made pretty complete arrangements for a long stay.
> The noble army of peacemakers even included a doctor – a noted
> Mayfair accoucheur [male midwife], whose presence suggested to
> the Parisians that we had come to stay for nine months at least...
> The Majestic was filling up with a vast assemblage, drawn from ev-
> ery corner of the Empire, of delegates, negotiators, experts, tech-
> nicians, clerks, advisers and hangers-on, all bursting with enthusi-
> asm to make the world safe for Democracy. Most of them brought
> their wives (or some substitute therefore), some their children and
> some again their cousins, sisters and aunts.[66]

It probably came as a relief to learn from the politicians that no meaningful dialogue would take place until 13 January 1919. One factor in the delay
was Lloyd George's decision to hold a snap election after the Armistice so
that he could negotiate with a clear national mandate. This was scheduled to
take place on 14 December but because of the large number of votes cast by
returning troops, the official count could not take place until 28 December.
This was the earliest date that the beleaguered Parker thought that the Hôtel
Astoria would be ready for the various staff, although he was already trying to
put off Penson and his intelligence clearing house until 2 January 1919. Their

offices had already been moved up to the seventh floor of the Astoria in a final bid to accommodate everybody below.

It is easy to dismiss Antrobus's observations about the nature of the diplomatic corps that began to descend on Paris from 8 January onwards, given his track record for acerbic commentary, but a more sober and senior member of the Foreign Office, Stephen Gaselee, confirmed that there was already a pessimism amongst the clerical staff about the outcome of a process bloated by 'experts':

> Immediately after the War the Foreign Office had to spare for the Versailles Conference something like half the Office while many of the temporary clerks were transferred to Paris, where a huge office was set up. Among them were an army of experts on every subject that was likely to be discussed. I gather that those in the highest places were at times bewildered, to repeat a word already used, by the multitude of counsellors. The 'hands' that Lord Salisbury disliked were so numerous that it seemed impossible ever to reach a correct conclusion on questions, for instance, of nationality and frontiers. Those matters, however, are, in Queen Elizabeth's phrase, 'too great' for the writers of this book.[67]

Nevertheless, the diplomatic perspective was slightly more optimistic, with seasoned professionals excited by the opportunity that Paris represented for their careers, given this was a once in a lifetime chance to forge a new world order. In the words of senior Foreign Office mandarin Robert Vansittart:

> I was notified that I should attend the Peace Conference… for a moment I felt a cockiness which I had not experienced since my small boyhood… I became briefly 'brilliant'… this conference was the finest and most promising thing in the world.[68]

Vansittart would continue his rise through the Foreign Office off the back of his presence in Paris, eventually ending up Permanent Under-Secretary in 1930 and playing an important role in Oldham's life.

To echo Gaselee, a full rendition of conference proceedings is outside the scope of this book, so a summary of the key points shall suffice as they directly shaped the world in which Oldham worked. Once the delegates had started to arrive from 8 January, an inter-Allied preparatory meeting was held on 12 January to decide the shape of the main Peace Conference. It was agreed that there would be an initial Plenary Conference on 18 January at the Salle de l'Horloge at the French Foreign Ministry on the Quai d'Orsay; 70 delegates representing 27 countries attended. Expectations were wildly optimistic, as there was no real consensus about the remit of the conference or the mechanisms for reaching decisions. However, from the outset, the proceedings were dominated by the main powers – Britain, France, the USA and Italy – who had their own agendas and quickly framed the parameters for the other countries. Indeed, Clemenceau's attitude was described by Foreign Office delegate Harold Nicolson as:

> High-handed with the smaller Powers: 'y-a-t-il d'objections? Non?... Adopté'. Like a machine gun.[69]

The American position was for a wider settlement, underpinned by a new 'world governance' in the form of the League of Nations championed by President Wilson. For Clemenceau and the French, the main aim was to completely dismantle the German military machine and ensure it was not rebuilt; harsh reparations, territorial gains and acceptance of the blame for starting the war were their objectives. The British position was somewhere in the middle. Lloyd George wished to ensure Germany paid reparations and disarmed, whilst redrawing the world map was an opportunity not to be missed. However, he also realised that the Germans needed to be able to pay their debts and should not have access to free trade markets restricted. Lurking in the background was the spectre of the revolutions in central and eastern Europe, with fears that too harsh a settlement would drive Germany into the arms of the Bolsheviks. Russia had not been invited to take part in the Allied conference, as the new regime had already made peace with the Central Powers at Brest-Litovsk. In the eyes of many

British delegates, their omission from the peace talks was a mistake – Nicolson wrote in his diary on 9 January:

> We hear that the Russians are constituting a committee or 'confer-ence' of ambassadors…This will be highly awkward for those who wish to ignore Russia. I am delighted. After all, we are dealing with Russian interests behind their backs and the above committee have only to formulate a protest in writing for the [Paris] conference to be branded, in the history of a future Russia, as having deserted her in her trouble.[70]

Also excluded from the process were the Central Powers of Germany, Austria-Hungary, Bulgaria and the Ottoman Empire, who had to wait until the conference concluded before they heard the terms they would be offered if they wished to secure peace. In many ways this was diplomacy down the barrel of a gun, since the Allied forces had an army of occupation in place in the Rhineland, waiting to resume hostilities at the first sign of disquiet.

The conference proceeded in stages, with a Bureau de Conference or 'Council of Ten' formed by two delegates from the main powers, including Japan. Britain was represented by Lloyd George and Balfour. However, it took another week to set up five general committees to look at specific issues – the League of Nations, reparations, the responsibilities of the authors of the war, international labour legislation and an international regime for ports, water-ways and railways. Delays, plus a refusal by the politicians to communicate with the Foreign Office staff, led Hardinge to comment on 24 January that:

> A precious fortnight has been wasted, our great men having thought that they could settle everything themselves, even to the smallest details, and that such things as committees were childish inventions of the FO [Foreign Office] or of the devil.[71]

Matters went from bad to worse. Territorial committees were set up at the end of January to deal with regional discussions but it wasn't until

27 February that a central territorial committee was established to coordinate discussion across the others. By then, most of the work had been done in isolation. Headlam-Morley observed that:

> The result was that week after week went by, each of the sections continued working by itself and no official arrangement was made for communication and consultation. Practically, owing to the fact that we were working in the same building and living in the same hotel, a great deal of informal and personal consultation took place, but this was at the beginning only very partial and, as far as I could make out, some of the sections – especially the economic and the financial which were of very great importance – continued to work on their own without any consultation or communication with others.[72]

The results were potentially catastrophic. As Nicolson put it:

> We were never for one instant given to suppose that our recommendations were absolutely final. And thus we tended to accept compromises and even to support decisions which we ardently hoped would not, in the last resort, be approved.[73]

Despite a warning from Hardinge against 'indiscreet talk' at the Hôtel Majestic, most of the important business was conducted outside the official meetings – over dinners, in the bar or between sessions. In fact, the clerks where Oldham was working were almost certainly more aware of the bigger picture than some of the delegates themselves, as they saw a far wider range of material pass before their desks. However, the Foreign Office delegation felt increasingly frustrated by the lack of consultation, with Sir Eyre Crowe grumbling that:

> I see no object in our collecting reports and information. Nobody wants or uses them, and our pigeonholes are being filled with masses of papers which represent nothing but wastes of energy.[74]

Matters became even worse when the Council of Ten became the Council of Four in March, when Japan dropped out and the leaders of Britain, France, USA and Italy met informally to speed things along – although Italy also walked out over a territorial disagreement. Thus even Balfour was excluded from the decision-making process, with Hardinge complaining that:

> I cannot help feeling that things here are going very badly. The set-tlement of the terms of peace is now in the hands of the four Prime Ministers who meet and draw up terms without expert advice and without any record being taken of what passes.[75]

The pressure on Hardinge eventually told as he found himself 'for the first time in my life on the verge of a breakdown from overwork and over strain'. He began to suffer acute insomnia caused by:

> Annoyance at the way I saw the negotiations being conducted here in Paris, regardless of the knowledge and experience of foreign affairs of which there were plenty in the British delegation, but which was absolutely ignored by the negotiators as being inconve-nient towards some of their projects.[76]

There was also the stress of keeping things ticking over in London. Balfour commented in early February that, 'I confess to find it very difficult in all cases whether a subject is being dealt with in London at the Foreign Office or in Paris or both.'[77] Nicolson wrote in his diary on 17 April: 'How they must hate us over there, poor people. We never tell them what is happening and we nev-er answer any of their letters.'[78] This was a pertinent remark; after all, junior staff such as Oldham were faced with the challenge of re-integrating amongst their colleagues in Whitehall after the conference concluded.

The length of time it was taking to resolve the various issues was not lost on the watching world, who were suspicious that everyone was enjoying themselves a little bit too much. The Foreign Office had already turned down an offer from Thomas Cook in December 1918 to help with various tours of Paris – 'excursions in and around Paris are not contemplated for the British delegation to the Peace Conference, who will all be engaged on urgent official work'[79] – but it was unreasonable to expect that Paris would be all work and no play. Everyone who was anyone could be found on the fringes of the conference. Nicolson noted a typical evening's entertainment:

> Saturday 15 February: dine with Lutyens at the Meurice and back to the Majestic where they have a dance on. Prince of Wales there – still shy and sad.[80]

It was not long before the press picked up on extra-curricular activities. *The Times* reported on The Majestic at play in March 1919.

> Visitors to the Hotel Majestic in Paris may sometimes come away doubting whether everybody in it is as anxious as the rest of the world for the peace conference to do its work and to disperse. When one sees the dancing room, the theatre, the restaurant, all crowded with interesting figures and when one compares the lot of a secretary in ordinary life with the lot of the 140 efficient people who aid the delegates and the sub-delegates and the co-opted experts and the secretaries to the delegates and sub-delegates and experts, it is impossible to believe that the conference turns to the staff at the Majestic the same face that it turns to government potentates and ordinary citizens.[81]

In particular, the report drew attention to an evening entertainment put on by the British delegation's dramatic company, which packed out the theatre situated in the basement. The first play was in French; the second was a typical piece of British self-mockery – a series of skits in which all aspects of the conference were gently ridiculed.

> It was a pity that Mr Alwyn Parker was not present to hear
> the reference to *'Ali Parker and the 140 Clerks'*... A government
> department which was not laughed at could be safely pronounced
> a 'dud'.[82]

As the conference dragged on into yet another month, the *Times* correspondent summed up the mood back in England:

> It is a happy family at the Majestic: and it would be a good idea to
> give them all pensions to keep them there. Could we at the same
> time pension the Conference to go somewhere else?[83]

This was a little unfair on the '140 clerks' whose workload was relentless while the committees sat, continued to discuss and produced ever more paperwork – all of which was categorised, indexed and filed for reference. Yet men like Oldham, involved at the heart of the bureaucracy and thus privy to the multiple lines of negotiation, would still have had time to join the throngs of diplomats and politicians mingling in the foyer of the Majestic for the various receptions, as well as their counterparts from other delegations and countless international lawyers who regaled them with tall tales over dinner or at the bar. Such conversations and contacts could make or break careers – especially if the right information was passed to the correct interested party who could return the favour later on. It is hard to describe this 'below the counter' diplomacy as espionage, as technically everyone was on the same side and working towards a common goal. However, a large amount of horse trading was conducted at the Majestic and elsewhere that would decide the fate of millions, as borders were drawn and redrawn based on subtle negotiations outside the committee rooms. It was in this environment that Oldham saw how diplomacy worked at grass roots level, despite Hardinge's reminder to delegates and support staff against 'indiscreet talk'.

Then, suddenly, a new pace was injected into proceedings in mid-April when the Council of Four invited the Germans to hear their peace terms, summoning them to attend the conference at the start of May. A quiet panic gripped the Foreign Office staff as they redoubled their work in the hope that they could iron out all the issues with the proposed treaty. Headlam-Morley expressed his grave concerns on 21 April:

> I am getting hopeless about the whole business; there is no fully responsible control exercised from the political side. Many things have been left until the last moment; the work is very much in arrears and I do not see how it is possible to have the treaty ready by the end of the week. What I fear is that the Germans will be able to put their fingers on a great number of points which show bad workmanship. Throughout, nothing has been thought of in advance and points of the greatest importance have been postponed until the last moment.[84]

The final push brought most of the delegates to their knees – Nicolson confided in his diary on 13 May that he was 'nearly dead with fatigue and indignation'.[85] Nevertheless, a draft treaty was ready to present to the Germans on 7 May. Gallic desire to weaken Germany as much as possible had largely won the day. When rebuked over the severity of the terms, Clemenceau scolded Lloyd George that Britain had the safety of the Channel to protect it whereas France had to share a land border. This paranoia lay behind huge territorial demands and continued occupation of the left bank of the Rhine, coupled with stringent financial reparations to the Allies in compensation for damage caused during the war and a wider demilitarisation of the German state. Equally contentious was the admission of German war guilt. Needless to say, when the German delegation was invited to Versailles to hear the conditions that were to be imposed their Foreign Minister, Graf von Brockdorff-Rantzau, declared:

> We know the full brunt of hate that confronts us here. You demand from us to confess we were the only guilty party of war; such a confession in my mouth would be a lie.

The Germans protested that they had not been permitted to take part in the negotiations and therefore that the terms they were being asked to accept were unjust – exactly what many Foreign Office staff had been concerned about. Despite a deep aversion to the conditions, which had provoked wide-spread condemnation back home, they were given no choice but to sign – although this only took place on 28 June 1919 under the threat of renewed hostilities, with Allied troops prepared to march out of the Rhineland to force compliance if the final deadline was not met.

If the aim was to humiliate Germany, then the Versailles ceremony was a success – the acknowledgement of war guilt was still in place. The ceremony took place in the glittering hall of mirrors in Louis XIV's palace at Versailles, with hundreds of dignitaries present to watch the historic moment. Nicolson was one of them and he vividly recalled when the time came for the Germans to sign:

> Through the door at the end appear two *huissiers* [officers of the court] with silver chains. They march in single file. After them come four officers of France, Great Britain, America and Italy. And then, isolated and pitiable, come the two German delegates. Dr Muller, Dr Bell. The silence is terrifying. Their feet upon a strip of parquet between the Savonnerie carpets echo hollow and duplicate. They keep their eyes fixed away from those two thousand staring eyes, fixed upon the ceiling. They are deathly pale. They do not appear as representatives of a brutal militarism. The one is thin and pink-eyelidded; the second fiddle in a Brunswick orchestra. The other is moon-faced and suffering: a *privatdozent*. It is almost painful.[86]

Later that night he added that there were:

> Celebrations at the hotel afterwards. We are given free champagne at the expense of the taxpayer. It is very bad champagne. Go out on to the boulevards afterwards. To bed, sick of life.[87]

Although the main work was done, the peace process continued beyond Versailles as, one by one, the Central Powers were brought to account. Austria signed the Treaty of Saint-Germain on 10 September; Bulgaria agreed to the Treaty of Neuilly on 27 November while it took until 4 June 1920 before Hungary was able to sign the Treaty of Trianon, given internal upheavals and war with its neighbours throughout most of 1919. The last peace agreement was concluded with the dismantling of the Ottoman Empire at the Treaty of Sèvres on 10 August 1920. However, by this date the British secretariat at the Majestic had long since disbanded and drifted home. By the end of June 1919 the hotel was virtually empty. Oldham and his associates had played their part in making history and with some regret returned to London to face their abandoned colleagues in a vastly different Foreign Office to the one they had left behind.

Chapter five

DECIPHERING THE NEW WORLD ORDER (1920–1924)

Coolness of head and temperateness of action were not at that period at all characteristic of the Foreign Office... From 1922 onwards crisis succeeded crisis in a hideous, unending chain... The world was upside down and any attempt at reconstruction could be nothing more than empiric.

GEORGE ANTROBUS, KING'S FOREIGN SERVICE MESSENGER, WRITING IN 1940

Caught up in the greatest diplomatic event the world had ever seen and having witnessed at close quarters how the 'other' side of the service worked, Oldham's appetite for a similar career was truly whetted. No doubt numerous conversations at the Majestic with consulate staff had fired up his enthusiasm for a peripatetic life in far-flung embassies situated in exotic climes. So, on 12 April 1919, during a crucial phase of the conference, he reactivated his application to join the consular service that had first been submitted back in 1916.

Given the focus of attention on Paris and then the subsequent process of finalising treaties with the other Central Powers, it is not surprising that it took the best part of a year before a meeting of a small Foreign Office Departmental Committee could be convened. On 26 January 1920, the committee considered the applications of 40 hopeful candidates who had been granted either temporary or honorary posts and whose claims were still pending.

At this stage, Oldham was very confident of success. Not only had he been part of the peace process, working tirelessly behind the scenes gathering first-hand experience of diplomacy in action but also he had been formally recognised for his role in the process – earning promotion to junior executive grade on 1 January 1920. Sir John Tilley, who had signed Oldham's release papers into the army and supported his career throughout, was one of the board members – but crucially he had not been present in Paris to witness Oldham operating under the daily pressures of the conference.

Of the 40 candidates, 15 were accepted and 14 rejected. Oldham was one of 11 left in limbo with applications held over, pending further inquiries. Nevertheless, he was nominated to a permanent post in the consular service on 29 January 1920, upheld by a promotions board on 10 February. His languages, which now included French, Spanish, Italian and German, had earned him a position as the Third Vice Consul in Rio – an admittedly junior role in an embassy, supporting the consul, but about as far away from the European battlefields as it was possible to get.

However, his dreams of an exotic posting to South America were cruelly dashed. The promotions board met again on 18 February and made various changes to the proposed list of new appointments, including the note that 'a fresh proposal to be made for the appointment of Third Vice Consul at Rio, as Mr Oldham is not to be taken into the Consular Service.'[88] The recommendation was placed on file to this effect on 26 February, but it would take until 15 March before a letter was sent to Oldham to put him out of his misery:

> With reference to Foreign Office letter No 515146/250K of 12 April past in which you were informed that your application for permanent employment in the Salaried Consular Service was being reserved for further consideration, I am directed by Earl Curzon of Kedleston to inform you that your case has been carefully reviewed and that he regrets to be unable to accept your candidature for admission to the services.[89]

With his hopes of a diplomatic career dashed by the new Foreign Secretary who replaced Balfour in October 1919, Oldham was faced with a return to mundane duties within a reformed Foreign Office. His bitter disappointment perhaps made him miss the fact that his superiors within the Chief Clerk's Department fully appreciated his work – hence his promotion – and that he was transferred to a key position within a new Communications Department, created as part of a wider restructure of the Foreign Office.

The Foreign Office had already taken charge of Britain's Diplomatic and Consular Services. Among other changes, the Central Registry and sub-registries were overhauled and replaced by a single Registry with three branches. In addition, a temporary Historical Section, set up during the war, was made permanent and transferred to the Librarian to manage and the Parliamentary Department was disbanded, with the King's Messengers and cipher clerks moving to the new Communications Department. The Foreign Office also took over the responsibility of the Government Code and Cipher School from the Admiralty in 1922, with oversight of the Secret Intelligence Service. These were important changes and reflected the way in which the work of the office had grown during the conflict and continued to expand with Britain's role within the new League of Nations. However, the general antipathy felt by the Foreign Office towards the League, its international rival, was reflected in the fact that only a sub-section of the Western political department was initially assigned to League business.

The origins of the new Communications Department lay in earnest attempts to provide a career for both messengers and cipher staff alike. A note placed on file in March 1919 sketched out the thinking behind the proposed merger of the two units, at the express wish of Lord Hardinge, the Permanent Under-Secretary at the Foreign Office whose experiences in Paris made him realise the importance of a unified system. The unnamed author was blunt to the point of insulting about the calibre of recruits:

> One difficulty about forming a cipher department is how to make it a tolerable career. No young man ought to settle down to a life of ciphering just as no young man ought to settle down to a life of carrying bags. Moreover, we could not expect to get the Treasury to sanction a new service with an inferior

entrance exam calculated to meet the requirements of people
with no sufficient brains for the diplomatic or consular services
but with qualifications which would make them absolutely trust-
worthy. They might however sanction an extension of an existing
service such as the Messenger Service. For that there is no exam
worth mentioning.[90]

It is worth bearing in mind that Oldham was now categorised amongst those
'with no sufficient brains' for the Diplomatic Service and was selected for the
new department, albeit in an elevated position as one of the permanent clerical officers. The aim of the merger was to ensure the maintenance of a body of
men who could undertake both ciphering and message deliveries:

I think the two services would fit in with each other: occasional
journeys would relieve the monotony of ciphering and teach the
cipherers a good deal that would be useful about places and things.
The messengers would be employed during their spells at home
and would be more in hand.[91]

The finer points of recruitment to the new combined group were then discussed further, with new admissions limited to British subjects – men, of
course – between the ages of 30 and 40 who had previously served in one of
the Armed Forces.

It is essentially a service for men who have done something else
and not one which should be used for giving soft jobs to young
men. Two or more experts now serving in Cipher Department
might be taken on although they have not served.[92]

Some degree of qualification was required, with the introduction of an exam
covering English, French and arithmetic which was to be 'rather more severe
than for messengers', followed by a selection board from within the Foreign
Office. However, pay was to be less than permanent staff, initially proposed at

£300 rising £20 per year to a maximum of £500, with a compulsory retire-ment age set at 60 and – crucially – no pension. The four remaining King's Messengers were brought across, with the temporary cipher staff. It was ini-tially envisaged that even junior diplomats 'should have a turn in the depart-ment, vice consuls also, even if only for a month or two,' so that they gained valuable insight into the way communications were managed at the centre before they were given a post overseas.

So what exactly did the new Communications Department do? In the words of Sir John Tilley:

> The primary duty of the Communications Department is the ci-phering and deciphering of telegrams and the arrangements for the transmission of written matter to and from our posts abroad. A lifetime entirely spent on the latter work must necessarily be rather dull and perhaps trying to the eyesight and brain; it is clearly better that a man should have occasional respites from work on telegrams by going on periodical journeys abroad as King's Messenger.[93]

However, to *really* understand the work we need look no further than George Antrobus, who served in the new department and described the intricate workings that took place behind the walls of the Foreign Office in Whitehall, largely in the functional spaces where Oldham and his co-workers were situ-ated, away from the grandly furnished state areas reserved for the politicians and visiting dignitaries.

> The inside of the building is a hodge-podge of amorphous rooms and dark, straggling corridors… The visitor is still struck with… the smell of Irish stew… I have often savoured steak-and-onions, and sometimes even roast pheasant, in the Foreign Office. These gastronomic odours, presumably from the housekeeper's kitchen, are not made easier to endure by the fact that there is no canteen or restaurant within the office.[94]

The Communications Department's premises consisted of a good-sized room for the ciphering and coding, a similar room for typing and copying, a small room known as the Distribution Room, another small room for the administrative and clerical work of the department, and a slightly larger room for the chief. They were very conveniently placed, close to the entrance, and all but one faced northward over the Horse Guards Parade. A north aspect, as artists know, is by far the best to work so long as the windows are ample, as it avoids the direct sunshine but gives a good light.[95]

Given Antrobus's criticism of the 'dark' and 'cramped' Foreign Office described earlier, he changed tack when justifying his own space and put a rather hypocritical brave face on his own working conditions:

There is a good deal of nonsense talked about office accommodation; vast and palatial rooms are often a great mistake and lead to more physical exertion owing to their size; cramped quarters – and ours were decidedly cramped – frequently give the best results.[96]

Yet he provides an insider's view of some of the most secretive and important rooms in the UK's entire diplomatic network – the fabled Room 22 where messages were coded and despatched around the world.

The cipher room itself, on which all others depended, was numbered 22; Room 22 will be a familiar title to many civil servants, both of the Foreign Office and of other Departments. It was a room with an atmosphere of its own – bare, gaunt, exceptionally lofty and lighted by two vast, rattling, plate-glass sash windows, it had no pretensions to art or beauty.

At the heart of the process lay the ciphering and deciphering of letters and telegrams. To do this, the temporary clerical officers would make reference to the official code books which were used in standard form across Britain's diplomatic networks so that only personnel with access to them could decipher the messages. To have the official cipher code books fall into enemy hands would compromise the entire communications operation, leaving Britain's diplomatic correspondence open to interpretation by others. Nothing short of a full reissue of new code books would ensure that a leak was closed – a costly and time-consuming business.

In theory, according to Antrobus, the process of coding was simple.

> A code book... is nothing more than a dictionary in which you look up the equivalent in the code language of an English word or phrase. The only difference between a code book and an ordinary dictionary is that the code words are usually limited in number so that each one of them has to serve for two or more English interpretations in close alphabetical proximity.[97]

Thus several words of similar spelling could lead to accidental confusion when interpreting the message – as indeed happened on occasion:

> There have, of course, been many improvements in code books since the days of which I am speaking... But even in 1915, I do not think the decoder had much excuse for making a perfectly respectable consul say that the distance between his residence and his office was four miles as Sir Eyre Crowe flies.

Antrobus described the daily bustle of activity in Room 22 in vivid detail, as staff coded and decoded the various telegrams piled high in the respective out- or in-trays – square and deep tin trays sitting on a small table beside the chief's desk.

> Picture to yourself a room about 25 feet by 20, furnished with half a dozen tables, a dozen chairs of a plain office pattern, two big ranges of cupboards 9 feet high, a rather more elaborate desk for the chief, and the inevitable water bottle and glass without which no Whitehall room is complete.[98]

The atmosphere in the room was a heady mix of noise and smoke:

> The smoke comes from the pipes and cigarettes – the pace is too
> hot for cigars – of those who write; the noise comes in a rhythmi-
> cal roar from the lips of those who read. For the whole secret of
> really high-speed working is cooperation; you work in pairs, one
> reading from the code book and the other writing. A good coder
> can dictate from the code book as fast as a good writer can take it
> down, that is to say at the rate of 25 to 30 code words a minute. In
> decoding, this means that the writer must be able to take down, in
> reasonably legible longhand, a good 50 words a minute and keep it
> up hour after hour.[99]

In charge of Room 22 was Algernon Hay, who possessed 'the supreme art
of making others obey him without knowing they were obedient'. Antrobus
wrote fondly of his former boss, commenting:

> He knew how to talk, not merely to those in his own station of life
> but to everyone, from a royal duke to a scullery maid. He never
> let anyone down or gave anyone away – things which are much
> easier to do than the uninitiated may imagine; true loyalty, such as
> his, needs qualities of the head as well as of the heart. He had all a
> Scotsman's mixture of shrewdness and generosity.[100]

Under Hay, what went on in Room 22 stayed in Room 22, a code of silence
that ensured that any problems were resolved within the closed circle of the
King's Messengers.

Once the correspondence had been coded or decoded, it was taken next
door to the typists' room, where up to 16 girls worked where there is 'less
smoke but even more noise'.

> They are all working on wax stencils, as the copies have to be du-
> plicated afterwards and the clatter of the ribbon-less machines is

deafening. We notice that the girls, even at the feverish pace they
have to work, are in no wise [sic] discomposed.[101]

Next, the typed up material needed to be copied.

In a little room adjoining are the duplicators, three or four machines operated by as many girls. These young ladies are, strange
to say, not Foreign Office employees; they are on the staff of the
Stationery Office and only temporarily attached. They are skilled
experts in the manipulation of their machines, each of which is
now a producing a snowstorm of foolscap sheets. The standard of
work is very high; the paper is of the best, and the quality of the
typing is a joy to behold.[102]

Once the copies had been completed, the final stage of the process got under
way in Room 5.

The next room, which is called the Distribution Room,
offers perhaps the most animated spectacle of all. Here the
typescript of every telegram is checked against the manuscript,
the duplicated copies are sorted out and distributed among
the pigeonholes of a gigantic cabinet and the finished products
enclosed in despatch boxes for conveyance by the home service
messengers to their destinations. Every important telegram
goes not only to the various departmental heads of the office, but
to the King, the Cabinet – a separate copy for each member –
and to various important personages in any other office that may
be concerned.[103]

Antrobus also sketched the role of the various clerical officers who worked in
the department – not involved with the ciphering process as such, but ensuring the smooth running of the operation as well as tackling any wider issues
as they arose:

> He reads the telegrams and marks them but he has no time to di-
> gest them; he has an automatic eye for an error, for both coders
> and typists make mistakes… he blue-pencils a line and rings a bell.
> 'Take this,' he says to the girl who answers, 'back to Room 22 and
> ask them what the hell they mean by this tripe. And when they've
> put it right you'll have to do an amended copy.' He has to shout, for
> all the while another girl is slamming down the lids of a series of
> despatch boxes, locking them, and crashing them down on a table
> near the door.[104]

Across the passage was another room that Oldham and his colleagues would
have been familiar with. Administration for the travelling arrangements of the
King's Foreign Service Messengers was carried out here. It included the itin-
eraries for all journeys to be undertaken, complete with timetables and any
necessary directions.

> It is a small room, cumbered with a good deal of large furni-
> ture in the severest official style. Every unoccupied space, on the
> floor, the tables and even the one chair that is not being sat on,
> is crammed with a miscellaneous collection of parcels, boxes,
> envelopes, bags, cases, sacks, cartons, pouches, wallets, locks,
> keys, cipher books, code books, waybills, schedules, rosters
> and a job lot of large and small objects including a safe, a pair of
> antlers from some exotic beast, an opera hat and three dozen tins
> of bully beef [corned beef].[105]

Thus, amid the clutter and chaos, it was easy for important items to go missing. It is fair to say that security within the Foreign Office was somewhat lax,
despite office keepers and a locksmith whose presence was designed to ensure
that a semblance of order was enforced and that the presses in which documents were kept remained locked when not in use. The senior staff officer
would preside over all these areas, an important role:

He distributes all the cipher and code books, special circulars, and instructions – in itself a vast and complicated task. Moreover, he superintends the locks, keys, safes, strong rooms – in a word, the security of British Diplomatic and Consular property throughout the world. It is no wonder that he looks a little careworn.[106]

The pace of work was often frenetic, as the aforementioned passages would suggest – with the urgency of messages increasing the pressure was on the cipher staff to come up with the goods. As a result, there was always the potential for mistakes to be made, or – even worse – to unwittingly 'leak' sensitive information to the press.

Unlike other departments, ours was open on Sundays. We then suffered much interruption from various outside sources with which we did not come into contact on weekdays. Newspapers, who knew well that the regular channels of information were less easily accessible on Sundays, often rang us up and tried to extract details of some particular event. They were, of course, fully aware of what they ought to do: the News Department always made thorough and complete arrangements for such emergencies when the office, as a whole, was closed; but Fleet Street guessed rightly that any news there was must come to us first and I daresay they hoped to entrap one of us into an indiscreet disclosure.[107]

This was one of the reasons behind the strict application process – to ensure the recruitment of the calibre of person who could be trusted with sensitive information.

We can discern glimpses of Ernest Oldham's work during this period and it is clear that he enjoyed considerable influence over the future direction of the Communications Department, especially the King's Messengers. For someone acting as a clerical officer, he certainly appeared in some exotic locations in the early 1920s – there is no way he can be described as a desk-bound civil servant. In 1921, he was charged with undertaking a round trip to Constantinople, with the outward journey by sea and the return leg overland via some of the key drop-off points on the King's Messenger itinerary. The purpose of his mission was to explore ways in which the routes could be reorganised. Oldham left London on 4 February 1921, returning home two months later on 3 April. However, it took him the best part of a year before he submitted his expenses to the Claims Department on 17 March 1922, asking for £18.16.1½ that was due to him. He added an explanation of various items that he'd included in the account along with his report on the messenger service.[108]

To get a sense of the journey Oldham undertook that spring, we can turn once more to Antrobus, with an occasional aside from Wheeler-Holohan, seasoned travellers who independently captured some of the excitement Oldham must have felt as he set out for the first time. This was a major undertaking for Oldham, taking in some of the more exotic parts of eastern Europe as well as the jewel of the Bosphorus, Constantinople.

> Picture, then, the vestibule of the Foreign Office. It is a rather forbidding looking place… There are some massive columns and arches, there is a large weighing machine; oil-paintings hang on the walls; boxes, parcels and crates litter the floor. Near the back, under the arches, stand two rows of bags, confidential and non-confidential, the former distinguished by the black crosses on their labels.
>
> It is the eve of the King's Messenger's departure. The bags are sealed by four o'clock in the afternoon and an hour or two later the Messenger appears, glances over the bags he will have to take and makes a rough mental estimate of just how much room will be left for himself in the Wagon-Lit's compartment [sleeping carriage].[109]

Oldham would have travelled on the train with the bags in the compartment at all times, often crammed into the space under his feet. The first task was to take the uncrossed bags containing regular post to Victoria station for storage in preparation for the boat-train to the coast which would leave the following day. The next morning, Oldham returned to the Foreign Office to pick up the crossed bags containing secret or sensitive material. Having collected his waybills, special red courier's passport and any last-minute instructions, Oldham jumped in the waiting car, followed by the traditional refrain of the doorkeeper to send him on his way – 'A good journey and safe return, sir.'

At Victoria, Oldham embarked on the boat-train to Dover and locked himself in the special compartment reserved for the King's Messenger, having asked the porter and inspectors to help him load the heavy bags into the compartment. This would have been the first of many cash 'tips' that Oldham was entitled to distribute, all part of the routine and ritual of the journey.

> You have got to tip the right people at the right time and on the right scale – no more and no less; and you have to bear in mind that you must render an account of all your disbursements against the advance you have received. This is very nicely calculated to cover, not the whole of your living expenses, but the additional ones entailed by the journey.[110]

A few hours later on arrival at Dover, the porters would load the bags onto his cabin.

> At the Channel, he scores heavily over the ordinary traveller. He is in no hurry, everyone knows he is coming and his cabin on the steamer and his compartment on the continental train are reserved for him. He can, and if he is wise he does, take his time in getting both on to and off the steamer.[111]

According to Wheeler-Holohan, the experienced King's Messenger would lock his cabin and then settle down for the journey

> [in the] smoking room, gazing reflectively into the amber of a glass of beer or a whisky and soda.[112]

On landing at the port, Oldham would have secured the services of another porter to disembark the bags, make his way through passport control and customs showing his red passport marked *courier du Roi* and found his reserved sleeper car for the long journey across Europe.

> The great European express trains have an air of mystery and romance about them. Truth to tell, this is but ill-deserved... They are slow, they stop often and they have the irritating habit of traversing the finest scenery at night.
>
> The King's Messenger has a comfortable journey. His main temptation is to eat too much on the first day; lack of exercise and the strange cuisine of eastern Europe will then land him at his destination in the full glow of indigestion. Time hangs heavy on his hands... You read and you sleep, you sleep and you read; at the frontiers you rouse yourself for the passport examination and at intervals you are met by branch couriers or Chancery servants (the office-keepers of diplomatic missions) and hand them the bags they have come to collect.[113]

Wheeler-Holohan described the final leg of Oldham's journey, one that he had taken many times.

> In those days the Orient Express had not been re-established. The Messengers went via Paris to Rome, thence to Brindisi, whence they sailed on one of the Lloyd-Triestino steamers. The next call was Corfu, then came the journey through the Corinth Canal to the Piraeus: here one disembarked and went up to Athens, in a few hours returning to the ship and so on to Constantinople through the Dardanelles. With what mingled feelings did those who had served on that ill-omened peninsula gaze on the place again! Constantinople was reached in the early hours of the morning; here the ship lay to, and a naval tug came alongside to take the King's Messenger ashore and so avoid the delay of *pratique* and customs.

> Constantinople from the sea in the early morning, almost veiled in
> the mist rising from the water, with its domes and minarets gleam-
> ing in the sun, what it promised the imagination and what a sink of
> a city one found it to be when, after landing at Top Hani, one drove
> up to Pera through the filthy and smelly back streets![114]

According to both Antrobus and Wheeler-Holohan, at journey's end the
King's Messenger would have some time to himself for a few days.

> During this time his services are 'at the disposal of the ambassa-
> dor', though as a rule he has his time as much to himself as social
> functions will allow.[115]

As a first time visitor, Oldham probably undertook some sightseeing in
Constantinople, but equally given his status as a King's Messenger he would
have been required to mix and mingle with the varied British diplomats, press
representatives and secret service officers who congregated at the various bars
and hotels such as the Club, a favourite haunt for international travellers.

> His discretion is thoroughly tested, for he is the link between the
> diplomatic missions; he hears all the gossip; he knows what is going
> on in London and his acquaintance with Whitehall and Downing
> Street is up to date and first hand. A fool or a talker could make
> untold mischief.[116]

Alternatively, he could meet some very interesting people and it would
appear that Oldham struck up a friendship with Harold Courtenay
Armstrong, a former Indian Army officer who had a colourful campaign in Mesopotamia, suffering capture and imprisonment at the siege
of Kut-el-Amarah before subsequently escaping from captivity. After the
war, Armstrong was posted to Constantinople as military attaché to the
British High Commission, where he stayed on the staff of the Allied Forces
of Occupation in Turkey after the break-up of the Ottoman empire; he

would eventually write a series of books about his time in Constantinople, including a biography of the great Turkish leader Mustapha Kemel Ataturk, *Grey Wolf*, in 1932. Oldham considered Armstrong as one of his closer associates.

The return journey was by train and took in all the key European capitals so that Oldham could examine the conditions under which the King's Messengers operated, as well as the costs, risk and dangers in the upturned post-war world of the 1920s. One of the places that Oldham visited was Bucharest, where he was issued with a new passport on 17 March. As with Constantinople, it would appear that he made some important connections while in Romania that would serve him well in later life.

This was a period during which alliances between the expanded Kingdom of Romania, the newly formed Czechoslovakia and the Kingdom of Serbs, Croats and Slovenes were drawn up, known as the Little Entente. This followed wars with the Hungarian Soviet Republic in 1919. The new alliances were of interest to Britain as a counterweight to the threat of Communism that, as we will shortly see, was gripping the attention of many post-war states. Once again, the King's Messenger had a pivotal role to play in passing on information – formal and often more importantly informal – to various classes of folk – lawyers as well as diplomats.

Given the travelling, interspersed with bursts of sociability with strangers wanting to make his acquaintance because of what he represented as much as who he was, this would have been a gruelling month for Oldham. Added to this was the burden of his assignment – to assess, analyse and improve upon the system.

> He is probably rather jaded and weary. The mental strain of keeping watch over the bags is beginning to tell; and the monotony of the Wagon-Lits, the lack of exercise, and the hasty meals necessitated by guarding the bags have had their effect on his temper and his optimism… He arrives in London and drives to the Foreign Office, where he deposits his bags and hands over his waybill.[117]

Oldham's mission was clearly a success that brought him even greater prominence within the department – because a month after his return from main-
land Europe, he was given an assignment of the highest prominence imagin-
able. On 9 May 1922, an urgent message was sent through to the Foreign
Office on behalf of the King, who was in Belgium visiting the newly laid-out
Commonwealth war cemeteries. A document was requested without delay.
The only way to transport the material during the King's visit was to despatch
a King's Messenger by plane and Oldham was the man chosen for the job.

While his colleagues made the necessary arrangements with Instone Air
Line Limited, Oldham was handed the relevant envelope and rushed to the
airfield. He donned flying gear and jumped on board a de Havilland DH.18 –
a single-engine biplane made predominantly of plywood and wire that was a
larger version of the planes he had first seen fighting to the death over the skies
of France in 1918. This time Oldham was himself a passenger, seated inside
the enclosed cabin whilst the pilot navigated his way across the Channel to the
landing field on the other side. On touchdown, he would have been whisked
off to hand the paperwork to a high-ranking dignitary, most likely the ambassador or one of his staff. All told, the emergency trip cost £40 in airfares – a vast
amount for the time – as well as £4.13.0 in sundry expenses and 12 shillings
worth of tips. Oldham was the hero of the hour.[118]

However, Antrobus recalled the incident slightly differently, albeit nearly
two decades after the event:

> Some time ago a King's Messenger was hurriedly summoned and
> despatched to Paris in a special plane. It was a record job and the
> Communications Department was rather proud of it. With an
> air of modest triumph the Messenger handed an envelope to the
> grateful ambassador and returned to London in a glow of duty
> well done. Unfortunately, the vital document was left behind and
> the envelope – on whose transport such care and cost had been
> lavished, contained – if I remember right – an information from
> a London club that the prices of the members' luncheon had
> been raised by sixpence. I need hardly add that neither the King's

Messenger nor the Communications Department were responsible for the accidental substitution, and that the little comedy led to no tragic result.[119]

Oldham was involved in other last-minute and sensitive journeys as well. For example, in December 1920 he submitted an expenses claim for two recent journeys, one to Lucerne and the other to Brussels. The first was almost certainly linked to the ratification of the Treaty of Sèvres which was held at Lucerne in late August 1920, while the second was associated with the Council of the League of Nations meeting in Brussels that mainly focused on the wars that had erupted between Poland, Russia and Lithuania in 1919.[120]

On 23 and 24 September 1922, he was travelling to Calais via Boulogne to meet 'Mr Gascoigne', who had 'special minutes of the conference' – probably a reference to the frantic negotiations to end the Greco-Turkish war in which Britain was involved following the collapse of the Treaty of Sèvres and the rise of the Turkish independence movement led by Ataturk. Oldham was required to explain various extra items of expenditure 'which were owing to the time of the journey', suggesting it took place outside normal hours and therefore at relatively short notice.[121] Having been involved at various stages of the framing, ratification and collapse of the Treaty of Sèvres, there is a neat symmetry to the fact Oldham was summoned in September 1923 to undertake three journeys in short succession between London and Dieppe.[122] It is likely that it was in connection with the conference at Lausanne, where the Treaty of Sèvres was finally amended to take account of the conclusion of the Turkish wars. No wonder Oldham was so interested in Harold Armstrong's insights into the career of Ataturk.

When he wasn't dashing around Europe on urgent business himself, Oldham was involved in organising the routes of others. It was not just regular King's Messengers that undertook journeys on his behalf. The use of unofficial messengers to carry diplomatic despatches was not uncommon. During the war, officers of the army and navy were detailed by the Admiralty and War Office to carry bags, as indeed were trusted captains in the merchant navy. The practice was continued in the years following the Paris Conference and

the day books of the Foreign Office are littered with requests from men of
military rank or status claiming for their travel expenses as King's Foreign
Service Messengers. However, men such as Antrobus, who considered themselves the real King's Messengers, appointed through open competition, grew
quite irate with the number of men outside their ranks who falsely laid claim
to their title. According to Wheeler-Holohan,

> Some of these gentlemen were called, or used to call themselves,
> 'King's Messengers'. I knew two of them personally and remem-
> ber that they used that title. This caused intense feeling as far as the
> real King's Foreign Service Messengers were concerned.[123]

But like it or not, a separate system was indeed in place, and Oldham built up
a network of trusted men to send, often junior staff such as Raymond Oake,
who regularly appeared in the Foreign Office day books, claiming expenses
that Oldham would authenticate. Tensions between the official and unofficial
King's Messengers never really abated.

Therefore by the mid-1920s, Oldham enjoyed an influential position within
the Foreign Office – he was the puppet-master, pulling the strings of Britain's
communications network with Europe and the near east, ensuring the most
expedient routes to destinations both close and distant. As part of the team of
permanent officials entrusted with ensuring the safety of both message and
messengers, Oldham found himself acting for King and country in the front
line once more, albeit in a very different struggle. Instead of facing German
machine guns in the woods at St Quentin, a more subtle foe lay in the shadows. This enemy could strike at home or abroad at any time – agents of the
Bolshevik revolutionary forces that were sweeping out of Russia, a communist
menace that sought to gain access to the heart of Britain's diplomatic network
in whatever way they could.

Chapter six

THE MARCH OF THE BOLSHEVIKS (1924–1927)

Bolshevism is moving steadily westwards, has overwhelmed Poland, and is poisoning Germany.

US PRESIDENT WOODROW WILSON, 1919

Within a year all Europe will be communist.

GRIGORI ZINOVIEV, PRESIDENT OF COMINTERN (COMMUNIST INTERNATIONAL), 1919

If the Russian revolutions of 1917 sent a shockwave through the world, then the brutal murder of Tsar Nicholas II and his family on 17 July 1918 was met with revulsion and disbelief, as well as realisation that the Bolshevik movement was prepared to do whatever it took to preserve its hold on power.

Ernest Oldham's life and work in the Communications Department were directly affected by events in Russia after 1917. Without spending too much time on the details, it is important to understand just why European states were so concerned about the impact of the Russian revolutions. First, and perhaps most importantly, the collapse of the Triple Entente had ushered in a new era where ideological class warfare – communism against capitalism, the proletariat versus the privileged bourgeoisie – created international tension in a post-Versailles world shattered by the recent global conflict. The threat of armies clashing along geo-political lines was replaced by fears of communist agents of change operating within states to foment revolution, fears which grew more hysterical throughout the 1920s and 1930s.

At the time of the Versailles Treaty, this was not a baseless concern; all across Europe, new countries were born while old ones were torn apart as the effects of Versailles were played out. Germany itself had witnessed this first-hand with its November revolution of 1918 being followed by the rise of socialist politics that stopped just short of embracing communism. The establishment of the Weimar Republic in 1919 ended any further movement in that direction. Hungary was also torn apart by internal protest driven by the working classes and the Hungarian Soviet Republic was established in 1919. However, the regime collapsed within months without support from their comrades in Russia.

Russian inability to assist another nascent communist regime was due to the increasingly brutal civil war being fought between the revolutionary Red Army of the Bolsheviks and the anti-communist White Army. The latter were initially aided by Allied troops, which increased the hostility of the Bolshevik leaders towards western states thereafter. However, western enthusiasm for prolonged military involvement waned in 1919 and by 1920 the White Army was defeated in most of Russia's associated provinces. It would be a further two years before Siberia and the far east were fully under Red control. Nevertheless, many former Russian provinces gained independence – Poland, Finland, Latvia, Lithuania and Estonia – while others were only subdued through the Red Terror. Oppression and atrocities such as torture and massacres were employed in places such as the Ukraine to ensure compliance to the new political system. It is not officially known how many people died, but a conservative estimate put casualties in the hundreds of thousands.

It was the Bolshevik state security organisation, the Cheka, which undertook the repression. Created by Lenin on 20 December 1917 as the 'All-Russian Emergency Commission for Combating Counter-Revolution and Sabotage', its role was to fight any attempt to undermine the communist system at home, with local Cheka established in all the major cities and regions to suppress political opposition and persecute deserters from the Red Army. The result was many thousands of people fled Russia during the civil war, ending up as refugees in places such as Constantinople.

Internal security through fear and violence was one thing but it was the stated intent of the leaders of the Russian state to export the Bolshevik revolution to the rest of the world, especially as Russia was faced by, in the words of Lenin, 'hostile capitalist encirclement'.[124] Alternative mechanisms were needed to spread communism within other nation states and thus the Soviet Communist International (or Comintern) was founded in 1919 to struggle 'by all available means, including armed force, for the overthrow of the international bourgeoisie and for the creation of an international Soviet republic as a transition stage to the complete abolition of the state'.[125] Comintern essentially encouraged and provided support for revolutions in other western countries. One immediate outcome was the formation of the Communist Party of Great Britain in 1920, a merger of several smaller Marxist groups, labour movements and socialist parties, which was then re-founded in 1921 when more organisations joined.

The leaders of the Russian Soviet Federative Socialist Republic also saw diplomacy as another way to achieve its goals, by keeping its enemies – which pretty much consisted of the rest of the world – divided. The main drawback to employing diplomacy on any scale was that by 1920 only Estonia, Finland, Latvia and Lithuania formally recognised the new country and then purely out of expediency as a means of confirming their own independence. The fact that the Bolsheviks had signed the Treaty of Brest-Litovsk meant exclusion from the Paris Peace Conference, the Treaty of Versailles and the League of Nations. They had also earned the growing distrust of America, which was gripped by the first red scare in response to communist ideals. The Russians were isolated from the diplomatic community and were unable to operate consulates and embassies across the world.

Nevertheless, there were some signs of a thaw in international relations, particularly on humanitarian grounds during the great famine of 1921–23, during which several million people perished. Organisations such as the American Relief Association, under the control of future US President Herbert Hoover, provided food and support when Lenin softened his stance towards outside assistance. At the same time Lenin introduced his New Economic Policy – a form of 'state capitalism' that was deemed necessary to breathe life into a moribund economy shattered by constant warfare since 1914.

Yet one thing that did not soften was Lenin's determination to continue the revolution abroad. In an attempt to exert even greater control, the State Political Directorate – abbreviated to GPU from the Russian *Gosudarstven-noye politicheskoye upravlenie* – was formed on 6 February 1922 to supersede the Cheka. The GPU acted as a combination of intelligence service and state police within Russia, and also had a foreign department involved with overseas intelligence.

At the same time, in a move designed to consolidate the political gains of the 1917 revolution within existing Soviet republics, delegates from the Russian, Transcaucasian, Ukrainian and Byelorussian governments agreed to create a new federal state. They approved the creation of the Union of Soviet Socialist Republics on 28 December 1922 with Lenin at the head. The GPU was transferred from Russian control in 1923 and became the All Union State Political Administration of the USSR – or OGPU (*Obyedinyonnoye gosudarstven-noye politicheskoye upravleniye*). Part of its remit was to operate agents on foreign soil, establishing *rezidentura* or a base of intelligence operations, usually within an official organisation such as an embassy. OGPU would place key staff in prominent positions, thus giving them a legal reason to be there. The *rezident*, or head of the operation, would also run a series of 'illegal' (the term for covert) agents, who would often pose as disaffected emigrés or businessmen – any cover story that would suit their needs. By the late 1920s, many of the most professional of these agents would move from country to country when required, earning them the nickname the Great Illegals or the Flying Squad. OGPU was also involved with preventing western counter-espionage operations within the USSR. The seeds of the Cold War were sown.

As we've seen previously, British intelligence services were reorganised after the war – mainly to deal with the post-Versailles international situation. A Secret Service Committee chaired by Lord Curzon, the new Foreign Secretary who replaced Balfour in October 1919, met later the same year and published a report that identified Bolshevism as the greatest threat to the fabric of British society. It recommended changes to the existing and some-what complicated structure.[126]

The Secret Intelligence Service (SIS) was given a remit to gather intelligence overseas and placed under Foreign Office control.[127] It certainly had its work cut out handling the rise of communism. Desmond Morton was placed in charge of Section V, dealing with counter-Bolshevism activities in the 1920s. A network of field agents existed, mainly from military backgrounds working under the cover of diplomatic status on missions in Russia. These included men such as Robert Bruce Lockheart, Acting Vice Consul to Moscow; Captain Francis Cromie, naval attaché to the British Embassy in Petrograd; Captain George Hill and 'ace of spies' Sidney Reilly who, with Lockheart and Hill, had been involved in a failed attempt to assassinate Lenin in 1918. Reilly was sentenced to death in his absence, having escaped in a desperate flight across Russia, while Lockheart was lucky to avoid trial and was swapped for his counterpart in the UK, Maxim Litvinov. Within days of their return to Britain and after a debriefing with the Head of SIS, Sir Mansfield Smith-Cumming, both Hill and Reilly returned to Russia under cover of a British trade delegation to continue their espionage work. Reilly was officially dismissed from SIS in 1921 but continued to work with counter-revolutionaries and enjoyed a freelance relationship with SIS. Still a wanted man by the Bolsheviks, he was duped into returning to Russia in 1925 by the OGPU-led Operation Trust, captured, and shot.

Closer to home, MI5 continued to investigate the threat of espionage and sedition on British soil although Sir Vernon Kell's resources were severely limited after the war.[128] MI5 was largely restricted to gathering evidence of Bolshevism in the armed forces, reflecting its roots as a military intelligence organisation. One of his key recruits was Jane Sissmore, placed in charge of MI5's Registry in 1922 and destined to rise still further within the organisation. In order to specifically tackle Bolshevik activity, a new Directorate of Home Intelligence was established under the control of Sir Basil Thomson, given his success in maintaining security in Paris. The directorate had the power to arrest potential spies identified by MI5. However, the arrangement was not deemed to be a success as the directorate clashed constantly with

MI5 and the police. Thomson's ego was another problem and he soon lost the confidence of his political masters. The Secret Service Committee was reconvened in 1921, including Sir Eyre Crowe to provide the perspective of the Foreign Office. The Directorate of Home Intelligence was disbanded, Thomson removed and the responsibility for both domestic and military intelligence passed to Kell at MI5.

This was a period of turmoil and upheaval within Europe, when borders and regimes changed overnight and revolution might only be round the corner. Add to the mix the 1919 to 1923 Turkish War of Independence that followed the break-up of the Ottoman Empire under the terms of the Treaty of Sèvres and it is easy to see why the politicians placed such importance on accurate intelligence. The work of the Communications Department in the Foreign Office was all the more important in preventing counter-espionage, taking a front line role to ensure the secure delivery of British messages to embassies around the world. Given his report on the reorganisation of the King's Messengers and growing influence in the cipher room as one of the permanent clerks, Oldham played his part in the defence of diplomatic material throughout this period.

It is worth pausing briefly to reflect on the League of Nations, which was created by the Treaty of Versailles with its own permanent secretariat under the command of former Foreign Office official (and champion of Esperanto, among other things), Sir Eric Drummond. The intention was to continue the diplomatic work begun in Paris with the agreement of all major powers to respect the territorial integrity of each other. Their work would be upheld not by military force but by a Permanent Court of International Justice. Indeed, the League of Nations wished all member states to disarm 'to the lowest point consistent with domestic safety'. A General Assembly was established, plus an Executive Council formed of the major world powers. In reality, there were concerns that the League was a device to ensure the hegemony of France and Britain over Europe given the rather surprising failure of the Americans to sign up. Yet not everyone in the UK was keen on the new world order – especially in the Foreign Office, where there was great concern that its century-old monopoly on the diplomatic process was under threat. Crowe wrote to Hardinge on 9 December 1919 about his fears that the League of Nations secretariat might try to 'perpetuate and extend the system which has unfortunately prevailed very largely at the Peace Conference and of which I feel sure both you and Mr Balfour will have realised the grave inconveniences from the point of view of the proper conduct of business'.[129]

As a result, Drummond's attempt to recruit members for his secretariat from the ranks of the British Diplomatic Service were treated with suspicion, as indeed were his requests for access to sensitive British political information that might assist the work of the League. Curzon suggested that he should perhaps request them 'informally' but, when he did this in 1920, Hardinge refused on the grounds that he could not release sensitive documents. It was a stance that gradually softened on the grounds of expediency – the League moved permanently to Geneva in November 1920 and was seen as a 'clearing house of ideas' from which Britain would equally benefit. It is therefore possible that 'informal' King's Messengers such as Oldham were used to transport documentation to League meetings that the regular King's Messengers, with their closer allegiance to the Foreign Office, would not feel so comfortable in delivering. Oldham would become a regular visitor to League meetings in Geneva over the next decade.

Back home, Oldham also played a prominent role inside the Foreign Office as fears of Bolshevism continued to increase. Lenin died on 21 January 1924 and power transferred to Joseph Stalin, who spent the next few years consolidating his position. Britain formally recognised the USSR on 1 February 1924 and agreed to lend it money, with a motion placed before Parliament for an Anglo-Soviet trade agreement. This endorsement was primarily a consequence of the general election held on 6 December 1923 that saw Ramsay MacDonald's Labour party take power, albeit in a hung Parliament and despite gaining 67 fewer seats than the outgoing Conservative administration.

Given the 19th century roots of the Labour movement among the underrepresented working classes and its professed socialist ideals, it is no surprise that the new government was keen to make common cause with the USSR without embracing the communist ideology of revolution as an agent of change. Labour preferred instead to follow the democratic parliamentary route eschewed by the Communist Party of Great Britain. This was Britain's first taste of socialist rule, but it did not last long. Minority government had proved hard enough in the past, let alone when undertaken by an inexperienced party reliant on the support of Liberal opponents who seemed willing to give Labour enough rope with which to hang themselves.

Despite demonstrating a level of competency thought beyond them by their political rivals, the Labour administration was brought down by its handling of the Campbell case – the intended prosecution of John Ross Cambell under the 1917 Incitement to Mutiny Act for publishing a letter in *Worker's Weekly* that encouraged soldiers not to fire on their fellow workers in the event of class war in Britain. Although the Attorney General recommended that Campbell be brought to trial, the Labour government withdrew the prosecution. This sparked a vote of no confidence which MacDonald lost and a new election was held on 29 October. Suspicions of Bolshevik elements existing in socialist parties were heightened sharply when a letter appeared in the *Daily Mail* a few days before the vote, purportedly from Grigory Zinoviev, Head of the Executive Committee of Comintern and its British representative, Arthur MacManus. The letter was addressed to the Communist Party of Great Britain and exhorted them to instigate a proletariat uprising in British industrial cities. The letter caused an outcry, least of all from Zinoviev himself who strenuously insisted it was a fake. He indignantly claimed that:

> The forger has shown himself to be very stupid in his choice of the date. On 15 September 1924, I was taking a holiday in Kislovodsk, and, therefore, could not have signed any official letter.[130]

He had a point; it has since been proven that the letter was indeed fabricated, most probably by an intelligence source working outside the UK. It was leaked to the press and Conservative Party central office with the complicity of MI6 – either Desmond Morton or one of his associates, including Major Stewart Menzies, who later admitted sending a copy to the *Daily Mail*. Either way, the damage was done. Although it is doubtful that the letter impacted on the core Labour vote, it certainly damaged the Liberals who had supported the

MacDonald regime. A decisive Conservative victory ensued, bringing Stanley Baldwin back to power. The trade agreement with the Soviets was swiftly cancelled a few weeks later.

Throughout 1924, measures were taken within the Foreign Office and Diplomatic Service to tighten security – just in case. Oldham was charged with the task of ensuring official safes were distributed to consulates around the world; his handwritten notes can be found within the National Archives in some of the few official papers preserved from the Communications Department. A memo survives from April 1924 in which a certain confidence bordering on pomposity is displayed in the way that he comments on the fact that 'the Treasury have misread our letter', before reiterating his point to demonstrate that any consular officer in charge of holding cipher code books should have 'combination lock safes' regardless of their status and that security should trump economy if an existing safe was not deemed to be of sufficient standard.[131] However, he was clearly in a position of trust; in May 1924 he compiled a revised list of holders of the *Government Telegraph Code* (1922), mainly because 'a considerable number of additions and corrections have been made since the volume was compiled'. His draft was stamped for approval by Hubert Montgomery, Chief Clerk, on the direction of Mr Ramsay MacDonald – who had assumed the role of Foreign Secretary as well as Prime Minister.[132]

There were also changes in personnel within the Foreign Office, in particular a new Head of the Communications Department. There had been regular change at the top with each incumbent lasting around two years apiece, including the steady Howard Smith and more flamboyant Duff Cooper who left to further his political career. On 19 May 1925 the decision was taken to promote from within and one of the King's Messengers, Harold Eastwood, was given the position – much to the delight of Antrobus:

> Not only was the new head thoroughly acquainted with the departmental work, but he was temperamentally well qualified for the post... he adopted, and rigorously adhered to, the traditional Foreign Office principle of giving orders and trusting to the loyalty of his staff to see that they were carried out.[133]

His deputy was Commander Ralph Cotesworth, who had also risen through the ranks – moving from the Royal Navy into the Foreign Office as a temporary clerk, before becoming one of the new King's Messengers after the war.

> Cotesworth had one advantage over Eastwood in that he had a thorough and expert knowledge of the technical side of the work, the use and management of the ciphers and codes.[134]

Under the Conservative regime, fears of the communist threat deepened as relations with Germany normalised. The Locarno Treaty was signed at the Foreign Office on 1 December 1925, with Germany admitted to the League of Nations amid real hopes of lasting international peace. This was hailed at the time as a major diplomatic coup and the discussions that took place between 5 and 16 October in Locarno, Switzerland, were important for fixing the borders of to the west of Germany but leaving those to the east open to further interpretation. The Soviet Union was excluded from discussions, exacerbating feeling within the isolated country that it was being undermined from the west and heightening paranoia over German territorial interest.

Oldham was the man in the Foreign Office to whom responsibility was delegated for organising transport to and from Lorcarno. He reserved the requisite number of berths from the Sleeping Car company – a special coach of 16 together – when the British delegation left on 3 October, at the cost of £108.6.7. Only 11 people actually travelled, necessitating a great deal of work for the home messenger service to sort out the logistics. Oldham was forced to dip into his own pocket to the tune of £3.5.11 to cover some of their expenses which he claimed back from the office.[135] At least he was not in charge of the refurbishment of the suite of rooms which were especially redecorated for the signing of the treaty in December once the conference had concluded – that was expenditure on an altogether different scale.

Meanwhile, steps against Bolshevism were being taken back home. On 14 and 21 October 1925, MI5 raided the headquarters of the Communist Party of Great Britain, seizing various documents and arresting officials including Albert Inkpin (who had been charged during an earlier raid in 1921),

Tom Bell, Ernie Cant, Harry Pollitt, Bill Rust, Arthur MacManus and, once again, J R Campbell. The following year, Soviet intervention was blamed for inflaming tensions between the Trades Union Congress (TUC) and the government over the miner's dispute, which led to the General Strike.

This was a period of general economic hardship, exacerbated by the re-adoption of the gold standard in 1925 and falling wages in many industrial sectors including coal mining. Initially, the government agreed to support the miners by providing a nine-month subsidy of their wages – a decision known as Red Friday, as it seemed to be a victory for the working classes. However, when they subsequently accepted the recommendation of a Royal Commission to introduce widespread change and greater national control, the Miner's Federation of Great Britain refused to accept them and a lock-out of miners ensued on 1 May 1926. The TUC then called a general strike from 3 May onwards in support of the miners and targeted transport workers, dockers, foundry workers and printers to cause maximum disruption. The Tory press saw industrial action as tantamount to revolution, but the *Daily Mail* was unable to produce an editorial to that effect as their printing staff would not print it. Incidentally, King George V refused to condemn the strikers as 'revolutionaries' with the comment, 'Try living on their wages before you judge them.'[136]

The strike lasted until 12 May and affected all government departments including the Foreign Office. With transport largely paralysed, alternative arrangements were made to ensure key staff could get into work.

> On the Monday evening before the strike, a skeleton staff of men and women went home for their clothes after office hours and returned, some with great difficulty, prepared to sleep on the floor in the office for as long as they were required to do so. Fortunately, owing to offers of hospitality, all the women were, by the end of the week, sleeping out in various houses, but the men slept at the office during the whole period.
>
> Arrangements were made to fetch as many as possible of the rest of the staff by cars, but a large proportion were left to find their own way to the office. Except in one or two cases where

there was literally no means of transit whatever to bring them the
30 miles or so to London, the whole staff made every effort to attend regularly, some walking distances of eight or nine miles each
way – five miles being quite a common occurrence, both for men
and women.[137]

Those with cars were expected to provide transport for their colleagues
– and it is with some surprise that we find Oldham listed amongst those
who were giving lifts in an early form of car pool. He had been assigned
the Enfield, Barnet and Finchley region where his parents lived and provided transport to shorthand typists Miss Grace Madeline Painter and Miss
Florence Dorothy Good, along with Miss Hilda Emily Holdway and Mr
Rance from the Chief Clerk's Office (though he was only able to provide the
service one way after 10 May).

More specifically, Oldham was involved in ensuring that the King's
Messenger service continued to function so that diplomatic bags containing
correspondence and suchlike could be safely transferred to the relevant ports
before they were taken to embassy and consular staff overseas. On 10 May,
he drew up a report showing how certain of the bag services have been maintained by the use of cars supplied and driven by volunteer friends of members
of the Communications Department.[138] This was a clear reference to the trust
mentioned by Antrobus – not just within the department, but extended to
friends and acquaintances. Given the ongoing security risk, plus potential un-
rest at the ports:

> It was considered desirable that the drivers should be accompanied
> by guards, who would also help as porters etc, and in the case of
> each messenger on the Bucharest and Constantinople journeys it
> has been necessary to send two cars.[139]

By this method, services were maintained for Newhaven to Paris, Dover to
Bucharest and Constantinople, Harwich to Brussels and trips to Southampton
for services to Washington and South America, for example. Various members

of the Communications Department, such as Thomas Kemp, were involved as well. All volunteers received a letter of thanks on behalf of the Foreign Secretary, Sir Austin Chamberlain, signed by Hubert Montgomery. However, some staff found themselves out of pocket and wanted to claim back their expenses, including Ernest Oldham. His request, received on 29 June, was rather unusual:

> Encloses a statement of expenses incurred during the strike and enquiries how much is due in respect of his car. Explains that he was working late on several nights and had to have dinner, which cost about 5/- a night at his club. Enquiries whether he can claim any allowance for that.[140]

There are several points of interest here. Leaving aside the question about how a permanent clerk on £150 a year could afford a car which would have cost his annual salary or more, it is clear that Oldham had designs on stepping up in the world. He was perhaps mindful still of his humble background compared to some of his colleagues – possibly the factor that had tipped the balance against him when applying for the Diplomatic Service. One way to gain standing was to become a member of a London club, a reliable badge of honour among those who had gone to university or worked in the City. St James and Pall Mall in particular were at the heart of club-land, where over 200 establishments vied to attract members. At the very top, leading establishments where ministers would talk politics, such as the Carlton Club, would have prohibitively long waiting lists and recommendation rules for potential applicants, so many junior or specialist clubs were formed at more affordable prices.

For a man such as Oldham, still living in his parents' terraced house in north London, the appeal of membership at a club to enhance his career prospects would have been compelling. It seems as though he was a member of the Junior Carlton Club, associated most strongly with the Tory party. The club had impressive premises at 30 Pall Mall, complete with dining and coffee rooms, a lounge for 'strangers', a smoking room and library. Many of Oldham's associates were members of clubs, allowing him to mix in a different social circle

– exactly the sort of environment where an up and coming Foreign Office hopeful could entertain diplomatic guests, for example.

It is strongly suspected that Oldham's maternal uncle, Henry George Holloway junior, first introduced him to the club scene. Holloway was a member of several clubs in his own right and was an intriguing character, who, as mentioned in an earlier chapter, had a range of occupations and turned a profit from most of them. By the 1920s, cinema had outstripped music hall and theatres as the entertainment of choice for a younger audience and Holloway had taken a financial interest in several cinemas. With the glamour of the silver screen came the taste for a luxurious lifestyle – for example, in 1936 he splashed out for a state room on the maiden voyage of the *Queen Mary*. Holloway cut an impressive figure and took the young Oldham under his wing as he made his way in the world.

Yet whilst Oldham enjoyed his time in London society and left his cares behind, security within Whitehall remained an issue and members of staff were expected to be ever-vigilant. An example of lax office-keeping was brought to Montgomery's attention on 29 November 1926:

> One evening recently the safe containing the confidential keys in
> Room 18 was found open at about 7.45 pm. This is believed to
> have been due to the inadvertence of a member of the office and it
> is therefore considered desirable to remind those who are respon-
> sible for taking out or returning keys that the greatest care must be
> exercised in ascertaining that the safe has been properly closed.[141]

Those fuelling the growing paranoia about Whitehall security were correct to be worried, as disturbing evidence emerged in 1927 about the level of Soviet infiltration within British society. On 12 May the headquarters of the All Russian Cooperative Society (ARCOS) at 49 Moorgate Street were raided by police following a surveillance operation by MI5 and SIS agents. It was the culmination of several years' work by agents such as Jasper Harker, Herbert 'Con' Boddington and John Ottaway. Since 1924 they had intercepted communications between William Norman Ewer, foreign editor of the

Daily Herald and former police officer Walter Dale, who was tailed to both ARCOS and the offices of the Federated Press. Phones were tapped and it became apparent that seemingly legitimate organisations were a front for subversive Soviet activity. When it emerged in March 1927 that a classified signals training manual from the Aldershot military base had been copied within the ARCOS office, a decision was taken to raid the premises.

It was not an overwhelming success – apart from finding startled AR-COS employees frantically shredding documents, there was no smoking gun evidence of espionage. However the consequences were monumental. The Soviets were alerted to the fact that their surveillance operation in Britain had been compromised and changed their system of codes. This seriously hampered future British intelligence gathering operations, with the result that security services failed to spot other infiltrators. Two Special Branch officers, Sergeant Charles Jane and Inspector Hubert van Ginhoven, had already been recruited by Ewer and were also passing information to the Soviets from the inside.

The political fallout from the ARCOS raid was equally far reaching. Fuelled by scare-mongering newspaper reports, a furious British government severed diplomatic relations with the Soviet Union on 24 May 1927, with Stalin commenting that peaceful co-existence with 'the capitalist countries is receding into the past'.[142] The Soviet Union, still outside the League of Nations, had officially supplanted Germany as the main threat to global peace and once again the world seemed a much more dangerous place. However, by this date Oldham's own world had already been turned upside down by a very different event, in a very different way.

Chapter seven

LUCY
(1927–1928)

Since our discussion yesterday morning, I have been puzzling about... how in the first instance EO came to meet my mother. I think he may have been introduced by her friend, a Lieutenant Commander Billy Everett, sometime in the early 1920s. Everett, impecunious and I fear a sponger, claimed to be a King's Messenger.

THOMAS WELLSTED, 27 NOVEMBER 1974

On 9 July 1927, as the furore around the ARCOS raid and the cessation of Anglo-Soviet diplomatic relations started to abate, a wedding ceremony took place at Kensington Parish Church. This was the second marriage for the bride, who had been widowed in 1919. Her name was Lucy Wellsted, allegedly 40 years old with a deceased father named Frederick King. A married couple, Octave Count de la Chapelle and his wife Rachel, were the witnesses to the happy event. The groom, a 37-year-old civil servant who recorded his residence as the Foreign Office, Whitehall, claimed to be the son of a gentleman. His name was Ernest Holloway Oldham and this was about the only completely true statement recorded on the entire marriage certificate.

The wedding of Lucy Wellsted to Ernest Oldham represents a pivotal moment in his life. Of course, marriage is usually life-changing but in this case it was more than just leaving bachelorhood behind – it was a complete change in his social status. To understand why there were so many 'inaccuracies' on the certificate, we need to travel back in time several decades and across various continents to trace the story of his new wife, since she played a key role in the direction Oldham's life would take over the next few years. Indeed, the friends and acquaintances that brought them together give us an insight into the circles that Oldham was now moving in, far beyond his humble origins. US presidents, international lawyers and high finance would become part of his world as he mixed with an altogether more flamboyant group then his colleagues in the Foreign Office. The change in Oldham's circumstances is vitally important in understanding what happened thereafter.

Lucy Eliza's birth surname was Kayser rather than King – it is possible that she decided to anglicise her father's name when she remarried as a result of anti-German feeling caused by the war. Even nine years after the end of the fighting, suspicion still remained – a legacy of internment, as well as the sporadic violence and vandalism towards long-standing German communities that had taken place in the years following 1914.

Furthermore, Lucy Wellsted had not been not born in 1887 as she claimed, but five years earlier on 24 November 1882 in Waratah, Tasmania – making her 45 when she married Oldham, 12 years older than her new husband; no wonder he gallantly added a few years to his own age to help narrow the gap. For Lucy, it had been quite a journey from the place of her birth, a small Australian community almost entirely dependent on tin mining for survival, which, in turn, was almost entirely dependent upon her father, Heinrich Wilhelm Ferdinand Kayser. We may now consider America to epitomise the 19th century land of opportunity, but 'Ferd', as he was known to friends and family, showed that it was possible to prosper 'down under' as well. He had been born at Clausthal, Hanover, in 1833 – the son of a mining engineer – before leaving Saxony to find his fortune in Australia. He landed in Adelaide in 1853 but moved to Melbourne the following year to try his luck in the emerging goldfields – wild, frontier territory where men could make their fortune or end up dead. Kayser found the former; by 1863 he had become a mining manager at Bendigo, one of the emerging new towns that acted as a magnet for other speculators and workers.

However, Kayser did not stay with gold but turned his attention to tin mining, moving to Tasmania in 1875 to manage the Mount Bischoff Tin Mining Company at Waratah. It had only started operating two years before. If Bendigo was a growing frontier town in the 1860s, then Waratah was little more than a track leading to the mine – plus a post office, a few modest houses, a hotel and a road leading to Burnie, the nearest proper settlement perched on Tasmania's northern coast. Yet Waratah became home to Kayser. The following year he married Mary Elizabeth Druce on 4 March in Melbourne and together they raised seven daughters and a son. During his time as manager, Kayser transformed the mine, the town and his own fortune – by 1898, when he retired, he had been responsible for the construction of proper homes, not just houses, to encourage families to settle, a hospital to provide healthcare, an iron tramway to Burnie and the Falls Creek dam to provide hydro-electric power which was used to light the town and mine. The power came years before the growing north London suburb of Edmonton would receive street lighting, it should be noted. True to his Baptist roots, there was a temperance hotel and a church.

No wonder people called him the Chief – he held the positions of magistrate, coroner, registrar of births, marriages and deaths and owner of the *North-Western Advocate* and effectively had the power of life, death and opinion over the inhabitants of the town. He was a 'humane despot' in the words of the *Australian Dictionary of National Biography* – or a tyrant, according to disgruntled employees who resented the way he dictated the way they could live and even think. Beyond dispute, however, was the fact that his methods were successful; he claimed that by 1892 the mine had extracted 37,000 tons of ore, generated over £1 million in dividends for its shareholders and was the driving force of the Tasmanian economy.

We can catch glimpses of Lucy's childhood growing up in Launceston where the family had their main house on York Street. She appeared at the Fancy Juvenile ball on 3 September 1897, for example, disguised in costume to represent 'modern art', alongside her sisters Cissie in the robes of a Bohemian dancing girl, Edie dressed as *La République française* and Bertha pretending to be Lady Teazle from Sheridan's *The School For Scandal*. The following year, her eldest sister Agnes married politician George Crosby Gilmore

on 26 April at St John's Church, Launceston, which was 'tastefully and lav-
ishly decorated by the girlfriends of the bride' according to the local paper.
The reporter then provided an exceedingly detailed and lengthy account of
the bride's dress, and pretty much everyone else's:

> ...the misses Bertha, Lucy and Edith Kayser, sisters of the bride,
> were bridesmaids and wore white silk dresses, the skirts edged
> with two narrow frills and the bodices trimmed with violet silk and
> white chiffon; violet silk girdles finished the waists and were knot-
> ted at the left side, the ends being edged with pearl fringe; their hats
> were of white felt, with a cluster of white ostrich tips and loops of
> violet velvet at the side, the brims having a pleating of mousseline
> de sole laid upon them; shower bouquets of violets, tied with white
> satin ribbon, were carried and gold dagger broaches [sic] set with
> pearls, the gift of the bridegroom, were worn.[143]

Four years later, the Launceston *Daily Telegraph* reported another marriage for
one of the Kayser girls – this time second daughter Bertha, who married an
Englishman called Thomas Gibbons on 27 February 1902. However, the report noted that:

> As Mr and Mrs Kayser and family intend leaving for a trip to
> Germany early next month, the wedding was of the quietest de-
> scription and immediate friends only were present at the wedding
> luncheon, given at their residence.[144]

Sure enough, on 18 March the local papers – including the enchantingly
named *Emu Bay Times* – noted the departure not just of Ferd Kayser, but also
his family for a 'well-earned holiday' where he 'proposed to visit England and
to return to Tasmania via America in about six or eight months' time'.[145] As
if to justify this time away, the paper noted that 'during Mr Kayser's management, the Mount Bischoff mine had returned in dividends of £1,618,500'.
This was clearly a family used to enjoying the benefits of wealth, and Lucy had

developed an aspiration to live to these luxurious standards throughout her life, regardless of the cost.

As family trips went, this was pretty special. A typical voyage to Europe could take around a month, once the requisite trunks of clothes and personal possessions were loaded onto the boat and the final farewells to friends and family said at the harbour. This holiday lasted around four months and almost certainly included professional networking for Ferd, after which the family embarked upon the *Ophir* at London on 15 August 1902, bound for Melbourne and home. The first Australian port they reached was Fremantle on 12 September, and the *Western Australian* duly noted the names of some of the more prominent people on board, including Mr and Mrs Kayser and family. They had been joined by Thomas Wilhelm Wellsted, a young mining engineer and newly appointed partner to one of the oldest mining companies in the world. He had joined the party in London and was ostensibly travelling on business; in reality, he had fallen for Lucy's charm and beauty and the couple was soon engaged. Within six months, Lucy and her mother were repeating the journey back to Europe, sailing on the *Friedrich der Grosse* on 24 February 1903 from Melbourne to prepare for an April wedding in London where Lucy would make her home with her new husband.

Wellsted was a partner with Bewick, Moreing and Company, based at Broad Street House, 62 London Wall but with regional offices around the world, including Melbourne. The business was involved both with the technical development of mining operations and mineral extraction as well as purchasing and operating mines globally – in particular in North America, Australia and the far east, but also increasingly into the European markets and Russia, with a growing interest in the uses of oil. This was a period of upheaval, though; the partnership terminated the services of mining engineer Anthony Stanley Rowe through personal bankruptcy and a scandal involving forged cheques, as announced in *The Times* on 7 January 1903. However, the company was still able to draw upon the talents of one of the most remarkable men of his time – Herbert Clark Hoover. He had been hired in 1897 and enjoyed an adventurous career around the world – even if he did not think so himself – which resulted in his promotion to full partnership in the company on 18 December 1901, when he based himself in London although his new remit was to oversee the company's Australian gold mining operations. Thomas Wellsted and Herbert Hoover were close working companions and often dined together, although many associates noted the rather lifeless atmosphere of a Hoover dinner party. The events would often pass in virtual silence – 'never was he heard to mention a poem, a play, a work of art', wrote one attendee – which was hardly surprising as Hoover's whole focus was devoted to making money.[146]

Hoover took up residence in Kensington – Red House in Campden Hill – where his two children Herbert Charles and Allen Henry were born in 1903 and 1908. Although Lucy developed a lifelong association with Kensington, drawn perhaps by Hoover's regular updates from her homeland, the Wellsteds initially settled at 14 Lambolle Road, Belsize Park, where their first son Thomas Arthur was born on 3 April 1904. A second child, Ferdinand Edward Wellsted, appeared on 27 January 1907, the proud parents posting an announcement in *The Times* to let friends and family at home and overseas know the good news.[147]

Later that year, Wellsted was posted to Australia to visit his company's operations and he made the decision to take his family with him – a great opportunity for his wife to catch up with her relatives and show off her children. Unsurprisingly, given the distances involved, this was not a short trip. They arrived in Fremantle on 1 October, with Wellsted spending some time with his in-laws in Tasmania before heading west to the Gwalia mines in early November. They eventually returned home on 6 February 1908, having completed a first-class circumnavigation of the world via Hawaii, San Francisco and New York.

However, it was at this point that the careers and fortunes of Hoover and Wellsted started to diverge. Doubts had been growing about some of Hoover's other business interests that were too close for comfort to those of Bewick and Moreing, in particular his association with the Zinc Corporation at Broken Hill, New South Wales. He also started to extend his influence in China, becoming involved in the controversial supply of migrant labour to South African mines that eventually caused disquiet in parliament. He began to explore the possibility of Russian oil as a new venture – something that Bewick and Moreing were also interested in developing. By 1908, he was a director of 11 other companies besides his day job. Amid growing tension, a parting of the ways was on the cards and it was to no surprise that on 7 July 1908 *The Times* carried the announcement that the partnership had been formally dissolved. Hoover left to set out on his own as an independent mining consultant. Throughout this period of upheaval, Wellsted played little part in the boardroom politics, mainly because he faced a crisis of his own. After the family's return from Australia Ferdinand had contracted whooping cough, a disease that had only been discovered by scientists two years previously. He battled the illness for 21 days but developed complications – acute bronchitis and, for the final five days of his life, convulsions. He died on 2 April 1908, two months past his first birthday, leaving the family devastated.

On departing Bewick and Moreing, Hoover had given assurances that he would not encroach upon their business. However, the world was simply too small for them to peacefully co-exist. Matters erupted into a courtroom battle in 1910 when Bewick and Moreing filed a lawsuit against Hoover for infringement against the non-competition agreement he had signed, specifically related to his pursuit of oil interests in Russia. The case grew increasingly bitter, with personal testimony submitted about Hoover's 'disregard' for his former colleagues and 'treacherous involvement' in Russia. In turn, Hoover calmly claimed that he had strictly observed the covenant not to practice as a mining engineer on the business of the old partnership in London, Liverpool or Manchester for ten years but that he was now engaged in new activities.

Despite the legal animosity at boardroom level, personal friendships and professional connections were harder to break, especially if they were lubricated in the newly formed Mining and Metallurgical Club, located a few offices down from Bewick and Moreing at 3 London Wall in the City. The venue was essentially a gentlemen's club for the professional mining community with dining, music, socialising and entertainment – an industry equivalent to the sort of establishment Oldham would frequent in the mid 1920s. The two old friends continued to meet there whenever possible, but by this date Wellsted and his family had moved to Langley Park House,

Watford. Wellsted picked up some of the tasks that his more experienced colleague would previously have dealt with – troubleshooting the threat of industrial action in the Kalgoorlie mines in September 1911, for example. On a personal note, the Wellsteds were blessed with another child, James Raymond having been delivered into the world on 13 May 1913.

However, when war broke out in 1914, the contrast between the fortunes of Hoover and Wellsted could not have been more pronounced. A note in *The Times* showed that the Wellsteds had subscribed £21 to the paper's Red Cross Appeal, whereas Hoover earned his nickname as the Great Humanitarian by almost singlehandedly organising the relief effort and makeshift camps to ease the Belgian refugee crisis – at least, he certainly made sure he took all the credit. Perhaps less well known is the fact that during the war he continued to buy chemicals in Germany rather than in Britain as part of his business operation, because they were cheaper. Under the terms of the 1917 Trading With The Enemy Act, he could have been arrested for treason and executed.

With Hoover gone, Wellsted found the burden of global travel falling increasingly upon his shoulders. However, he was no longer a young man and found it much harder to manage the change from hot dry climates abroad to the damp and smoky City air, with the result that his health began to suffer. By 1919, after Wellsted had been afflicted by a particularly bad case of whooping cough that left his chest weak and prone to further infection, the family took the decision to move to Melbourne in the hope that the climate change would prove congenial. They ended up not far from St Kilda, where Lucy's father had relocated in 1908. Thomas's brother, Edward James Wellsted had already moved out to manage the Kalgoorlie operations for Bewick and Moreing. The remedy was unsuccessful, and on 30 April Thomas Wellsted passed away at their home on Collins Street, Lister House, aged only 54. Devastated by the loss of her husband, Lucy packed her bags, said her goodbyes to her family and returned home to England, arriving in London on 31 July 1919. Her departure was the last time she was to speak to her father. A few months later she learned that he had died on 12 October at home in St Kilda, aged 86.

According to later documents, Lucy was apparently well catered for by bequests left in both her husband's and father's wills. It is stated in private papers that she inherited a lump sum of £22,000 – over £1 million in today's money – and an annuity of £600 to cater for her sons, exactly four times what Ernest Oldham was earning each year at the Foreign Office.[148] However, closer scrutiny suggests that this was not exactly the case.

Lucy had been named co-executor of her husband's will, along with the National Provincial and Union Bank of England Ltd, so that a solicitor could deal with Wellsted's somewhat complicated financial affairs. She renounced her claim to probate – meaning that she was no longer a executor and leaving the financial administration in the hands of William Henry Sidebotham, who had been nominated by the bank to act as the administrator. Probate was duly granted on 24 October 1919, and it is apparent that once Wellsted's estate had been assessed, the net value was only £9,679.5.4.

Wellsted had drawn up his will the day before he died and made careful provision for his family. Lucy was to inherit all his personal trinkets and watches, plus a cash legacy of £1,000 to be paid to her as soon as possible after his death. However, the rest of his estate was to be invested in securities and trust funds to provide an annual income for his wife, on the understanding that she would use the money to provide an education for her children. She was also made their sole guardian. Thus £600 per year was likely to have been her living allowance.[149]

At the age of 37, relatively wealthy, still young and very attractive, Lucy decided to settle where her friends were congregated – Kensington. First she acquired accommodation at 6 de Vere Mansions, Queen's Gate, before moving to Lurgan Mansions, Sloane Square in 1923. She eventually settled at 79c Cromwell Gardens – a somewhat exclusive area of Kensington with views of the Natural History and Victoria & Albert museums.[150] Lucy began to re-establish herself amongst her old circle of friends. It is hard to imagine the circumstances under which the glamorous, well-connected widow would first be introduced to and then fall for a much younger civil servant who lived in a north London suburb with his parents. Lucy's oldest son Thomas, writing in the 1970s, tried to recall the circumstances under which her mother first met Oldham.

I think he may have been introduced by her friend, a Lieutenant
Commander Billy Everett, sometime in the early 1920s. Everett,
impecunious and, I fear, a sponger, claimed to be a King's Messenger and I remember his saying a visit he made to Constantinople, I
think in 1923, was as a King's Messsenger. He died 1924 or 1925.[151]

Thomas Wellsted clearly had a good memory, particularly when we dig a bit
deeper into the evidence. The person he was referring to was William Bos-
tock Everett, born in 1879 in Ashby de la Zouche in the Midlands. He seems
to have been a conscientious student – a report in the *Derby Mercury* on 9
February 1898 proudly boasts of 'a grammar school boy's success':

> Mr William Bostock Everett, son of Mr Everett, the stationmaster
> at Ashby, has been appointed English correspondent in Athens by
> a large London firm, who had 250 applications from all quarters
> for the position. Mr Everett was educated at the Ashby grammar
> school, after which he held posts in London.[152]

His overseas posting may have served to fuel his lust for travel and adventure,
as he became an assistant paymaster in the Royal Naval Reserves in October
1904, which suggests a prior career as a merchant seaman. During World War
I, he quickly rose through the ranks to become paymaster on 2 May 1917
and then lieutenant commander by 1920, a rank backdated to 15 October
1914, when the Royal Naval Reserve decoration was conferred on him by
King George V. On 31 December 1922, he was promoted to commander.[153]

From 1916 to 1918 he served on board HMS *Himalaya*, an armed merchant cruiser and mercantile conversion that formed part of the guard for the
Central and South Atlantic convoys. During this period, Everett sailed around
the Cape of Good Hope, visiting Guinea, South Africa, Mozambique and
Tanganyika (now Tanzania) before heading back home via Brazil. Thereafter, with his new rank he gained a position on the 'stone frigate' – or naval
land base on shore – HMS *President*, on the Victoria Embankment near Tower
Bridge in the heart of the City. Everett was assigned to President VI, which

handled transport service accounts and from February 1919 served as the base for the Murmansk tugs, while managing the accounts of officers assigned to northern Russia. At the end of the war, he took up residence at 29 Harrington Gardens in Kensington, though he habitually provided his address as the Cocoa Tree Club, 64 St James Street, in the West End.[154] This was one of the many clubs that were concentrated in the area where it was fashionable to be seen as a member, although the Cocoa Tree rather incongruously shared its premises with a gunsmith's shop.

Given the general use of Royal Naval Reserve officers for signals and light intelligence work, it is perhaps not surprising that many of Everett's colleagues regularly appeared in the records of the Foreign Office running diplomatic courier missions, as we've already seen. These included a messenger service three times a week from Paris to London. A King's Messenger travelling on overseas business would almost certainly have known or worked with Ernest Oldham, since he had been given the task of managing the service – including the unofficial King's Messengers that had so irritated men such as Antrobus and Wheeler-Holohan. Sure enough, an entry appears in the day books for the travelling expenses of Commander WB Everett, presented on 3 September 1923 and filed a week later, for his trip to Constantinople on official business between 21 August and 2 September. It showed a balance of £9.12.10 due to him. He even remembered to enclose the relevant vouchers, no doubt endearing himself to Oldham and his colleagues who had to process all the dockets. However he wrote later to say that he had 'destroyed' his note of expenses and had to contact the Wagon-Lit offices for confirmation of the amount. Such carelessness may explain why this was the only entry for his services on a long-haul journey.[155]

In any case, Everett's travelling days were drawing to a close. Eighteen months later he was dead, having checked into the Suffolk Victoria Nursing Home at 57 Fonnereau Road, Ipswich, for treatment for ulcerative colitis – severe inflammatory bowel disease. It would appear that the treatment was unsuccessful as this was listed as the cause of his demise, along with exhaustion which probably tells its own story. Interestingly, the informant was Everett's brother, who lived in Windsor Road, Finchley, only four miles from Oldham's home in Edmonton. However, while it is easy to tie Everett and Oldham together, it is much harder to see Everett's connection with Lucy Wellsted other than a vague residential proximity, presuming Everett even stayed in Kensington beyond 1918 given the more exotic address that he habitually provided. Far more likely candidates for mutual acquaintance are provided by the witnesses at Oldham's marriage in 1927, Octave Count de la Chapelle and his wife Rachel. But as with most strands in this section of the story, not everything was as it seemed.

Octave Count de la Chapelle was one of the most colourful characters of the time, whose full title – Victor Octave Xavier Alfred de Morton de la Chapelle, Count de la Chapelle – reflects both French and Scottish aristocratic roots. According to the *Dictionary of National Biography*, he was born in 1863 in Périgord, in the Dordogne region of France, the son of the Count and Countess de la Chapelle. He spent the first eight years of life on the family estates at the Château de Montcuque, Périgord, and at Château Giomer on the edge of the marshes at St Valéry-sur-Somme. His father, Alfred, was a staunch supporter of Napoleon III and had his estates confiscated when the emperor was deposed and exiled in the wake of France's catastrophic defeat in 1870 during the Franco-Prussian war. Humiliated at Sedan and captured by the Prussians, Napoleon was eventually released and chose to live in England – Camden Place in Chiselhurst, to be precise. The de la Chapelle family moved to Italy, before eventually also coming to England.

Elements of this are certainly true, but in reality Alfred had a thirst for adventure when younger which took him far beyond the confines of Europe. Initially, he headed for California in the early 1850s, drawn by the lure of the gold rush and became embroiled in a failed French military incursion against the Mexicans, which resulted in de la Chapelle being condemned to death and left *en capilla* – sharing a cell with his own coffin. However, he was pardoned by President Santa Anna (a man worthy of a book in his own right – known as the Napoleon of the West, he had one of his amputated legs buried with full military honours) and sent back to California in disgrace.

Given this experience, it is perhaps no surprise to find de la Chapelle appearing on the other side of world, chasing fame and fortune in Australia by prospecting the outback in search of gold. His base was Melbourne, where on 17 September 1863 his son, Octave Xavier Alfred, was born at St Kilda. It is almost certain that Octave's birth was illegitimate, as there is no record of marriage between Alfred and the mother, 20-year-old Kate Royal from Manchester. On his return to France, Alfred became close to the emperor, with Kate often staying at Camden Place during Napoleon's exile. Alfred continued to run errands abroad, with important papers hidden in his garments or hat and trailed everywhere by detectives from the French Republic.

With this glorious background, it is perhaps no surprise that Octave similarly threw himself into the world of international intrigue and shady connections, albeit through a more conventional route – the law. In 1888 he trained as a solicitor in London, eventually establishing his own firm based in Gresham Street, a short walk away from London Wall where Bewick, Moreing and Co. were located. Through his family background and equally flamboyant nature, Octave was able to build a reputation as a leading international lawyer with contacts across the world based in Paris, Geneva, Brussels, Berlin, Alexandria, Florence, Bucharest, Melbourne and New York – 'a popular figure in legal, City and social circles' and, according to his great friend the journalist James Wentworth Day,

> He made friends for life when he made them at all. And his choice, usually, was for those who appealed to his own nature, a dashing Gascon temperament, that had no use for men who avoid risk, who have not lived dangerously.[156]

Aside from holding 'many European secrets', he was particularly close to Romanian affairs. During World War I, he acted as the legal counsellor to the Romanian ambassador in London, and played a key part in persuading the King of Romania to enter the war on the side of the Allies in August 1916. He was certainly feted thereafter, receiving several decorations from the grateful Romanian authorities as well as the Portuguese, Japanese and Spanish Red Cross decorations in 1922. His company, La Chapelle and Co., was regularly listed in Foreign Office correspondence, mainly as 'lawyers in London with knowledge of Romanian law' and he clearly continued the family's business interests in Melbourne.

His private life was equally colourful – though not everyone was aware of this. To the outside world, his working life was spent in the City or attending to his European businesses. He retired to his weekend and holiday retreat in Tollesbury, Essex, to pursue his love of 'punt gunning' – shooting wildfowl in the Essex marshes. On one occasion just prior to World War I, he was mistaken for a German spy and arrested, and had quite a task to protest his innocence. Known to locals simply as the Count, he was regularly accompanied by his wife Rachel and his daughter to Tollesbury, where they regularly threw parties and entertainment.

However, all was not quite as it seemed. For a start, and following in his father's footsteps, there was no sign of a marriage to Rachel – probably because he was already married to a woman named Mary Evelyn Paddison, with whom he'd had a daughter in 1888. It looks like his first wife entered a convent in Stamford Hill, Hackney, where she was listed amongst the residents in the 1911 census. At the same time, Octave was living with Rachel and their four-year-old daughter, and claimed to have been married for five years. With no sign of a divorce from his first wife, who survived until 1950, the reasons for the deception – avoidance of bigamy – are perhaps clear.

Another of the Count's great loves was jazz – and this is where some of the disparate strands that tie Lucy Wellsted and Oldham start to come together. Octave funded his own jazz band that regularly played in some of the emerging London venues. The capital's jazz scene had really started to flourish after the war, especially when the Original Dixieland Jazz Band toured Britain in 1919. For those elements of society that could afford it, London in the 1920s was the place to socialise. Venues offering dinners, dancing and live music sprang up – tango teas at Murrays on Beak Street, cabaret and fine dining at the Café de Paris in Coventry Street or the Kit Kat Club in Haymarket – and the cares of the war were forgotten in a new breed of 'nightclubs' that drew the disapproval of more traditional elements of society who saw jazz as 'riotous' and thus dangerous. Many of the trends came over from Europe, so for a frequent visitor to Paris and similarly racy destinations like Oldham, they were a natural attraction. It is highly likely that Oldham's visit to Bucharest in March 1921 is significant in this context, either as the moment when they first met, or a mutual point of discussion thereafter.

Thus professional and social interests linked Oldham to de la Chapelle via the European legal and communication networks of the Foreign Office, while Lucy's former life among the mining magnates from Melbourne to New York and throughout the continent also brought her into de la Chapelle's circle. The appearance of the de la Chapelles at their wedding suggests a very strong bond between the two couples.

Whoever made the initial introduction, it proved to be successful. Lucy was strikingly beautiful and Oldham was handsome of sorts, judging by a family photograph from 1926 provided in the 1970s by Thomas Wellsted junior. They clearly had plenty to talk about, given their mutual connections, love of the high life and stories gathered from travelling the world. Oldham may well have regaled Lucy and the de la Chapelles with stories from Paris during the Peace Conference or snippets of gossip and overheard conversations from within the Foreign Office. It was the sort of harmless talk between couples that, in the wrong hands, could have been very useful if filed away by a legal mind with a sharp eye for business.

By this stage, Lucy's eldest son Thomas had already flown the nest – setting out on the SS *Raiputana* on 20 August 1926, bound for Bombay. Aged 22, he had decided to follow in his father's footsteps and become a mining engineer, practising in one of the few parts of the world where his ancestors had not set foot – India. Therefore the Oldhams' wedding was a rather small family occasion, graced by the presence of their closest friends.

It is clear that Oldham's relationship with Lucy had brought him not only a wife and new family, but also something that could not be obtained by his job and background – money. Certainly, some of his ostentatious mannerisms make more sense in this context, such as the ability to afford a car and the annual fee for his club. It also explains an interest in sartorial elegance bordering on the flamboyant. He dressed in matching brown suits, shirts, ties and shoes – many of which had an 'EHO' monogram stitched into them. Expensive taste could only be sustained through private funds, something which Lucy appeared to have in abundance, judging by the fact that the newly married couple purchased an upmarket house in Lucy's beloved Kensington.

This was a big change from the small terraced house of his childhood that Oldham had lived in so far; his new home, 31 Pembroke Gardens, had been built that year by the Prudential Assurance Company on the site of an old Wesleyan chapel. It was designed using an amalgam of styles that incorporated cutting-edge steel and concrete technology by the company's chief surveyor GA Coombe and built by James Smith and Sons. Two maids were hired to help around the house or walk the dogs that the couple owned. To complete the trappings of luxury, a Sunbeam Coupe, registration YH6368, was driven by their personal chauffeur Cowley. The car was parked in a basement garage with access to the street through a communal courtyard at the rear of the property. Today, 31 Pembroke Gardens is worth an estimated £3.5 million and even at 1927 prices it certainly put a dent in Lucy's dwindling inheritance.

As a belated honeymoon, the Oldhams took their beloved Sunbeam to the continent, in July 1928, covered by AA insurance for a 'tour abroad' during which they visited places such as Dieppe and Behobia, Spain. Upon their return, two surprises were in store. Perhaps most significantly, Oldham was appointed on 24 August as the Staff Officer for the Communications Department on the retirement of John Gritton. With promotion came a salary increase to the £300 to £400 band. This was a position of real authority within the office as the lynchpin of the operation that provided a connection between the Head and his Deputy – Eastwood and Cotesworth respectively – and the work of the cipher clerks and despatch messengers. It may well have been his rise in social status, coupled with an 'independent income' – albeit one that he had married into – that helped to secure a promotion that must have seemed forever beyond him in the rather static world of the civil service. The second surprise was the visit of his uncle Ern, who had arrived at Southampton from Cape Town on the *Glengorm Castle* on 27 August to see his family. To cap a stunning year for the Oldhams, on 6 November 1928 Lucy's family acquaintance Herbert Hoover secured a landslide victory in the US presidential election, winning 40 of the 48 states.

In the prime of life, with promotion, wealth, a glamorous (if somewhat older) wife and friends in the very highest circles in the world, Oldham must have thought that he was set for a glittering career. He was a trusted senior official, known to politicians and the Foreign Office hierarchy alike, and he played a pivotal role in enforcing national security through the smooth running of diplomatic communications. As 1929 dawned, further promotions were surely his for the taking; unfortunately, this was as good as it was going to get for Ernest Holloway Oldham.

Chapter eight

THE HUNT FOR 'CHARLIE SCOTT' (1929–1931)

In 1929 there was a similar incident in connection with a British code.
An unknown man offered Ianovitch the code used by the London Foreign
Office for its communication with the Indian authorities.

GRIGORI BESSEDOVSKY, *REVELATIONS OF A SOVIET DIPLOMAT* (1931)

On the morning of 2 October 1929, a fine crisp autumn day in Paris, tenants of a house in the Rue de Grenelle were startled to see a well-dressed young man scramble over the wall of their property, grazing his hands as he dropped into the courtyard below, and demand to be taken to the nearest gendarmerie. His name was Grigori Bessedovsky, the Soviet chargé d'affaires, and he was fleeing his own embassy in fear of his life.

As he explained to bemused officers at the gendarmerie, and later to various assembled journalists from the French press who scented a scandal brewing, he had been summoned from his work by a visiting representative of the Central Control Commission of the Communist Party, Boris Roisenman. In front of the embassy staff, Bessedovsky was told that he had to report back to Moscow immediately to give an account of 'politically heretical' views he had expressed about the poor treatment of Russian peasants. A heated argument ensued and Bessedovsky refused to comply with the demands to return, on the reasonable grounds that he would probably never reappear.

This was a period when Stalin was beginning to tighten his grip on the Communist Party and Soviet government, with the expulsion of Zinoviev and Trotsky in 1927 serving as a warning to all. Furthermore, Stalin's own personal assistant, Boris Bazhanov, had defected on 1 January 1928, eventually seeking asylum in France. Stalin had despatched OGPU agent Georges Agabekov to hunt him down and kill him, although Agabekov failed to achieve his mission. A British SIS agent stationed in Paris, Commander Wilfred 'Biffy' Dunderdale, had been granted an interview with Bazhanov from which he was able to compile 140 pages of notes about leading Communist Party members and the way OGPU operated.

Perhaps mindful of the damage caused by another defection so soon after Bazhanov, Roisenman drew his revolver and repeated his commands at gunpoint, instructing the embassy porters not to allow Bessedovsky or his family to leave – hence Bessedovsky's recourse to desperate measures, forcing his way past his would-be captors and scaling the wall of the residence. He persuaded the French authorities that he had

> …fallen out of sympathy with the domestic and foreign policy of
> the Soviet government and would tender his resignation to the am-
> bassador when he returned to Paris.[157]

In the meantime, a squad of gendarmes were despatched to the embassy to retrieve Bessedovsky's family; the officials were forced to comply, but with the utmost reluctance. William Tyrrell, by now the British ambassador to France and stationed in Paris, alerted the Foreign Office to the incident and sent note of the fact that Bessedovsky was planning to reveal further information about the Soviet regime. The way his family was held hostage was seized upon as evidence of Soviet tyranny, with the confirmation that OGPU were spying on their own officials received with particular distaste. On 6 October, the Soviets issued a statement of their own: Bessedovsky was wanted in Moscow for questioning about the alleged use of public funds for private use – embezzlement

– and that it was not as a result of any difference of opinion with the embassy or official government policy. When the Soviet explanation was also relayed to Whitehall by Tyrrell, it was greeted with the acerbic comment that it was 'a feeble explanation'.[158]

The timing of the incident was particularly unfortunate. Diplomatic relations between the Soviet Union and the UK had only been restored the day before Bessedovsky's flight, the result of months of negotiations following the return to power of a minority Labour government on 5 June 1929. To have such damaging revelations appear in the world's press could hardly help foster mutual trust and understanding. Nevertheless, there the matter might have remained – no more than a diplomatic storm in a teacup – if it were not for the fact that Bessedovsky, under the protection of the French authorities and being debriefed at the French Ministry of Foreign Affairs on the Quai D'Orsay, made good his promise to reveal more details about the way the Soviets ran their embassies. No wonder OGPU had wanted to shut him up given some of the intimate details Bessedovsky started to provide to the press within days, and later summarised in a book

> In Paris the work of the OGPU was actively pursued. Its director, Vladimir Ianovitch, was not a man of broad political views. In the old days he might have been a chief of judicial police in a small provincial town. He knew the tricks of his trade, however, and ran his section at the embassy well enough.
>
> The OGPU occupied four small rooms on the third floor of the embassy, with windows overlooking its garden and that of the adjoining house, 81 Rue de Grenelle. In one of these rooms there was some elaborate photographic apparatus with electric light powerful enough for all photographs to be taken with instantaneous exposures. In a room at the side, always kept locked, was a darkroom and chemical inks. The third room was Ianovitch's own office, and the fourth served as a meeting place for the typists and Ianovitch's subordinates but was, of course, only entered by agents with a definite position at the embassy or the consulate.[159]

Bessedovsky was able to provide notes about the way a legal *rezident* such as Ianovitch (real name Vladimir Borisovitch Wilenski) would operate:

> Ianovitch's activities came under several headings. First, he kept a watch on the whole embassy staff, including the counsellor and the ambassador himself, employing to this end numerous 'secret cooperators' recruited from the embassy officials. These secret agents listened at doors and gathered information about the private lives of their colleagues, sometimes acting as *agents provocateurs* by themselves initiating compromising conversations. Most of them worked in the Trade Delegation, the Petrol Syndicate, and the Soviet Bank. They had to take stock of the political opinions professed by the officials and of their personal relationships with French citizens.[160]

As well monitoring the activities of Russian refugees fleeing the revolution who lived in France, Ianovitch conducted other surveillance operations.

> The third branch of Ianovitch's work was to provide the Russian government with information on all that happened in France and her colonies. Here too he had the help of many secret agents, and certain officials in the Trade Delegation and the Bank were also made to report on everything they learned in their dealings with the French, on pain of dismissal.[161]

Ianovitch did not work alone. There was only one person he could trust with his secrets:

> Ianovitch was assisted by his wife, who was young and very pretty. I do not know whether she was really his wife or not but at any rate they simulated conjugal life to perfection. Although he only held minor appointments, Ianovitch nevertheless lived on a grand scale; officially a clerk, he occupied a fine apartment, and could indulge in the luxury of servants.

Mme Ianovitch had charge of her husband's personal code; she coded dispatches and the ambassador had to affix his stamp without their having been submitted to him previously so that he might have to sign a report which concerned himself. She also looked after the photography department and finances of the OGPU in Paris. Money arrived by diplomatic mail in large dollar bills and was paid into the embassy's treasury where dollars were exchanged for francs through our bank. She made appointments with the secret agents, wearing on these occasions one of her finest fur coats. She was regarded as one of the best intriguers of the OGPU and was entrusted with the most dangerous missions.[162]

As well as a talent for organisation, Ianovitch's wife was required to play a range of other roles during her career:

At Berlin she had played the part of a Hungarian countess, in Austria she had passed as the wife of a Persian diplomat, and in Czechoslovakia as the widow of a rich diamond merchant.[163]

Operations were not confined to Paris, though.

They frequently went to Normandy, staying on the coast near Trouville. They pretended that Ianovitch needed rest, though at the embassy he did nothing at all; from time to time he put in an appearance at the Chancellery, but this was merely a matter of form, and he spent the rest of his time in the secret rooms.[164]

Clearly, the Soviets were desperate for intelligence and were prepared to go to great lengths to secure it from within the countries where they operated embassies. Yet perhaps the most startling revelation of all was Bessedovsky's claim that the Soviets had obtained access to Italian cipher codes, which had been offered for sale at the Paris embassy the previous year. Bessedovsky recalled:

In the summer of 1928 a young man came to the embassy and
said that he was attached to one of the Italian embassies in Europe.
He was received by Guelfan [Helfand], the embassy secretary. He
explained that, being in great need of money, he was prepared to
sell to the Soviets a secret code which he had stolen from his chiefs.
Guelfan informed Ianovitch of this visit. The Italian was told that
before paying Dovgalevsky [the ambassador] would have to glance
at the key of the code and he duly brought them to the embassy.
While he was waiting Mme Ianovitch, in an hour and a half, photographed all that was needed and he was then informed that the
embassy did not buy stolen codes. Thus the deal was affected without any expense.[165]

More was to come, though; it was not just the Italians who had been compromised by the black market trade in official cipher codes:

In 1929 there was a similar incident in connection with a
British code. An unknown man offered Ianovitch the code used by
the London Foreign Office for its communication with the Indian
authorities. The same little comedy was played and Mme Ianovitch
again brought Ianovitch a substantial monetary reward.[166]

If the allegations were true, they represented a serious breach of British security. The India Office cipher codes had only been changed earlier in the year.
The new edition of the cipher and re-cipher tables were circulated to all official holders and acknowledgement of safe receipt was duly recorded with a
diligence and attention to detail similar to that demonstrated in the exercise
Oldham had coordinated in 1924.

The leak could only have come from someone with access to the codes,
which narrowed it down to three sources: a diplomat associated with
the India Office, someone within the India Office or a person within the
Communications Department itself, where the cipher codes were issued.
The British were duly alerted about Bessedovsky's claims and Dunderdale

was sent to interview him on 5 October. However, Dunderdale did not form a very strong impression of Bessedovsky, considering him to be 'smart and intelligent, but neither frank nor principled and quite possibly not honest'.[167] Perhaps it was the disbelief that anyone from the British civil or diplomatic services could betray their country in such a way, but despite the fact that a copy of Dunderdale's report was sent to Captain Hugh Miller of Special Branch, the allegations were not pursued.

Nevertheless, this was exactly the sort of problem that Oldham, as the new Staff Officer, and his trusted team of permanent clerks were there to prevent or, should the unthinkable have occurred, to investigate. However, the potential crisis coincided with a serious illness that incapacitated Oldham and prevented him from going to work. Although the nature of the illness was not specified, notes were placed on file in the Registry day books that he had been signed off work for a considerable period – initially for two weeks, from 18 to 31 October, with a further medical certificate issued on 7 December and a third on 23 January 1930, stating 'that it would probably be three months before Mr Oldham would be fit for duty'.[168] This was an extraordinary length of time to be away from work and the absence of the Staff Officer clearly contributed to the lack of official interest within the Communications Department.

However, Bessedovsky did not go away. A week after Oldham's absence from the office began, Bessedovsky's allegations began to seep out to the press in a series of articles reported in the *Telegraph*. On 25 October, he fuelled existing paranoia about Soviet activities by writing:

> The latest Anglo-Soviet agreement in no way modifies Stalin's plan
> to undermine the British colonial empire in order to achieve world
> revolution. Those who think Moscow no longer believes in the
> possibility of such revolution are mistaken.[169]

This, though, was only the beginning. He repeated his claims that Italian and British codes had been sold and copied, and the story was picked up around the world – not just major capital cities, but regional and local newspapers too. Faraway titles such as the *Townsville Daily Bulletin*, Queensland, published a syndicated summary of Bessedovsky's claims with the headline SOVIET POSSESSES INDIA OFFICE CODE:

> M Bessedovsky asserts that the Soviet also obtained by the same method the British government's India Office code, and since has been able to translate all British code messages to India.[170]

The *Canberra Times* added:

> The Foreign Office refuses to comment on the allegations concerning the Italian and British secret codes.[171]

The British newspapers were also strangely quiet on the matter, and in general the claim that British codes had been sold were ridiculed. *The Daily Herald* reported on 29 October:

> STOLEN CODE STORY REGARDED WITH DERISION IN
> LONDON
> The story of the acquisition by the Soviet Embassy in Paris of a British cipher 'used by the Colonial Office for communicating with India' is regarded here with derision.
> M Bessedovsky, the former Counsellor of the Soviet Embassy, who tells the story, has a great flair for the topical...
> An Italian cipher is stolen in Berlin; and promptly Mr Bessedovsky tells how a British cipher was stolen in London and taken to Paris.[172]

However, given the *Herald*'s role as the 'official' newspaper of the Trades Union Congress and therefore its greater sympathy to Soviet ideals and aims, their stance was perhaps understandable. The stories rumbled on for a few days and then gradually faded away. However, investigations and checks continued behind the scenes. On 6 December 1929, the SIS forwarded the report of Bessedovsky's statement to their counterparts in MI5, hoping that they would pick up the trail:

> Regarding the alleged sale of a British Foreign Office cipher to the
> Soviet embassy, Paris, in July 1929. According to Bessedovsky's
> statement, the Englishman who offered to sell the cipher and who
> gave his name as 'Mr Scott', was interviewed by the second secre-
> tary of the Polpredstvo [embassy], Gelfand [Helfand].

So Bessedovsky had provided a name for the British source of the leak, and
a rough date for the interview with Leon Helfand, nicknamed the 'Eye of
Moscow' for the way he passed information back home. Although a personal
file was raised on 'Scott', MI5 was unable to follow up on this lead – it seems
that suspicion had mistakenly fallen on William Arthur Scott – and with Oldham still absent, the Communications Department showed an equal unwill-
ingness to stir up any trouble. Indeed, it seems that internal security remained
sloppy in the wake of the affair, if a later entry in the day books is anything to
go by. A report filed on 12 March 1930 noted that a safe in the Passport Office
in Room 32 on the second floor had been found by the Office of Works, night-
watchman unlocked, albeit with the door closed. The incident had occurred
on 20 February, meaning there was an interval of nearly three weeks before it
was officially noted.[173]

The secret services were clearly concerned about Soviet attempts to intercept British intelligence. MI5 agent Jasper Harker noted in January 1930 that:

> We are in possession of information that [O]GPU agents received
> instructions during 1929 to watch foreign officials residing in
> hotels with a view to seizing any opportunity for ransacking
> their luggage.[174]

However, it took another defection to finally rouse the Foreign Office into action. Agabekov – the man who had been sent to eliminate Bazhanov and then,
it transpired, 'liquidate' Bessedovsky, before the mission was aborted – had
been acting as an OGPU illegal and head of operations in the near east since
the failed assassination attempt in 1928. However, he too sought asylum in
France in June 1930 for 'ideological reasons', although the fact he had fallen

in love with an English translator, Isobel Streater, played a large part in his decision to flee to the west. He was quickly expelled by the French – they were unconvinced by his information and were glad of an excuse to get rid of him – and deported to Brussels, where he caught the attention of the waiting British authorities.

Special Branch sent future MI5 agent Guy Liddell across to interview Agabekov, and he provided various written reports to MI5 and MI6. He also kept in close telephone contact with MI5's Jane Sissmore, by this date in charge of B Division (investigations and inquiries) with oversight for Soviet activity within the UK. Agabekov explained how his network of agents had operated whilst he was in Tehran and the near east, as well as the ways in which British telegrams were intercepted or copied. Amongst Agabekov's claims, many of which subsequently appeared in the papers, was the news that:

> Moscow is better informed at what happens in the British offices in Egypt than is Mr Arthur Henderson [the Foreign Secretary] himself... For the past few years, Moscow has received copies of all the secret reports of the British High Commissioner in Egypt and also copies of all the British Foreign Office correspondence with the High Commissioner.[175]

The repeated boasts of Soviet defectors – that they had access to restricted British codes or confidential information – could not be ignored indefinitely, especially as the security of the entire communications network would appear to have been breached. An internal inquiry was instigated within the Foreign Office, led by the Communications Department. We do not know what, if anything, the investigation uncovered or indeed who was in charge because the file no longer exists. All that remains is a line in the Foreign Office correspondence index that states that the department looked into Bessedovsky's claims that India Office ciphers had been compromised. In fact, all official Communications Department files have been destroyed for the crucial period from 1927 to 1935.

So what, if anything, occurred in July 1929? With the British files from the period missing, we have to turn to Soviet sources, specifically the personal notes and memoirs of a key illegal and man of many identities, Dimitri Bystrolyotov. He and his associates filed reports with OGPU which now form part of the archives of its successor body, the KGB.[176]

Born in Akchora, Crimea in 1901, Bystrolyotov had a difficult childhood and was caught up in the growing turmoil of the revolution and civil war. He fled Russia in 1919 and ended up in Constantinople where he spent the next few years struggling to survive before moving on to Prague in January 1922. It was here that Bystrolyotov came to the attention of OGPU operatives, who recruited him into their ranks in 1925. He began work as a legal *rezident* as part of the Soviet Trade Mission in Prague. One of his tasks was to secure the codes of a western power. Soviet intelligence networks had been severely damaged since the ARCOS episode in 1927 and in the wake of similar raids around the world against covert operatives in Poland, Turkey, France, Lithuania, Switzerland, Austria and Japan. The lack of information helped fuel Stalin's paranoia about enemy attacks against the Soviet Union and made him more determined to find out what was actually being discussed – hence the need for cipher codes to crack the traffic of messages flowing between governments and embassies.

The period from 1925 to 1936 saw the establishment of the network of operatives dubbed the Great Illegals – spymasters who established *rezidentura* in places such as Paris or Berlin and identified key targets who provided them with intelligence, either unwittingly or with complicity. These targets included people working for official organisations or institutions with access to useful information. Access could be achieved via exploiting a need for money, a shared political ideology or a weakness for sex. The role of the illegal was not only to gather intelligence from their targets but also after the early 1930s to establish 'recruitments in place' or double agents, such as the Cambridge spy ring in the UK. These would then carry on their work undetected by the establishment. Given the attempts to re-establish Anglo-Soviet relations, no *rezidentura* was initially set up in London but counter-intelligence activity continued, controlled from abroad and predominantly coordinated out of Berlin.

Since 1925, Bystrolyotov had developed a network of operatives in Prague and – despite being married – in his quest for codes he had been required to use his good looks and charms to seduce a young worker at the French embassy, Marie-Elaine Aucouturier, who had access to promising material. However, in the spring of 1930 he was suddenly transferred to the Berlin *rezidentura* headed by Boris Bazarov (codenamed KIN) and given his own codename, ANDREI, later changed to HANS. Bystrolyotov was provided with a false identity and passport, that of Greek businessman Alexander S Gallas from Salonika.

Bazarov controlled illegals in other countries as well, including England, and the role of his group was mainly to gather information on Anglo-German relations. However, there was a pressing case that Bazarov was dealing with – a mysterious man called 'Charlie' who had walked into the Soviet embassy in Paris in July the previous year, the same person that Bessedovsky had referred to as 'Scott'. Bazarov was able to brief Bystrolyotov on what had happened, providing us with an insider's account of the affair. According to Emil Draitser, Bystrolyotov's biographer who interviewed him in 1973:

> A modestly dressed short man, the cuffs of his jacket worn, paid a visit to the Soviet embassy in Paris and asked to see the military attaché.[177]

Second secretary Helfand was working in his office when a messenger told him that a stranger was asking to see a high official. Intrigued, Helfand asked the messenger to bring the man to him. The man walked in, speaking 'poor French with a strong English accent'.

> He introduced himself as Charlie, a typesetter in charge of printing copies of the deciphered British diplomatic despatches from around the world for distribution among the members of the British Foreign Office.[178]

Charlie was carrying a paper package under his arm which he placed on the desk in front of Helfand, asking if he wanted to inspect the contents. The

Oldham's personal passport photo.   (Courtesy of The National Archives)

Hotel Majestic, Paris. (Courtesy of Getty Images)

Hotel Beau-Rivage, Geneva. (Courtesy of Getty Images)

Oldham's house,
31 Pembroke
Gardens,
Kensington c.1974

*(Courtesy of Survey of London/
London Metropolitan Archives/
British History Online).*

a. Nos. 31–34 Pembroke Gardens (left) and Nos. 41A–41B Warwick Gardens in 1974. James Smith and Sons (Norwood) Ltd., builders, for Prudential Assurance Company, 1927–8 (p. 267)

Left: (From left to right) Oldham, his stepson James Raymond Wellsted, and 'Brand' c. 1926.

(Courtesy of The National Archives)

Right: Oldham's stepson James Raymond Wellsted.

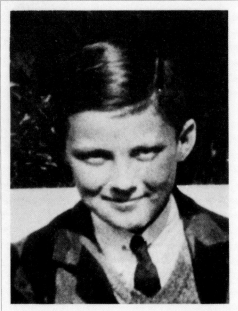

Left: 'Brand'.

Right: Ernest Holloway Oldham.

Sketch of HANS drawn by PIECK

Bystrolyotov aka 'Hans' as sketched by Henri Pieck. *(Courtesy of The National Archives)*

Extract from Tel. Check - Western 4571.

19.7.33. - 5.50 pm.   From - Thought to be from Call Office.

      Caller.(man)   Called

Is that you Lucy?
                                Yes.
Ernest speaking, can you bring
me some handkerchiefs, socks
and pyjamas?
                                Yes.
Joe is here, I hear KEMP has
been, what for?
                     What is that to do with you?
I suppose you told him
everything.
                     No I didn't but Its about time
                     I did. How long are you staying
                     there?
Not much longer.
                     Well you won't find me here. I'm
                     finished, you've done nothing for
                     me.
Oh yes I have. I will get
Joe down if you like and ask him.
                     I waited and you have done nothing
                     I have finished. Goodbye.

Intercepted call between Oldham and Lucy where she leaves him. *(Courtesy of The National Archives)*

When in drink he becomes talkative. He has told me of journeys he made to the Continent (when connected with the 'communicating' branch) with the late Earls Curzon and Grey, and, on one occasion, mentioned one JESSER-DAVIS, a King's messenger, with whom he apparently was frequently working.

He boasts of his friendship with Mr Harry Preston of Brighton, at whose hotel he frequently stayed with his wife. He often refers to his house in Kensington and explains his non-residence there to its being in the hands of the decorators and his wife being abroad with their son, who has just completed his education at Bonn University.

Each night, on leaving the Chequers, he visits Grays, the Chemist, of Duke Street, where Jock (a local character), the assistant, has ready for him a concoction for sleeplessness. He usually leaves Jock a bottle of beer.

In my opinion, OLDHAM is rapidly heading for a breakdown.

(Sd). H.H.

Report from Hunter, just before Oldham's final disappearance. (*Courtesy of The National Archives*).

package was placed on the table and unwrapped. It contained two books, one of which was bound in red buckram; they were entitled 'Foreign Office ciphers' and 'Colonial and Dominions Office ciphers'.[179] At this point, Charlie was instructed to leave the room so that Helfand could privately consult with his OGPU superiors, something that Charlie was incredibly reluctant to do without possession of the cipher books. Eventually, Charlie was ushered into a waiting room and Ianovitch was summoned by phone. He then took over the interview, albeit with a degree of suspicion fearing that the 'walk-in' was a trap. Charlie quickly set out his stall:

> For a fee of £10,000, he offered to make an extra copy of these despatches for the Soviets. He made it clear that, if the deal went smoothly, he would also be willing to serve as a middleman in selling copies of the British diplomatic codes and ciphers.[180]

Initially Charlie had demanded £50,000, a phenomenal sum worth well over £2.75 million in today's money, but £10,000 was still a substantial amount. It was noted at the time that Charlie wore a look of 'last and utter desperation',[181] suggesting he faced some unimaginable financial crisis that had brought him to this desperate resolution. Nevertheless, he remained determined and was not in the least bit reckless. In fact, in his dealings with Ianovitch he displayed a clear knowledge of the way intelligence agencies worked within the diplomatic services:

> Asked why he chose the Soviets as his potential customer, Charlie cited safety: in his view, unlike other embassies, the Soviet one was least likely to be infiltrated by British secret agents.[182]

Charlie was clearly more than a humble typesetter, something Ianovitch and his staff suspected when he made his one non-negotiable precondition to doing business: anonymity. Charlie said he would provide no further information for the Soviets if he suspected in the slightest that they were attempting to shadow him once he left. It seems clear that no transaction was agreed at that point; a further meeting was set up for the following month, again at the embassy in Paris, at which point Charlie would bring more material.

No attempt was made by Ianovitch to steal the codes that had been brought in by Charlie, despite Bessedovsky's claims. Bessedovsky had, in fact, mixed up Charlie's approach with events that had occurred exactly one year before in August 1928, when a short man with a red nose carrying a heavy briefcase had offered to sell Italian codes for 200,000 French francs. This was the occasion when Ianovitch deployed deception, taking the briefcase to the secure OGPU area within the embassy and passing the codes to his wife to photocopy. When this was complete, Ianovitch stormed back into the interview room and threw the case at the visitor in feigned rage, claiming that the attempt was a deliberate act of provocation and threatening to call the police. The visitor left angry and empty-handed, and Ianovitch was hailed as a genius for obtaining the codes for free. He was awarded $1,000 as a bonus.[183]

No wonder Ianovitch was nervous about Charlie. One walk-in was fortunate, but two seemed highly suspicious. Nevertheless, Charlie returned and provided more samples of his codes, as well as a variety of diplomatic telegrams and correspondence which he claimed he secured through a source at the Foreign Office. He insisted that he was only the middleman, taking a cut of the money on behalf of someone higher up. Satisfied that Charlie was genuine, a price was agreed; an initial fee of $6,000 was paid for the first instalment, $5,000 for the second and thereafter $1,000 per month depending on the quality of information provided. Charlie was assigned the codename ARNO, and at first all went well. However, the flow of information soon became patchy, as it was dependent on Charlie's ability to get to France to hand it over. Furthermore, the quality of material started to diminish, with much of the diplomatic correspondence of little use to the Soviets and seemingly picked at random. Charlie also prevaricated about the sale of diplomatic cipher codes. Given the potential value of Charlie as an intelligence asset, a decision was made by OGPU officials to track Charlie down and bring him under closer control, with the aim of facilitating less risky exchanges of documents away from the embassy in Paris and exerting greater leverage over the type of material that the Soviets needed. This required knowledge about who

Charlie was and what he actually did. This operation was assigned to Bazarov in Berlin, which he passed to Bystrolyotov to undertake. In a briefing note Bazarov wrote:

> At first we were quite satisfied… as long as we believed his story about being a typesetter. Then, as he seemed to delay the delivery of ciphers and failed to pass over top quality telegrams, providing only politically insignificant material, the issue of his true identity arose and we pressed him about the quality of the data. We were also concerned that the choice of the time and place of meetings was always his and it was clear that we had to take him in hand. The Centre has assigned you this task, ANDREI, and I shall direct the operation on the spot.[184]

Together Bystrolyotov and Bazarov decided upon a course of action that would help them establish Charlie's true identity and if necessary investigate the source of his information within the Foreign Office. To do this, they had to concoct a plausible scenario, based on various assumptions about Charlie's background. Most Foreign Office employees were thought to be of aristocratic stock, so Bystrolyotov assumed the identity of an impoverished Hungarian count by the name of Lajos József Perelly, based on a real person of the same name. To authenticate the cover story, he was provided with a passport and sent to Budapest to acclimatise himself in the role, visiting various haunts frequented by the local aristocrats and acquiring trinkets and paraphernalia with which they were adorned, including smoking pipes with the Perelly coat of arms and a little brush for his hat, as fashion dictated. He even managed to acquire a photo of himself with a Hungarian cardinal to whom the real Perelly was distantly related, along with other snaps taken in key landmarks to confirm his credentials. Meanwhile, Bazarov adopted the guise of a merciless Italian communist with the name of Da Vinci, a fanatic adherent to the Soviet cause who was pressuring Perelly for information on behalf of OGPU. The idea was that Charlie would sympathise with Perelly's situation, permitting him to establish a bond and win Charlie's confidence.[185]

However, before the plan could be put into action, Bystrolyotov was summoned to Moscow and interviewed by OGPU's deputy chief of foreign intelligence, Abram Slutsky. On arrival he was shown a copy of Bessedovsky's memoir written in Russian and his attention was drawn to the passage about the Italian cipher codes. A single word had been marked in the book against the description of the incident – 'restore' – which Slutsky revealed had been written by Stalin himself. In other words, the Soviet leader himself wanted them to track down the man they knew only to be short with a red nose. Instead of being pleased by Ianovitch's cleverness, it was perceived as a tactical mistake to have let such a potentially valuable intelligence asset go free and now Bystrolyotov was charged with tracking him down. This was a matter of utmost urgency; he was given no more than six months to complete his assignment. All he had to go on was the physical description.

Despite the odds being heavily stacked against success, Bystrolyotov first travelled to Paris to gather local information and then Geneva, home of the League of Nations where diplomats gathered for regular meetings. He brought across two of his former agents, Dr Joseph Leppin (codename PEEP) and his 'wife' Erica Weinstein (codename ERIKA), who scoured Italian embassies across Europe taking pictures of anyone who vaguely matched the description of the mystery man. In Geneva, he enlisted another illegal, Dutch artist Henri Christian Pieck (codename COOPER) and together they visited the two most popular haunts of the foreign diplomats – the International Bar and Brasserie Universal – and began sketching the patrons. The gamble paid off when a man fitting the description appeared in both locations.

Bystrolyotov knew a barman at the International Bar, Emilio Spada, who earned extra money selling snippets of information about his client's backgrounds – often gleaned when alcohol-loosened tongues. He immediately recognised the man in question and provided Bystrolyotov and Pieck with the name of their quarry: Swiss businessman Giovanni de Ry, known everywhere as Rossi (which was then used as his codename). It was only a matter of time before Bystrolyotov tracked down and confronted de Ry, securing his cooperation for the sale of further codes.[186]

This was a stunning success but had eaten up precious months. By the time he was able to join Bazarov in Paris towards the end of 1930, several meetings between Da Vinci and Charlie had already taken place to continue the handover of material, but Bazarov had made little progress in finding out any more about the mysterious Briton's background. He remained as cagey and elusive as ever. Bystrolyotov and Bazarov therefore hatched a plot designed to win Charlie's confidence – posing as Perelly, Bystrolyotov showed up at a restaurant where Bazarov and Charlie were meeting, claiming to have mixed up the time of his own rendezvous. Joining the two men, Perelly introduced himself and, when Bazarov made an excuse to leave temporarily, started to explain his own dealings with OGPU. Perelly claimed that he had been ruined by the Great War and turned to Bolshevism, eventually taking money from OGPU to maintain his lifestyle with the result that he was now beholden to Bazarov and could not extricate himself.

Thus the 'good cop, bad cop' dynamic had been established. Returning to the meeting, Bazarov assigned Perelly to work with Charlie and oversee the transfer of future information, with Perelly beseeching Charlie to help him deal with 'that cruel and angry Bolshevik, Da Vinci', and give him what he needed, otherwise Perelly would pay the price. However, Charlie refused to thaw during the next few meetings, held in Paris over several months.[187]

Frustrated that the Perelly story had failed to elicit the sympathy that he had hoped for, Bystrolyotov decided to break the cardinal rule that had been laid down by Charlie and brought in PEEP and ERIKA to help shadow him. Remarkably, despite several attempts to follow Charlie back to his accommodation, he gave them the slip every time – the man seemed to know the back streets of Paris remarkably well for a modest Foreign Office typesetter, leading Bystrolyotov to suspect that he possessed some form of counter-surveillance training.

In desperation, Bystrolyotov tried another tack at their next meeting and plied Charlie with alcohol. He certainly seemed to like a drink, but despite showing signs of inebriation when they parted, Charlie was still sufficiently possessed of his wits to be able to spot Bystrolyotov following him in the crowd. More amused than annoyed, Charlie told him to 'stop playing the street spy' and suggested a new venue for their next meeting – an address in Paris where he said his relatives lived. Buoyed by this apparent slip, rather than suspicious at the ease with which he'd secured personal information, Bystrolyotov raced to the apartment the next day only to find that Charlie had tricked him – it was the site of a demolished building.[188]

The game of cat-and-mouse continued throughout 1931, until one day ERIKA had a stroke of luck – she spotted Charlie dashing into the foyer of the Hôtel Napoleon, a rather grand establishment not far from the Arc de Triomphe. Mindful that this might be another attempt to shake any pursuers, she cautiously followed him inside where she spotted him requesting a room key from the main reception desk; he entered an elevator and disappeared out of sight. ERIKA approached the desk and asked which room the man was staying in, and was told he had booked into room 86 on the third floor. She slipped away to report her findings to Bystrolyotov, who returned immediately and checked into the Hôtel Napoleon himself. It did not take him long to extract the information he was looking for – Charlie had registered as Ernest H Oldwell.

With another meeting imminent, Bystrolyotov bided his time until the point when Charlie needed to leave the hotel to make his way to the agreed rendezvous and took direct action – adopting his Perelly guise, he burst into Charlie's room, asking him to forgive the intrusion on account of an emergency that had arisen which necessitated a change in the time and location of their meeting. Charlie was furious, but relented somewhat when Perelly explained that he was being sent to Turkey on an urgent OGPU mission. Perelly apologised profusely once again, bowing as he left the room – but in doing so, managed to spot Charlie's travel bag in the corner with the monogram 'EHO' embossed on the side.[189]

Initial checks showed that there was no-one with the name Oldwell in the Foreign Office but Bystrolyotov reasoned that EHO still represented Charlie's real name, given the monogrammed case. He also deduced that a Foreign Office employee in Paris was almost certainly connected with the forthcoming League of Nations meeting in Geneva, since the French capital was used as a base for daily diplomatic correspondence between London and Geneva. The most likely destination for EHO was therefore the Hôtel Beau Rivage, where UK delegates traditionally stayed. This was the perfect cover for Bystrolyotov. In the words of Antrobus, who regularly made the Paris to Geneva run:

> A vast concourse of politicians – for that is what a League meeting amounted to – is bound to bring all the ragtag and bobtail of the earth sniffing at their heels. Never, I suppose, were more secrets divulged than at one of these meetings. All the paraphernalia of leakage on a grand scale there assembled. The delegates were mostly amateurs, politicians or freelances, not professional diplomats; the press of every country was there in force, ready to extract the juices of their fat prey; worst of all, the place swarmed with spies and secret agents who, I imagine, got what they wanted handed to them on a plate.[190]

In this febrile atmosphere, Bystrolyotov stalked his target. It could not have been made any easier for him to find the identity of Charlie, as a list of delegates and attendees had been posted in the hotel lobby. Scanning the names, he located someone amongst the British delegation that was a perfect match for the initials EHO. Bystrolyotov did not have long to wait to test his theory, as he soon spotted the man he knew as Charlie take a seat at the hotel bar. Quietly, Bystrolyotov walked across the foyer and slipped into the seat next to him, without saying a word. The man's face drained of colour as he recognised Perelly and knew his cover as Charlie had been blown.

Unmasked as the mole in the Foreign Office, Ernest Holloway Oldham must have immediately realised that he was now in the clutches of OGPU. He could no longer rely on anonymity to protect him. In a blind panic, he dashed from the bar, gathered his things together and fled Geneva at the earliest opportunity.[191]

Chapter nine

AGENT ARNO
(1931–1933)

Attach complaint received from Commander Cotesworth regarding Mr
Oldham's behaviour in September and October last. Mr Oldham left
the office on 9 November and has not been seen since. He has neither
telephoned nor written to give any explanation for his absence. Suggest
that an official letter be sent to him asking for an explanation of absence
and failure to report the cause of it and telling him that he will be
required to send in his resignation if he takes further unauthorised leave.

ENTRY IN FOREIGN OFFICE DAY BOOK, 14 NOVEMBER 1931

Why? The burning question – why would Ernest Holloway Oldham risk his
career and freedom to sell codes to the Soviets? – is hard to answer. The risk
was indeed enormous.

By 1929 Oldham held an important position within the Foreign Office at
the heart of Britain's diplomatic network. He was responsible for the King's
Messenger routes across Europe and he was in control of the security of the
cipher codes for British colonies around the world. If caught, his actions would
at the very least warrant a criminal charge and it could be argued that they
were tantamount to treason, given he started selling information during a
period when Britain had severed its diplomatic ties with the Soviets precisely
because of this sort of activity. His actions do not appear to have been driven
by ideology – the lengths he took to preserve his anonymity were hardly consistent with a communist supporter. It leaves the main motivation as money.
This tallies with the obvious look of desperation painted across his face when

he first spoke to Helfand and the ludicrously high financial demands that he made in July 1929. However, this simply raises another question – what happened to Lucy's inheritance?

As we've seen previously, the remnant of Thomas Wellsted's estate was tied up in trusts to provide an income for his children, the £600 per year that Lucy received. If all factors are taken into account – global travel, overseas private schooling for her children, rented apartments in Kensington prior to the capital outlay involved with purchasing a new house in Pembroke Gardens and a penchant for luxurious living – then it is easy to see how Lucy's income may well have diminished quite rapidly. However, Wellsted had made other stipulations in his will. Lucy was to enjoy the proceeds of the trust fund set up for her children only until they reached 23, when they would receive the money directly, as well as their share of the investment fund.

In addition, her annual net income from the fund would only be paid on the condition that she remained unmarried. As soon as she married Oldham, the other trustee – the bank – would then have the right to administer the money as they saw fit, bound by a clause that the money should be expended for educational purposes. Her oldest son Thomas reached the age of 23 on 3 April 1927 and her marriage to Oldham meant that the other half of the estate ought technically to have been administered by the bank until her second son attained his majority in 1936. These conditions put Lucy's financial affairs in a very different light and indicated that the couple was deeply concerned about access to money. Indeed, Oldham was negotiating a loan of £2,000 with Eagle Star and British Dominions Insurance at an interest rate of 4.5 per cent, using 31 Pembroke Gardens as security for the mortgage. This suggested that they had seriously over-extended themselves.[192]

Records also show that Lucy and her husband had dabbled in the stock market. Their solicitors, Walbrook and Hoskens, used the brokers Messrs Laurence Sons and Gardner of 11 Copthall Court, not far from where Wellsted had worked in the City. At some point after her arrival back in England, Lucy had invested alongside Mr D W Rees in Port of London 6 per cent inscribed stock 1930/1940. She decided to take the earlier repayment option, cashing £951.8.9 in July 1930. Oldham had invested in a company called Visual Education Ltd in 1928, perhaps persuaded that this was a sensible move by his first-hand knowledge of his parents' teaching profession.[193]

This was a dangerous time to be speculating. Prior to the great Wall Street Crash, there were runs on the stock markets in March and May in 1929, but during the summer there were steady gains, peaking on 3 September – after Oldham's first contact with the Russians in Paris. Indeed, the London stock market only crashed on 20 September, while Wall Street suffered increasingly severe crashes on 24, 28 and 29 October (Black Thursday, Black Monday and Black Tuesday respectively) under the weight of of panicked selling. Lucy's former dinner companion, President Herbert Hoover, was powerless to prevent the economic catastrophe that marked the end of the roaring twenties and the start of the Depression.

It is likely that these global events greatly exacerbated the Oldhams' financial discomfort from risky stock market speculation, as well as the impact of the market turmoil on the trust fund, which would have further diminished their income. Perilously close to the brink, Oldham may well have been mindful of the rules governing bankruptcy in the civil service, which were circulated several times during his tenure in the Foreign Office. The general Treasury Chambers guidelines stated that:

> A civil servant who becomes a bankrupt or insolvent must, under pain of dismissal, at once report the fact to the Permanent Head of his Department.
>
> In such cases, the officer concerned should be required at the earliest possible moment to submit a complete statement of the facts of his case to the Head of his Department who will decide, in his discretion, whether the circumstances are such as to call for disciplinary action, it being understood that, if the officer who has become bankrupt or insolvent has committed any act of dishonesty or has otherwise acted discreditably he will be dismissed. The Department should take steps to prosecute the offender if there is evidence of the misappropriation of public monies.

> Pending the result of the Departmental Inquiry into his case, the officer concerned should be continued in his post, unless there is *prima facie* reason to believe that public monies have been or are likely to be involved, in which cases he should be suspended;
>
> Provided always that in no circumstances can a Civil Servant who is bankrupt or insolvent, continue to be employed on duties involving the handling of money.[194]

Under these guidelines, Oldham would have been suspended and – even before his illegal activities in France – have faced demotion to a position of lesser importance or even dismissal, bringing to an end his career and flamboyant lifestyle. Perhaps it was a fear of losing everything that drove him to roll the dice in one desperate gamble, trying to remain anonymous whilst he rebuilt his finances so that he could break with the Soviets on his terms at a time of his choosing. It certainly seems to be the case that Lucy's determination to cling to her luxurious lifestyle was a key factor.

Given the enormous pressure this deception placed upon him at work, as well as the professionalism of the agents he was pitted against, an even harder question to answer is how Oldham managed to get away with leading a double life for so long. From July 1929 to September 1931, he was able to not only obtain cipher codes and important communications from his own department, transport them to France and find the time to deliver them initially to the Soviet Embassy and then to his handlers, but he also kept the OGPU illegals at bay without detection. No wonder the Soviets suspected him of being more than just a clerk, although it was his familiarity with the streets of Paris during his time at the Peace Conference as well as in support of the League of Nations that clearly paid off. Furthermore, it is possible that he had retained his knowledge of basic spy craft from his abortive attempt to join Military Intelligence in 1918, honed through a long working relationship with various security officers within the Foreign Office, along with a good knowledge of the importance of personal safety while travelling in Europe on King's Messenger business.

Clearly, Oldham knew how to look after himself in a foreign country and possessed more than sufficient language skills to get by; the 'poor French' deployed in 1929 was almost certainly a ruse to support his own masquerade as a humble clerk, an ingénue abroad. Furthermore, it is highly likely that he came up with his desperate plan on one of his earlier trips to Geneva on League of Nations business, the place where De Ry returned in foul spirits after he had been deceived by Ianovitch in 1928. Given the way 'private information' had a habit of spreading around Geneva's bars and restaurants, Oldham would have picked up details of the attempted sale and deception fairly easily, possibly over a late night drink at the International Bar or at the Beau Rivage when the flawed plans of others could be refined in alcohol-fuelled conversation. Doubtless, Oldham thought that he could do better than de Ry and would not make the same mistakes – his reluctance to leave the code books unattended on his first visit to the Soviet Embassy was born partly out of natural caution, but also shows some prior knowledge of the way de Ry was tricked out of his material by the Soviets.

However, what is certain is the strain that Oldham felt as a result of his duplicitous behaviour. His first bout of sick leave on 18 October 1929 can probably be explained by the shock of Bessedovsky's revelations – after all, he would have had prior warning about the nature of the claims before they hit the press and his prolonged absence meant that any internal investigation was seriously hindered. Intriguingly, the Oldhams' good friend Count Octave de la Chapelle suffered a nervous breakdown at around the same time, ostensibly due to a 'misappropriation by a trusted member of staff'[195] that affected his legal business. It took him some time to return to work. However, given the sensitive nature of his legal business and close connection with key Romanian politicians and diplomats, it is tempting to speculate on what, exactly, was misappropriated.

In 1931, Bessedovsky finally published his book in English about his time in the Soviet diplomatic service and provided far more detail about the ways in which Ianovitch and his associates obtained codes – in particular, through agents carefully placed in Romanian circles:

> I remember a conversation I had during a poker party given by
> Dovgalevsky. This game occupied a great deal of the time of the

higher officials at the embassy; Dovgalevsky and Piatakov were both enthusiastic card players. I won a fair amount of money and eventually stopped playing, as I found my continual wins embarrassing. One day Ianovitch was playing. He had just lost some thousands of francs to Dovgalevsky and was very nervous. I said to him ironically:

'What does it all matter? There are plenty of fools wanting to sell codes'.

'I like that,' he replied. 'What have I made out of these codes? Scarcely a few thousand dollars. I know a fellow who has had some luck with the Romanians. He has managed to place a woman near one of the heads of the Romanian Siguranza [Special Branch] and now he has all the Romanian codes at his fingers' ends and knows their inmost secrets. *He* has made some money!'

'How is it', I said, 'that the Romanians can't see that the chief of their police is working for the OGPU?'

He laughed noisily.

I was astonished and asked some questions. A few glasses of vodka made him talkative.

'He's an ace. His whip has been felt by nearly all Bessarabia. When he arrests Romanian communists he tortures them in his office. How could the Romanians believe that he is in league with us?'

I was horrified. Here was an agent of the OGPU who tortured Romanian communists. It was diabolical. I said that the thing was a disgrace to the Soviet government. None of the political police of former regimes had ever used such abominable methods.

'Don't be so simple,' replied Ianovitch. 'Don't you know the value of the services of an agent of that stamp? We should be willing to send him communists to flog ourselves so that he can carry on with his work. And if revolution breaks out in Romania let him be shot with the rest! *We* shan't intervene. The effect of his activities is clearly revolutionary – he gives us information and flogs Romanian peasants. Thanks to him we even know the names

of the people who dance with the ambassador's wife in Paris'.
Dovgalevsky flushed. 'Remember that the Romanian Siguranza
exchanges its information for counter-espionage abroad. Thanks
to that we have had tips worth tens of thousands of dollars – hundreds, perhaps. A few peasants flogged in Romania – well, that's all
in the day's work!'[196]

Such news would have been deeply unnerving to anyone connected with the
Romanian diplomatic service, given the way in which communications had
been compromised, although no connection to de la Chapelle or his immediate associates can be proven. On 9 June 1931, de la Chapelle shut himself in
his office in Gresham Street. A few hours later his secretary heard a loud noise
from his room and rushed in to see if he was alright. She found him slumped
at his desk with a bullet wound to his head and a revolver by his side; the
coroner's verdict was suicide. On 13 June, the Count's funeral was held in his
beloved Tollesbury and he was laid to rest at West Street burial ground, facing
the sea. Significantly, it would appear that the Oldhams were not present.[197]

By this stage, Oldham was facing demons of his own. It is clear that a major
cause of his lengthening absence from work was a growing alcoholism, ref-
erenced by Bystrolyotov when he tried to get Oldham drunk, and no doubt
exacerbated through 1929 and 1930 by the double life that he was leading.
Nonetheless, the root cause of his fondness for drink can be traced to one of
the hidden pleasures of the Foreign Office – 'the Mine', as the basement bar
was referred to – presided over by the head office keeper 'assisted by his el-
egant and charming wife and daughter'. Antrobus described the setup:

> The bar was quite a picturesque place and looked more like a wine-
> shop in the south of France than an English public house; the bar
> itself was a couple of broad planks on a foundation of upended
> barrels and the stock-in-trade was on view behind it, in the shape
> of half a dozen puncheons of ale, sundry cases of bottled stout and
> soda water and a goodly selection of stone jars and bottles of whis-
> ky, gin and brandy.[198]

For someone with a weakness for drink, this was a dangerous lure and can help explain how Oldham slipped into bad habits; there was something of a drinking culture in the Communications Department. As Antrobus explained:

> Ciphering is thirsty work and although the true, bred-in-the-bone cipherer has a strong head, we were obliged in times of pressure to reinforce our numbers with selected amateurs. Some of these gentlemen, I regret to say, had not acquired so great an imperme-ability to the effects of strong waters as to justify them in drinking so much as they did.... I have certainly seen temporary gentlemen emerge from the Mine'... with their faculties sufficiently impaired to make the reading of what they subsequently wrote a task beyond human powers.[199]

Drink clearly affected staff in different ways, and not all of them were tolerated:

> One young gentleman, I remember, specialised in bumpers of port and amused himself by discharging the empty glasses at the heads of those who entered the room; another repaired to the basement at an early hour of the evening and drank himself into a complete coma; while a third, less immoderate but more volatile, became so amorously inclined towards a dark-eyed damsel in the adjoin-ing room that his advances led to an active repulse from the lady concerned and his consequent ejection from the department.[200]

Not all of Oldham's first period of absence can be blamed on the booze. He was clearly well enough to accompany his wife on a trip to Algiers by boat, de-parting from Southampton on 30 January 1930 having booked passage on the *Johan de Witt*, a vessel owned by the Nederland royal mail. This choice of trans-port suggests an attempt to avoid the more popular liners that they would normally have considered. Also on board was a young lady from Glasgow with the rather exotic name of Yolande Gabrielle Jeanne Elizabeth Mauboussin, the daughter of a French-born language teacher. She was to become the Old-hams' daughter-in-law later in 1930 when she married Thomas Wellsted on 22 September at Kensington Parish Church.

Equally, Oldham's absence was a useful cover for his regular trips to Paris to deliver material. It may well have been necessary for Oldham to use his counter-surveillance skills to avoid detection by his own colleagues and associates in the diplomatic corps, given he was meant to be at home recuperating from his 'illness'.

Nevertheless, as the strain increased, Oldham's absences from work continued. He was signed off sick again on 23 January 1931, forwarding various medical certificates that extended his absence until at least 23 February and probably the end of March. A further entry in the Foreign Office day books, dated 17 April 1931, stated that 'after being at the office from 1 to 9 April after his last sick leave, he was taken ill with bronchitis' and 'hopes to return soon after 20 April.'[201] It is fair to state that he spent almost as much time away from Whitehall as he did in his office, taking into account his 'official' trips abroad on League of Nations business. Yet it was from Geneva that he fled when Bystrolyotov ambushed him at the Beau Rivage and his sudden disappearance landed him in hot water. The Deputy Head of the Communications Department, Commander Cotesworth, made a complaint 'regarding Mr Oldham's behaviour in September and October'.[202] So where had he gone?

Having unmasked Oldham, Bystrolyotov and Bazarov planned a trip to London in early September to thoroughly research Oldham's identity and background. This did not take long. It was a relatively simple task to discover his true position within the Foreign Office by consulting the *Foreign Office List* and *Imperial Kalendar* while Oldham's address was readily available in the published electoral lists. The next step was to visit in person, to reinforce the fact that OGPU could gain access to Oldham whenever and wherever they chose – a gesture that would make it abundantly clear that the nature of the relationship was firmly out of Oldham's hands.

The OGPU agents returned to London. Adopting the Perelly guise once more, Bystrolyotov modified his dress code to reflect his location – dark grey suit jacket, striped trousers, a bowler hat – and set off for Kensington, with a last exhortation from Bazarov praying for a successful outcome to the mission, 'May God be with you.'[203]

Once again, we are indebted to Bystrolyotov's vividly written memoirs and OGPU reports as an account of what happened.[204] On his arrival at 31 Pembroke Gardens, Bystrolyotov was greeted at the door by the Oldhams' maid, to whom he presented a calling card that had been specially designed to contain his Perelly crest, as well as false credentials that identified him as a representative from a Dresden bank. The maid took the card – as well as a £1 tip, a large amount for the time – but informed Bystrolyotov that her master was not at home. This was a surprise and he was even more unnerved when Oldham's wife – 'a beautiful woman around 50 years old who tried to look younger than her age' – came to the door to demand to know what he wanted with her husband. Thinking quickly, Bystrolyotov explained that he was there to provide some advice about Oldham's investments, which were at risk due to the volatile stock market. This shows some knowledge of Oldham's affairs – it is possible the two men had discussed financial matters during their meetings. At any rate, Lucy's attitude to the handsome stranger relaxed somewhat, she confided that her husband was out of town and asked whether she could help. This provided Bystrolyotov with a perfect opportunity to find out more information before he confronted Oldham.

Playing the part of a confused foreigner, he explained, 'I'm sorry, I'm not very familiar with British etiquette, but I hope it's not out of line to invite you to lunch with me at the Ritz hotel?' Duly impressed at his choice of expensive venue, Lucy agreed and they arranged to meet the following day.

Over a lengthy lunch, washed down with 'a bottle of high-priced burgundy and coffee with cognac', Lucy warmed to the handsome count and revealed that her husband was a hopeless alcoholic. She explained that his absence from home was due to ongoing treatment for his addiction in Rendlesham Hall, a large country house near Woodbridge in Suffolk that had been converted into a sanatorium in 1923. Commenting on her husband's position at work, she noted that he was in poor standing with Monty, who she claimed was the head of the intelligence service at the Foreign Office.[205] It is not certain whether this topic of conversation was an attempt to impress the count by a bit of shameless namedropping or to issue a subtle warning that the Oldhams were under the scrutiny of security forces – it would appear that Oldham's liaison with Perelly was still a mystery to her, though Bystrolyotov was later convinced that she had been the driving force behind her husband's actions in July 1929. Either way, she was being disingenuous. Sir Charles Hubert Montgomery was the Chief Clerk in the Foreign Office and, by 1930, the Deputy Under-Secretary of State; he would have known about Oldham when the Communications Department was set up. To have fallen out of favour with such an important figure within the Foreign Office did not bode well for Oldham's prospects.

In a desperate attempt to help her husband, Lucy asked the count if he would visit Oldham at Rendlesham and ensure that he completed the treatment. She indicated that he had failed in previous attempts at rehabilitation – most notably during his major period of absence from work between October 1929 and April 1930. This presented Bystrolyotov with a golden opportunity to exert his influence over the stricken Oldham, one that was made easier by Lucy's offer of the family car, complete with chauffeur.

The following day, Bystrolyotov was picked up from his London hotel and driven for several hours to the countryside retreat, 90 miles away. The house was situated off the Woodbridge Road in its own secluded parkland, with the tree-lined gravel drive sweeping to the front of a grand 1870s exterior. Rendlesham Hall was run by the Norwood Sanatorium Limited, which advertised a restorative, holistic and recuperative approach to alcohol addiction – an approach that its tranquil setting in the Suffolk countryside seemed to support. However patients were treated with chemical purges and drugs, including injections of strychnine, as set out in the official publication of Norwood Sanatorium in 1932 that reflected on a quarter of a century of work in this field. Financial worry was listed as one of the principal causes of alcohol abuse.

When Bystrolyotov arrived, he found Oldham slumped in an armchair in the hallway, sleeping. He was either drugged or seemed to be drunk, in line with standard practice in the sanatorium as recorded in one of its annual reports.

Having decided the patient's degree of tolerance to alcohol, he is tapered with a sufficiency of this drug and for a sufficient length of time until there is a complete absence of deprivation symptoms and sleep is obtained without hypnotics.

When there is no tolerance, the alcohol is cut off at once and the specific treatment is commenced. This is known as the strychnine and antropine treatment and is given by subcutaneous (hypodermic) injection in ascending doses until a maximum is reached. Then there is a general reduction to the original dose.[206]

Regardless of the cause of Oldham's catatonic state, when he finally roused himself he was treated to the sight of Bystrolyotov sitting opposite him, which must have sobered him up sharply. His flight from Geneva had been in vain and he knew that the game was up. 'God damn you', he cursed but Bystrolyotov stayed with him as he had promised Lucy.[207] Over the next few weeks he learned more about OGPU's new agent, ARNO. Oldham continued the treatment for a month, during which time Lucy – who had formed a strong attachment to the count – insisted that Bystrolyotov stay with the Oldhams in their Kensington residence. As Bazarov reported back to Moscow on 9 October:

The improvement in the relationship with ARNO is beyond doubt. ARNO's wife suggested rather insistently that HANS should stay at their house. ARNO suggested the same. Incidentally, ARNO's wife told HANS that when HANS came to them she would introduce him to many colleagues of ARNO, who is known to all the chiefs of the Foreign Office.[208]

This was too good a chance to ignore but Bystrolyotov was somewhat startled when, on the eve of Oldham's return from Rendlesham, Lucy made a pass at him with the 'spirited gesture of a seaport hooker, rolling up the hem of her dress, spreading her legs and begging him not to waste any time.'[209] This was not part of his plan but with only a split second to decide on the right course of action, Bystrolyotov did not resist – he realised that Lucy

was too important in maintaining control over Oldham to alienate with
rejection. Afterwards, wracked with shame, he was worried he had made a
terrible mistake; his mission was precariously poised and the slightest wrong
move would jeopardise everything. 'I looked in the mirror. I'm sweaty; my
tie shifted to one side. My God, what do I tell my superiors?'[210] However,
the news was well received, and Lucy was assigned the codename MADAM,
perhaps as a result of this encounter.

Nevertheless, Oldham was not out of the woods. His activities in September
and October had indeed attracted the attention of his superiors and the trip to
Rendlesham was apparently unauthorised, which landed him in further difficulty. In a note placed on file in the Foreign Office Registry on 14 November:

> Mr Oldham left the office on 9 November and has not been seen
> since. He has neither telephoned nor written to give any explana-
> tion for his absence. Suggest that an official letter be sent to him
> asking for an explanation of absence and failure to report the cause
> of it and telling him that he will be required to send in his resigna-
> tion if he takes further unauthorised leave.[211]

The Head of the Communications Department, Harold Eastwood, consulted
with the Government Medical Referee, Dr Turney, about the situation and
reported back on 30 November:

> Doctor Turney considers that Mr Oldham's absences from duty on
> the grounds of ill health have been so frequent during the past two
> years that Foreign Office should press for his retirement for medi-
> cal reasons.[212]

The seriousness of the situation required the intervention of Oldham's own
medical advisor, Dr Henry Rowan of 33 Onslow Square, Kensington, to reas-
sure the officials about Oldham's condition. Writing on 5 December 1931
in response to a request sent two days previously from the Foreign Office to
provide an accurate assessment of Oldham's condition, Rowan stated that he

> ...considers that there is every prospect of his making a recovery which will enable him to carry on with his work regularly and efficiently.[213]

The crisis was averted by a whisker, but alongside growing interest in his attendance record, a further investigation was started about his personal affairs – in particular the fact that 'no income returns have been received from him for the years 1928–29 to 1931–32'.[214] This was, in many ways, more challenging to deal with than the issue of his sick leave, as full disclosure of his financial affairs during this specific period would have raised serious questions about where his money had come from. It was not illegal for staff to enjoy private income streams – after all, it had been actively encouraged until recent years – but it would have been difficult to explain the regular appearance of payments in dollars from overseas sources. Nevertheless, it would appear that he was able to dodge these inquiries, as the question was not raised again when he finally returned to work.

During the winter of 1931–32, Bystrolyotov increasingly based himself in London and became integrated into the Oldhams' family life – witnessing first-hand their financial hardship and forming the opinion that it was Lucy who had driven Oldham to take the desperate measures in 1929. She was reluctant to give up her lifestyle even though the money had gone. However, despite Bystrolyotov's presence to ensure Oldham complied with the delivery of material, it was far too risky for Bystrolyotov to take it across the Channel, so Oldham was still required to travel abroad. A range of locations were used as well as Paris, such as Madrid, Trouville-sur-Mer, and a Swiss resort near Brienz, in the canton of Bern, where technical bases were set up to process the material and ensure its safe despatch back to the OGPU centre in Moscow.

Given the increasing concern about Oldham's performance at work, a cover story was required to explain the trips overseas, so Bystrolyotov arranged for Lucy's youngest son, James Raymond Wellsted, to be placed with a German family near Bonn to undertake his schooling, giving the Oldhams a reason to travel to see their son. Bystrolyotov also assisted with somewhat darker aspects of family life. According to his notes, he arranged for Lucy's daughter in law, Yolande, to visit a clinic in Berlin to have an abortion, since she had exceeded the legal time limit for the operation in Britain.

To help him travel, Oldham applied for a new passport on 16 February in his rather blunt, almost arrogant, style; he claimed he had lost the old one, but it might have been part of a ploy to create a new identity for himself or Bystrolyotov:

> Dear Holloway,
> Would you like to issue me with a new passport?
> I am unable, at the moment, to lay my hands on the old one, No 151, issued at Bucharest on March 17 1921; it is not here, and a hurried search at home last night failed to bring it to light.
> I will send it over as soon as possible.
> Yours ever
> EH Oldham[215]

Included with the papers was a declaration signed by Oldham that the passport was needed for travel to Europe for the purpose of 'duty'. Rather disingenuously, given the covering note, he declared that all previous passports granted had been surrendered for cancellation to a British Passport or Consular office. The counter-signing officer was his Communications Department associate, Thomas Eldred Kemp, who was to play an increasingly important role in Oldham's life. He was happy to state that he could vouch for him as a fit and proper person to receive a passport, having known Oldham for 13 years. The order to issue the passport was initialled by 'PCH' on the same day as Oldham submitted his application – presumably Percy Clarence Holloway, another war veteran and one of Oldham's cronies who had worked with him as a temporary clerk after the war before switching departments to find employment as an examiner in the Passport Department. A replacement was issued immediately, entered on the Passport Office register that no fee was paid as it was 'gratis – FO'.[216]

By this stage, Bystrolyotov was regularly joined by his colleagues Bazarov, Leppin and Weinstein in London, as well as another Great Illegal, Theodor

Mally – just in case further pressure had to be exerted on Oldham, who was still insistent that he was acting on behalf of a 'source' within Whitehall. The deployment of so many key operatives in London as a functioning cell shows the importance with which ARNO was held within OGPU and the Soviet hierarchy as an intelligence asset. Yet the strain on Oldham was beginning to show once more.

Shortly after he gained his new passport, with Bystrolyotov breathing down his neck, and worn out from over two-and-a-half years of deception, Oldham turned to drink again with the inevitable consequences in his department. Discussions among his superiors took place between 2 and 9 March about his 'irregular attendance at the office'.[217] For the first time the spectre of dismissal was raised with him directly, when he was brought in to be 'interviewed on the question of his proposed resignation'[218] – the sort of proposition in which he had little choice but to comply.

In the world of the Foreign Office, where the gentleman's code of conduct still operated, openly discussing the retirement of a 39-year-old permanent official was an extraordinary step and demonstrated just how much trouble Oldham was in. The patience of his superiors had been tested to breaking point by his lack of attendance and served notice that everything Oldham did was now under microscopic scrutiny. Oldham was not helped by the actions of Bystrolyotov, who himself was under just as much pressure to ensure Oldham did not fall apart and thus expose the cell.

As a result, mistakes crept into Bystrolyotov's work; on one occasion Oldham brought cipher codes and correspondence to Paris for Bystrolyotov to copy, but when pressing the material under glass to enable easier photography, he cut his finger and a drop of blood stained the paper. Despite his best efforts, he was not able to remove the stain and was forced to hand it back to Oldham in the damaged state. Remarkably, no-one noticed, demonstrating the amazing lack of security or scrutiny within the Foreign Office as well as the trust placed in civil service colleagues.[219] Other cracks in Bystrolyotov's once meticulous cover were gradually exposed as he became more jaded.

One evening, Oldham and Bystrolyotov took some time out to socialise together by watching a film in the local cinema. 'God Save the King' was played

– a standard custom to demonstrate loyalty to the Crown – but Bystrolyotov failed to rise from his seat. This gaffe reduced the panicked Oldham to a state of near hysteria for fear their fellow patrons might think they were spies.[220] Nevertheless, he continued to do his best for Perelly and we can discern a glimpse of Oldham's relationship with Bystrolyotov from a report sent from Bazarov back to the OGPU centre on 18 April 1932:

> ARNO sees in him an aristocrat, a Hungarian nobleman who im-presses him very much (he seems to have seriously believed his legend), who somehow found himself a Bolshevik, but since he is not Russian he is far more acceptable. How exactly he imagines it in his mind is not clear. Obviously, he thinks that either HANS was our prisoner of war or had got lost in Europe. HANS only asks for something, explains the pressure on my part, as if he himself were placed in such as position in which lack of success in the work means transferring him to another, non-European section.[221]

With great effort, Oldham pulled himself together after the 'final warn-ing' from his superiors and resumed work back in the Communications Department – as well as his covert activities on behalf of Perelly. Having gath-ered together more material, he sailed to Calais twice in April and flew to Paris in May and Amsterdam in June with Imperial Airways,[222] but his real value to the Soviets came with the Lausanne Conference that was convened between 16 June and 9 July.

Representatives from Britain, France and Germany met to discuss Germany's reparation payments under the terms of the Treaty of Versailles. These had been suspended the previous year due to the global economic cri-sis post-Wall Street Crash and much depended on whether Lucy's old friend Hoover would accede to European demands for a relaxation in the terms of the loan repayments to the USA. The negotiations had repercussions beyond the nations in attendance; the Soviet Union was fearful about any diplomatic agreements between Germany and France that might threaten their security and were desperate for access to the conversations that were taking place.

The exact details concerning the material that Oldham provided from Lausanne is open to interpretation by historians, but what is beyond doubt is that he was able to pass across some very valuable documents. According to the OGPU files, and the notes compiled by Bystrolyotov, these included a Foreign Office cable dated 28 June in which Sir Horace Rumbold, the British ambassador to Berlin, stated that he obtained information about the intentions of the newly appointed German Chancellor, von Papen:

> To reach a compromise with France at all costs about all points of contention even at the price of sacrifice on the side of Germany.

Other useful pieces of information were obtained:

> On the day of von Papen's return from Lausanne, during the cabinet meeting before signing the treaty, a secret session took place during which General Schleicher insisted on the necessity to come to an agreement with France on the question of armament, stating firmly that Germany cannot exist any longer with an army of 100,000 serving a 12-year stint.[223]

Bystrolyotov provided unsubstantiated intelligence back to his masters within OGPU, including various informal conversations between the British Prime Minister, Ramsay MacDonald, von Papen and the French Prime Minister, Édouard Herriot – with von Papen taking the negotiating position that military concessions were required to enable him to halt the rise to power of Adolf Hitler and the National Socialists. The official British papers from Lausanne are housed at the National Archives and provide ample corroboration for Bystrolyotov's access to the most secret conversations in Europe. For example, the MacDonald–von Papen–Herriot summit took place at midday on 28 June and the following notes were sent back to London:

> Herr von Papen said that the task of his government was to prevent a social revolution inspired by the nationalists. How could he do

that? These people were moved by the discrimination which they thought was directed against Germany. They felt that she was being treated as a nation of second rank. If reparations could not be wiped out and if Germany could not feel that she was a nation having equal rights with the others, it would be impossible to restore confidence. All this could be covered up in a general plan for the restoration of Europe.[224]

This was not an idle threat; Adolf Hitler, leader of the National Socialist (Nazi) party had been defeated in the presidential elections in April, despite polling nearly 13.5 million votes in the final run-off, but the party's popularity had been growing rapidly in the years since the Wall Street Crash had exacerbated German economic crises.

Herriot's response was also recorded:

The second means of disposing of the reparation question was to make it an occasion of reconciliation between France and Germany. The Franco-German dispute had poisoned history and was poisoning Europe. The French delegation clearly understood that if the end of reparations could be made the occasion of Franco-German reconciliation the disappearance of the solde [payments] would have little importance... He understood that if they could bring back from Lausanne a Franco-German reconciliation that would be more important than any solde.[225]

All official communications were ciphered and sent back to London, usually by the secretary to the British delegation, Victor Perowne, who was on secondment from the Foreign Office. In a series of accompanying letters, Perowne revealed the level of work undertaken by the secretariat to preserve security. On 27 June he wrote:

This has been a frightful day but there is very little to report that pertains to our own muttons. The cipher officers were working

from 3.00 am to about midday; I was up at 6.15 am to start typing
out their decipherages as the PM insisted on knowing what was in
the telegrams by 7.00 am if possible. It is a sad business this running reparations, European reconstruction etc, disarmament and
Ireland all from Lausanne![226]

On 29 June he noted that meetings with ministers from the French and
German delegations had taken place the previous day, and that transcripts had
been made, 'but the confidences exchanged on these occasions are regarded as
too secret for copies of these records to have reached me.'[227] Yet he was eventually made privy to some of the behind the scenes deal-making; on 4 July he
wrote back that:

I have now secured a copy of the record of the mysterious conversation which took place between the prime minister and von
Papen on 27 June and I enclose four copies herewith. One copy
has, on the PM's instructions, been sent to Herr von Papen.[228]

In this meeting, MacDonald revealed information on the French and British
negotiating position to von Papen 'in great confidence' to help the Germans
understand what was needed to reach a crucial consensus and ensure the conference was a success.

Clearly, Oldham gained access to a large proportion of this secret, coded
correspondence, as well as the despatches sent back to London in the official bags. This level of insight into the diplomatic position of three major
powers was invaluable to the Soviets, who were excluded from the negotiations. The information assisted them in developing their own diplomatic
responses. As it transpired, only an informal agreement to remove German
war debt and suspend reparations was announced, contingent upon agreement from the USA. The proposal was rejected by Hoover's administration in December. After the Conference, Oldham was able to extend his
usefulness by providing another key resource for Bystrolyotov – a British passport under the name Sir Robert Grenville, delivered on 27 July.

Oldham claimed that it was signed by the Foreign Secretary, Sir John Simon, who was a personal acquaintance. Bazarov reported the acquisition to the OGPU Centre, in doing so revealing his ignorance of the way Britain's passport system operated:

> Charlie has brought a book for HANS. This book has been issued not by the Ministry of Home Affairs, as is usual, but by the Foreign Office. This book is British and not Canadian, as originally intended, it is like the one Charlie has.[229]

However, Oldham's exertions at Lausanne had taken a huge toll on his physical and mental well-being and drink once again took hold. He failed to make appointments with Bystrolyotov: the delivery of the passport took place ten days after the scheduled meeting date and it is clear that Oldham had started to deteriorate physically. As Bazarov reported at the time:

> HANS has just come back from his trip; this time his partner made him wait for as much as ten days. He has brought nothing interesting. I think this is explained by his careless attitude to his job. He keeps convincing us that his partner was extremely busy in connection with the Lausanne conference so he had no opportunity to interest us in different matters which are of significance to us.[230]

Far more seriously, though, Oldham's mistakes at work were becoming increasingly obvious and far too serious to avoid. Among other things, he failed to respond to the inquiries of other officials within the Foreign Office, possibly linked to the fact that a code book had gone missing from the safe in the basement of the Foreign Office in which Oldham had been seen wandering during periods when he had been officially signed off on sick leave. In addition, he had been spotted using the ambassador's side entrance to leave the building rather than the front door, thus avoiding security in the form of the door keepers. Add to this the fact that he was often found drunk or even asleep and it was clear that he had become a dangerous liability.[231]

The final straw came on 12 September, when yet another medical certificate was issued in regard to a leave of absence on the grounds of sickness.[232] Although he had been considered a capable official and every effort had been made to give him chance after chance, the impact of his alcoholism upon his work had grown too serious to ignore any longer and made his position within the Foreign Office untenable. On 30 September, Oldham was summoned to see his superiors. He was told that his work over the last two years had been unacceptable and a litany of mistakes was used as evidence. In addition to the issues described above, Oldham was blamed for the loss of confidential papers which he had unaccountably taken home over the previous six months and he was equally unable to explain unauthorised visits to the cipher room. Rather than formal dismissal, he was instructed to:

> ...submit his resignation on account of ill health. As his doctor is
> of the opinion that he will in due course regain his normal health,
> Mr Oldham is not in a position to put forward, for submission to
> the Treasury, a claim for pension on the grounds that he is perma-
> nently unfit for duty. Enquires whether some form of gratuity can
> be applied for in the circumstances.[233]

The failure to grant a pension or gratuity was a particularly devastating blow on two accounts. Not only did this further compromise the Oldhams' parlous financial affairs but it also raised the chilling prospect that the Foreign Office suspected him of wrongdoing or illegal activity rather than simple incompetence caused by his alcoholism. On the handful of previous occasions when a permanent official had not been awarded their pension, the person removed had been under suspicion of espionage.[234]

Rocked by this catastrophe, but compelled to continue the charade that they still had access to sensitive material of value to the OGPU, the Oldhams travelled to Croydon Aerodrome and flew with Imperial Airways to Berlin on 18 October on the 9.20 am flight to meet Bystrolyotov as previously arranged. They failed to mention Oldham's dismissal although, from his poor physical condition, it was clear that Oldham was in the grip of alcohol addiction once more.

According to Bystrolyotov's biographer Draitser's account of the meeting:

> Although he swore he would continue to bring British diplomatic
> mail in the future, in Dimitri's [Bystrolyotov] judgment, he couldn't
> last more than a few months before becoming fully incapacitated.
> During their meeting, ARNO was totally apathetic, vomited and
> often couldn't even move.[235]

Three days later, Oldham booked a flight to Berlin but cancelled at the last
minute, choosing to travel to Cologne instead before returning to England.
He rearranged his meeting with Bystrolyotov but in the end only Lucy made
the journey, flying back to Berlin on her own and confronting Bystrolyotov
with the true extent of Oldham's decline and fall on 11 November. As with
previous dealings, there was a mix of truth, half-truths and outright lies.
Bystrolyotov digested the shocking news and sent a report back to Bazarov:

> In the middle of October, that is, a week before his arrival in
> Berlin, ARNO was dismissed from the service. How greatly the
> chiefs were prejudiced against him is indicated by the fact that not
> even a partial pension was granted to him. The reason was that for
> the past two years he had been drinking heavily and he had been
> working carelessly. For the past six months he has ceased working
> entirely and had not appeared at the office. He had taken official
> papers home and lost them and had failed to answer urgent inqui-
> ries. His colleagues had tried to reason with him but to no avail, so
> they had given up, with the exception of his former assistant Kemp
> who still visits him.
>
> ARNO's financial situation is bad. He had some money in the
> bank, but not much. MADAM intends to leave him, to sell the
> house and car and take her share. She intends to settle in some
> French resort where there are plenty of Englishmen and work as
> a housekeeper or companion. If this fails she will become a prosti-
> tute. She has asked me not to leave her without support.

ARNO's physical condition is poor. He will take a rest after the Berlin trip and will recover some of his cheerfulness and capacity for work but in the end his strength will not last for long and complete disablement will follow in a few months.

ARNO declared that he will continue to maintain contact in the future and we agreed to meet in Germany next week. There was no deterioration in our relations because of his abnormal condition. Complete apathy, heavy vomiting and the inability to speak or move has made him impossible to talk to.[236]

Bystrolyotov's mission as Oldham's handler was in crisis. He proposed an exit strategy, which he revealed to Lucy – namely, to offer Oldham a life pension on the sole condition that he put Bystrolyotov in touch with his 'source'. It is staggering that, even after his engineered sacking, Oldham had clung to the original cover story that he was merely an intermediary for a 'retired captain from the Foreign Office' whose name he would not reveal and on whose behalf he was selling material. When pressed on this by Bystrolyotov, Lucy denied any knowledge of such a person. She also stated that her husband never went abroad on Foreign Office business – clearly untrue, given his presence at Geneva in 1931 – and that nothing Oldham said could be trusted.[237]

Unsure of what to believe, Bystrolyotov decided to return to London and find a solution – an extraordinary risk to take, given it was entirely possible that Oldham was suspected of treason and therefore under surveillance. As a mark of appreciation for the work he was undertaking, on 17 November Bystrolyotov was bestowed with a personal gun:

For successfully carrying out several assignments of major operative value and exceptional persistence in doing so.[238]

It bore the inscription:

For a merciless fight with the counter-revolution from the OGPU collegium.
OGPU Deputy Chairman Balitsky[239]

After a brief sojourn to the continent to sort out a few personal issues, Bystrolyotov finally made the trip to London just before Christmas. Not even two years spent working as ARNO's handler could have prepared him for the terrible scene that lay in wait behind the genteel façade of 31 Pembroke Gardens. Oldham had been on a non-stop drinking binge, with Lucy unable to restrain him as he grew increasingly violent.

> [On] 22, 23 and 24 December, ARNO drank more and more; our entreaties and reproaches irritated him with no result. Finally, I decided to take the matter into my own hands and demanded that he go to the country for treatment. On the evening of the 25th I went to his house and found ARNO dishevelled and asleep in an armchair, an alcoholic who had completely gone to pieces. I shook him awake, but without opening his eyes he reached out for a bottle and drank, thinking that I was his wife. 'Go away, you bitch,' he said, before falling asleep again. I persuaded MADAM not to give him any more brandy and urged her to call a doctor when he awoke. When he did so, that night, her refusal to give him a drink prompted him to try and strangle her and she was only saved by the doctor who gave him medication and arranged for him to be taken to the country unconscious. ARNO looked awful and MADAM was shattered and wanted to do away with herself. I spent three days persuading her not to commit suicide while she lay sedated in bed with the marks of ARNO's fingers very evident on her throat.[240]

Thus 1932 closed with Oldham once more in Rendlesham sanatorium, undergoing more treatment for his alcoholism and his suicidal wife on the verge of leaving him, still battered from the attack at Christmas. This was Bystrolyotov's worst nightmare, but still he persisted with his work when common sense dictated that Oldham had become more of a liability than an asset.

Changing political circumstances on the world stage also played an important part in Bystrolyotov's decision. With the rejection of the Lausanne agreement by the Americans in December, the prophetic words of von Papen came to pass as Adolf Hitler was made Chancellor of the German Republic on 30 January 1933 in place of von Papen. Hitler's international stance was clear; alliances with Britain and Italy were desired to provide security against France, considered to be Germany's 'unrelenting mortal enemy'. There was also to be an enlargement of Germany's *lebensraum* ('living space') at the expense of territory seized from the Soviet Union. In German elections on 5 March, the Nazi party won nearly 44 per cent of the vote and Hitler used his populist mandate to exert even greater authority over the state. The Reichstag passed the Enabling Act on 23 March, effectively ending democracy and making Hitler a de facto dictator in Germany. This made the calls from Benito Mussolini – already leader of a Fascist state in Italy – on 19 March for the creation of a Four-Power Pact even more alarming to the Soviets, as they were not included.

Yet the faith placed by Bystrolyotov in Oldham's powers of recovery rather improbably paid off when, in May 1933, Oldham arrived in Paris with another packet of documents for the Soviets, just when they needed access to diplomatic correspondence the most. He claimed he did not know what was inside the packet, only that he had paid for them in full. Furthermore, Oldham said that he was in negotiation for the purchase of a Foreign Office code book called 'C' plus various other cipher charts, though the price that his source required was much higher than before. It was clearly a ploy to extract more money from the Soviets. Bystrolyotov countered by asking once again for direct access to the source, which Oldham refused to provide. Yet whilst the cover story provided some legitimate explanation for how he could still gain material from the Foreign Office, it was completely untrue – so how had Oldham managed to obtain new material?

The answer is staggering: Oldham was able to stroll through the front door. Antrobus recalled that 'an official could bring a friend in with him without hindrance or comment'[241], and even a former employee such as Oldham, who had left under a black cloud less than a year before, was able to enter unchallenged. It transpired from later accounts that Oldham had been a regular visitor to his old office on several occasions, mainly to see friends like Thomas Kemp as well as King's Messengers with whom he was close, such as Raymond Oake and Charles Jesser-Davies.

However, he had another legitimate reason to request entry; incredible as it may seem, he was allowed regular access to the Foreign Office because he was permitted to keep a safety deposit box on the premises. Perhaps more than anything else, this revelation should remind us that Oldham and his associates were living in a different age and, despite some of the changes in attitude and culture that have been described in earlier chapters, the Foreign Office still at times resembled a 19th century gentleman's club, with its natural assumption that everybody played by the rules.

We are fortunate to have an account of the episode, provided by one of the assistant clerks, Herbert James Bindon, a few months later.

> He has only just retired and has been in to look over the papers in his box two or three times. On the last occasion – something like May – he came in about the same time (nearly 6.00 pm). I had not finished my work and the presses were unlocked.[242]

The presses were where confidential material was stored – exactly the sort of thing that Oldham was after.

> He sat down at his old desk, chatted for a moment, and then got out his box. I think he said 'I am just going to run through my box and look out papers, and I must also write to Bell at Jeddah.'
>
> I was of opinion that he was not in possession of all his faculties and was rather thick and heavy. I cannot say if he took any papers away.
>
> I wondered if he ought to be left there and I discussed with Mr Roberts. He had previously said, 'I shall only be about 20 minutes,' and when I went back he was writing to Bell (I could see the heading of the letter) and I asked if he was going to be much longer. He offered to lock up. However, I said I was not going just then. He was left alone but there was nothing important he could get at.
>
> After about five or six minutes I went back and he said he had not yet finished. He asked who was on duty, and I said Roberts would

be there until 7.45. He said he would give the keys to Roberts. I therefore told Roberts, who said he would look out for him.

On the last occasion I went in, he said, 'I ought to be finished by 7.45, but in case I am not, what is the combination?' (meaning the combination lock of the safe in which the keys are kept at night). I said, 'I don't know'. He asked if Roberts knew and I came to discuss it with him. I then told Oldham that I could not find out about it. He said, 'Isn't there anyone in Room 22 [cipher room] or Central Department who would know?' I said I did not think so and he had better give the keys to Roberts.[243]

This is astonishing – even accounting for the fact that Oldham was still permitted access to his possessions, there was no justification for granting him access to the keys to the presses, even if the combination to the safe was not revealed.

When I got home I phoned Roberts, who said he had got the keys back but had had some trouble with Oldham. It seems that when he went to look for Oldham he had gone and Roberts had caught him in the hall and found Oldham just going out with the keys. He was a bit 'funny' over Roberts asking for the keys and said it was a lot of unnecessary fuss. He also tried to find out the combination from Roberts.

He was not left alone for more than ten minutes at a time and in Room 5 he could have had access to nothing except the Inter-Departmental book giving a list of holders.

I checked the stock after his last visit and found it correct.[244]

The office keeper, Mr Roberts, corroborated this version of events.

In May, Oldham borrowed the keys from Bindon and when Bindon went home about 7.00 pm, he asked me to look out for Oldham.

As Oldham did not come over to me with the keys soon after 7.00 pm, I went down and found he had gone out to get a drink

and when he came back I asked him, 'What about the keys?'
I found he had been out and taken the keys with him and was
coming back to return them. I rang up his house during his disappearance to see if he had gone home but he came in while I was
waiting to be connected.[245]

Clearly, the lax security – and residual deference to a former senior colleague,
even after his 'retirement' – explains how Oldham had managed to obtain
confidential documents for so long. However, he had already drawn sufficient
attention to himself to rouse the suspicion of his long-time friend, Thomas
Kemp, who had been instructed to keep an eye on Oldham whenever he
visited the Foreign Office. Indeed, he had been concerned by reports from
Lucy over Oldham's drinking. She claimed over £3,000 had been spent in
three weeks the previous October. It was Kemp who discovered that a bundle
of telegrams had disappeared from the duty cipher's desk. According to the
OPGU file, Kemp 'rushed round to ARNO's house but discovered he had
already left for the continent'.[246]

After delivering the new package, Oldham went back to England on
12 May, but soon afterwards returned to Paris on 25 May via Le Bourget
airport accompanied by his wife, where they remained for three days. According to flight and passport records, they visited the French capital once
again on 2 June. While Oldham spent most of the remainder of the month in
England, Lucy continued to travel back and forth to Paris on a regular basis,
flying out on 7 and 14 June, presumably to keep lines of communications
open with Bystrolyotov.[247]

Having risked a visit to the Foreign Office in May, Oldham was perhaps
understandably reluctant to chance his arm again and was therefore just
as unwilling to see Bystrolyotov without anything new to deliver. Lucy informed Bystrolyotov that Oldham had started drinking heavily again, and that
Dr Rowan suspected he was showing symptoms of delirium tremens – hallucinations and violent shaking related to alcohol withdrawal. Furthermore,
he was suffering from severe heart pains, which in Dr Rowan's opinion was a
sign that he might expire at any time.

Yet Bystrolyotov could not be put off indefinitely and so on 20 June Oldham was forced by his wife to fly out to Paris to confront him, though Oldham arrived empty-handed and claimed he did not have enough money to pay his source. Once more Bystrolyotov demanded to know who the source was and once more he was rebuffed. Oldham's dire physical prognosis meant that Bystrolyotov's hand was forced. If he wanted to retain any chance of restoring his line of communication with the Foreign Office he had to involve himself even more closely in the Oldhams' affairs, so he planned a trip back to London to push Oldham back into rehabilitation and Lucy overseas to recover from the strain of the last few months.[248]

The Oldhams travelled back via Cologne, taking a short break at the Excelsior Hotel and landing in London on 22 June. Bystrolyotov arrived the following day only to be greeted by yet another alcohol-fuelled domestic fight. Worse, Lucy claimed that Sir Robert Vansittart had taken an interest in Oldham, possibly after the May visit that he'd made. She claimed Vansittart was chief of intelligence or counter-intelligence – he was actually the Permanent Under-Secretary and therefore Head of the Foreign Office. This was terrible news and Bystrolyotov feared that Oldham was about to be uncovered. He alerted the OGPU centre, who were so alarmed at the prospect of exposure that they gave the order to withdraw all illegal operatives from the country including Bazarov and Mally.[249]

Meanwhile, Bystrolyotov still had Oldham to deal with, who once again had grown violent. Bystrolyotov called for medical help. While he was waiting for an ambulance to arrive, he gave Oldham two glasses of gin to quieten him down and then, with Lucy's help, dragged the insensible man upstairs. As at Christmas, when the doctor arrived Oldham was drugged and taken away by ambulance with Bystrolyotov accompanying him to hospital. This was Bystrolyotov's chance to escape as well, but he remained to see his mission through to the end – extraordinarily brave or extremely foolish.

Just when it seemed things could not get any worse, Lucy decided that she had finally had enough and wanted to file for divorce. She removed her valuables from 31 Pembroke Gardens and hired a lawyer to start proceedings against Oldham. This meant exposing Bystrolyotov to a high-ly difficult interrogation, in his guise as Count Perelly, as an official representing a company through which Oldham had claimed to have made £2,000 in commissions. This was a tight situation; anything Bystrolyotov said could be quickly checked, and Bazarov was genuinely concerned about Bystrolyotov's safety. OGPU believed that Britain's counter-intelligence services included execution squads, even though none existed in reality. But Bystrolyotov insisted on staying to conclude one final mission, to obtain the cipher codes for the following year. Reluctantly Bazarov agreed, and the OGPU Centre was informed of the appalling risks that were being faced by Bystrolyotov:

> It is possible that ANDREI will be liquidated by the enemy. None-theless, I have not given any order for his immediate departure. For him to depart now would meant the loss of a source of such importance that it would weaken our defence and increase the power of the enemy. The loss of ANDREI is possible today, as is that of other colleagues tomorrow. The nature of their work makes such risks unavoidable.[250]

When Oldham was released from hospital, Bystrolyotov beseeched him to gather the codes that he had promised and so Oldham tried to gain access to the Foreign Office, often waiting until nightfall before making his entrance. According to Antrobus:

> It is a grim place after dark. I have often, when on night duty, had to traverse its long and echoing corridors in the still watches. When you are alone in a big, silent building you always feel you are not alone; you start at fancied sounds and you quiver at imaginary shadows; suddenly, you see two great gleaming eyes staring at you from the blackness and you think of bogles and hobyahs and things that go bump in the night – till you realise that it is only the office cat on her nightly rounds.[251]

According to the OGPU file, the cat was not the only creature that unsuspecting officials might encounter. Oldham could also be found prowling the corridors, muttering to himself in Gollum-like fashion:

> ARNO resumed his visits, making up to three a day, and even appeared after working hours, moving from room to room in an agitated state, obviously anxious to be left alone.[252]

Another attempt to get the codes was made on Thursday 6 July. One of the office keepers, Mr Wilson, later recalled that the housekeeper, Wright, had informed him on Friday 7 July that Oldham had been found in Room 5 and the cipher room the previous evening at around 11.00 pm, having been spotted by the night staff. However, security had been tightened, with staff instructed not to give Oldham any of the keys to the safes.[253] Furthermore, a trap had been set by Kemp, who left a file unattended on his desk. Possibly sensing trouble, Oldham did not take it and, not wishing to draw any further attention to his presence, withdrew empty-handed.[254]

This meant that the conspirators had to change their plans. It was now imperative to obtain an impression of the keys so that a duplicate set could be made before any further attempt to steal the cipher code books could be undertaken. On Thursday 13 July, Bystrolyotov took Oldham to Hyde Park and, sitting on a bench, Oldham practiced making impressions of keys in dentist's paste, used in a similar way for creating moulds of teeth. Bystrolyotov then explained what Oldham had to do, before he 'blessed him for his last battle'.[255] Steeled mentally, Oldham left the park and set off towards Whitehall in the early evening sunshine, striding in determined fashion towards the Foreign Office one final time.

Chapter ten

BREAK-IN AT THE FOREIGN OFFICE (JULY–AUGUST 1933)

He was quite sober, but I did notice that, when he handed the keys to me,
his head was bathed in perspiration and he could not keep his hands still.
I thought to myself, Guilty conscience.

HERBERT JAMES BINDON, FOREIGN OFFICE ASSISTANT CLERK, 14 JULY 1933

Break-in is perhaps too dramatic to describe the events that unfolded on the evening of Thursday 13 July 1933. Despite Bystrolyotov's preparations that made it seem as though a major heist was being planned, the least problematic element was gaining access to the Foreign Office – once again, Oldham was able to stroll right in through the front door. However, this time his former colleagues were waiting for him on a heightened state of alert and the element of risk was exacerbated by the fact that, in order to secure an impression of the safe key, he had to perform a tricky piece of spy craft with only limited practice.

We have several eye-witnesses from within the Foreign Office who provided their version of what happened that evening when interviewed the following day. The main account was provided once again by Herbert James Bindon.

> I was checking off the weights of the Paris bags as usual at about
> 5.50 pm on Thursday (13 July) when I saw Mr EH Oldham enter
> the Foreign Office by the main entrance.[256]

The timing of Oldham's entry is important; most of the key officials would
have left by around 5.00 pm, minimising the chances that he would be challenged. However, the cipher staff and other colleagues from the communications staff would still have been there, plus the door keepers and office keepers
to ensure security was maintained.

The strain that Oldham was under had clearly started to tell. According to
Bindon:

> When he came into the building, first of all in his usual manner —
> he is not a particularly healthy looking man — he explained a mark
> on his nose and dark marks under his eyes as being due to a fall
> from a horse, saying he had run into a tree. Personally I doubt it.[257]

On his way in, Oldham realised that he had been spotted and was forced to
come up with a plausible explanation for why he had turned up again.

> He noticed that I saw him and wandered round to where the scales
> were. He chatted to me for a few minutes and asked if Mr Kemp was
> still in. I said, 'No, he has just gone.' He said, 'What a pity. I wanted
> to see him. However, I shall pop down and leave a note for him.'[258]

Oldham's appearance the previous week had clearly put Bindon on his guard
and he was still mindful of the risk that Oldham posed given the incident in
May with the keys.

> Bearing in mind the circumstances which had occurred quite re-
> cently, I took no notice when he went away, knowing that the keys
> of Room 5 were in the safe in Room 19 and that the presses were
> locked, and that he could do no harm.

> I had to wait a few moments before the bags were ready and, instead of going back to Room 5 and perhaps indulging in some awkward conversation, I went to Room 19 and chatted to Mr Roberts for a moment.[259]

Charles Roberts was one of the temporary clerks in the Communications Department, someone who would have been familiar with Oldham.

> While I was in there Mr Hilbery came into the room with his own key, which is the key to the confidential presses in the bag room and which is normally kept on the bag ring and said, 'Do you know Oldham is in our room?'
>
> I said, 'Yes, I know and I really don't mind'.
>
> He said, 'He wants to get at something of his which is in the press'.
>
> I thought for a moment and then said to Hilbery, 'Well, you can take the keys but he is not to handle them. You are to open the press, let him get what he wants, close the press and bring the keys back to me.'[260]

Clearly security protocols had been tightened up since the previous week, possibly in consultation with the press keepers, men such as Alfred Norris, under the watchful eye of John Wright, the office keeper. However, Bindon was not expecting Oldham's next move.

> He [Hilbery] was gone about five minutes and then suddenly he dashed in and said 'He [Oldham] has got the keys and he has gone to the lavatory.'
>
> I did not quite know what to do. I went out of the room, went to the main door keeper and said, 'Oldham is not to leave the building until I have given leave.' I also went to the back door and Hilbery himself was down there by that door. I then waited in the vicinity where Oldham was, so as to prevent him getting out of the office with the keys.[261]

The chief door keeper was Sidney William Merryweather, and he would have alerted his associates William Dunkley and the rather aptly named Charles Lockyer. With the exits to the Foreign Office secured to prevent Oldham's escape, Bindon tried to work out from his colleague, Clarence Anderson Hilbery what had happened.

> Apparently when [Hilbery] went in to undo the press, the chair in which Oldham was sitting was almost touching one of the doors as it opened. This door has the lock on it. Hilbery naturally opened the press and as he was going to close it again shortly, he did not take the keys out. He had no sooner opened it than Oldham seemed to dash by him, saying where he was going. When Hilbery came to lock the press, he found the keys gone. He did not hear Oldham take the keys out of the lock.[262]

Hilbery confirmed that he had accompanied Oldham to the press and his testimony of what transpired confirmed that the new security measures had been authorised from the very highest authority in the department, Harold Eastwood.

> Last night I went into Room 5 to put the key on the bunch as usual and Oldham was there sitting down writing a letter. He said he wanted to go to his box and would I get the keys?
>
> I went to Room 19 and was told to let him have his things but not to give him the keys, as Mr Eastwood had given instructions. I told Oldham he could have his box, so I opened the press. Oldham said, 'Sorry, I must just go outside to the lavatory'. I then found the keys had gone.
>
> I told Bindon what had happened. It must have been quietly done as I did not hear the rattle of keys. I thought there was something peculiar about it, so I went and saw Bindon.[263]

Bindon confessed that he had not seen where Oldham had gone, but that Hilbery's suggestion seemed most likely.

> I did not actually see Oldham come out of the lavatory, but he had
> not time to go anywhere else. He could not have left the building
> in the 10 minutes he was missing.[264]

However, they did not have long to wait.

> In about seven or eight minutes Oldham appeared again, went
> down to Room 5 and I followed him and immediately asked for
> the keys which he handed over. I said, 'Have you got all you want?
> I am going to lock up.'
>
> He said, 'Just one moment, I want to get something else, I will
> be in tomorrow to see Mr Kemp.' Then he left the building. I no-
> ticed on the table that he had started to write a note to Kemp; it
> was evidently left there so that I should see it and there was really
> nothing in it. Just as he was going he picked up the note and said,
> 'Well, I won't leave this now as I shall see Kemp in the morning,'
> and destroyed the note.
>
> He was quite sober but I did notice that, when he handed the
> keys to me, his head was bathed in perspiration and he could not
> keep his hands still. I thought to myself, Guilty conscience.[265]

With Oldham gone, Bindon brought in another colleague and together they
inspected the keys for any sign of tampering. Their suspicions were quickly
confirmed.

> Roberts and I examined the keys and found particles of wax or
> soap; as I had only just used the keys, there was no possibility of
> their having come into contact with anything of this nature during
> the last five or ten minutes. There were particles of wax on the
> ward, which – had it been there before – would have been one of
> the first places to get it removed. I reported to Mr Eastwood that
> he might have taken impressions.[266]

Given that Eastwood had already tightened security and Oldham had still managed to outfox them, it was time to call in the professionals. The Director of Security Services at MI5, Vernon Kell, was notified the next morning about what had happened and Kell immediately passed all relevant details to B Branch, which conducted investigations and inquiries relating to domestic security.

The case was taken up by B Branch Head, Oswald Allen 'Jasper' Harker. He was an intimidating figure who listed his recreations as big-game hunting, riding and fishing, reflecting his earlier career in the Indian police. He moved quickly to place Oldham under surveillance. Under direct instruction from Kell, Harker applied for a Home Office warrant (HOW) which authorised the interception and subsequent reading of 'all postal packets and telegrams addressed to EH Oldham or any other name, 31 Pembroke Gardens, W8'. This was supported by a decision to monitor all phone calls to the property, sent to the Director of Investigations at the General Post Office (GPO), Mr CF Wavish, so that the line could be tapped. Ominously, the justification given on the warrant was that Oldham was 'suspected of offences under the Official Secrets Act'.[267] Due to the urgency of the situation, the applications were made by telephone with the relevant permissions subsequently put in writing a few days later where Harker was more specific:

> The subscriber to this number is an ex-employee of the
> Foreign Office and, owing to his recent very suspicious actions, he
> is strongly suspected of attempting to commit offences under the
> Official Secrets Act.

Harker also arranged for Oldham's movements to be monitored by his small team of agents in Section 11 of MI5, including inquiries officer John Ottaway, who took up position outside Oldham's home under instruction to maintain 'close observation day and night'. Meanwhile, the keys and waxy substances were sent to the Chemical Section for analysis by the Head of Security Research, H Smith, while interviews with Bindon, Hilbery and Roberts were arranged for the same afternoon. Oldham's passport application from February 1932 was retrieved, complete with photograph for identification purposes and a file was opened on him by MI5 which was to grow rapidly over the coming days.

That same day, Oldham met Bystrolyotov and reported that he had been unable to get near the safes, given the new levels of security that were in operation. The stress of the mission had clearly taken its toll on the former civil servant. According to Bystrolyotov, Oldham's face was 'sallow grey' and his health was worse than ever. Pity did not come into the equation. Bystrolyotov needed Oldham to see this through to the end, so he arranged for him to enter another clinic, this time the Queen's Gate Nursing Home, run by Miss Lucy Hopkins at 31 Queen's Gate, Kensington, to 'purify Oldham's brain from alcohol and spur his heart on so that he could extract the ciphers at all costs'.[268]

No wonder Bystrolyotov's OGPU superiors had used the word 'merciless' when inscribing his gun in November 1932, though Oldham's new accommodation was nowhere near as harsh as Rendlesham. Miss Hopkins 'was charming, tactful and skilful in the running of such an institution and she herself was quite a favourite… Her charges were quite reasonable for that part of London'.[269] However, the removal of Oldham from his home doubtless saved him from further scrutiny by the surveillance operation. Ottaway was forced to confess in a phone call to MI5 on 17 July that there had been no sign of Oldham at 31 Pembroke Gardens, though he confirmed the presence of Lucy along with two maids, a chauffeur and her pet dogs.

Nevertheless, MI5 was able to discern some aspects of the Oldhams' activities, thanks to the phone surveillance. On 15 July, Lucy received a call from Dr Rowan at 9.47 am. He was briefed about her husband's latest disappearance to a clinic. The conversation shows that Rowan had long been acquainted with Bystrolyotov, in his guise as Count Perelly, and that he was sufficiently trusted as a confidante to allow Lucy to reveal that money was excruciatingly tight once more.

> Things are in a terrible state. Joe came to see me. I don't know how you are going to get your money or how he will pay the nursing home. I had to pay an overdraft – he's quite bankrupt. I kept Ray [her younger son] in Germany seven weeks. I'm going to sell my furniture.[270]

The next day, Lucy started to look for alternative accommodation, preparing to make good on her earlier threat to leave Oldham. According to MI5's surveillance report, she was picked up from her home at 1.10 pm by 'a man aged about 38 – 40, 5 foot 9 inches, very bronzed, Jewish appearance'. They left in a taxi and Lucy did not reappear until 6.30 pm. The taxi driver was tracked down and in an interview he revealed that he had driven them to Brown's Hotel, Dover Street. On making further inquiries at the hotel, Ottaway established that Lucy had asked about hiring a suite of rooms but had found them too expensive. Intriguingly, her companion gave his name as 'McCormick' and claimed to be a journalist from the New York papers. This was all rather strange, as Brown's Hotel was where her son Thomas Wellsted and his wife Yolande were staying; Lucy had referred to the fact he was visiting from India during her conversation with Rowan the previous day.[271]

Lucy was not the only one on the move on Sunday 16 July. Oldham was not confined to his new accommodation at Queen's Gate as he had been at Rendlesham – something made abundantly clear when, out of the blue, he turned up at the Foreign Office again at 12.50 pm to request access to his belongings once more, possibly hoping that security would be less stringent on a Sunday. If so, he was severely disappointed; he was asked to fill out a form before permission to see his safe deposit box could be granted. At this point he grew suspicious and walked away, promising to come back the next morning – which he failed to do.

The encounter was only reported to MI5 by Eastwood the following morning, the day when the results of the laboratory tests on the samples and key were sent back to Harker at MI5. The analysis revealed nothing conclusive, other than ruling out wax and an observation that the material contained water, an insoluble gritty substance and red pigment. In conclusion, it was tentatively suggested that the material was a form of soap, certainly something in which impressions could have been made. Further comparison with the soap in the Foreign Office failed to reveal a match, strongly suggesting that Oldham had brought it with him deliberately.

Monday 17 July proved to be particularly active for operatives on the Oldham case. At 10.32 am, a male caller, hesitantly identified by the intercept transcriber as Monsieur 'Purrilli' or 'Joe', requested to speak to Mrs Oldham. Thanks to the phone tap, we have a full transcript of the conversation.

> Lucy: *Hullo Joe. Sorry I had to cut you off last night. I thought he was coming in, but it was only the dogs.*
> Joe: *I understood, your voice sounded unusual.*
> Lucy: *Dr Rowan rang up, he wants to see you.*
> Joe: *I'm going away tomorrow. Could you make an appointment for 5 o'clock today?*
> Lucy: *Yes. I will make arrangements. I am going to the bank to get an overdraft – next month will be better then I will go to Ernest to see if he will give me any more money.*
> Joe: *It is a waste of time, I shouldn't.*
> Lucy: *He's got money somewhere, he had cigarettes and I have not been near him.*
> Joe: *I gave him half a crown, he asked me for a bank note. Goodbye.*[272]

Two hours later, after a visit to the bank, Lucy placed a call to Brown's Hotel in the hope of speaking to her son, mainly to see if he would lend her some money, given the unlikely prospect of obtaining any from her errant husband.

> Lucy: *May I speak to Mrs Wellsted, Room 33?*
> [She is connected to the room by the receptionist]
> Lucy: *Lucy speaking, is Tommy there?*
> Yolande: *No, he has gone to the bank.*
> Lucy: *I have been to the bank this morning and the manager was very snorty and rude and would not let me have a penny, so will you ask Tommy to stand guarantee for £25? Can you come round this afternoon?*
> Yolande: *No, we are going out in the car.*
> Lucy: *All right, I have an appointment with Dr Rowan this afternoon at 5 o'clock. You must come round for dinner.*
> [Yolande agrees and says 'Goodbye'][273]

Whether either meeting took place is not recorded, but it would seem that Bystrolyotov turned his attention away from Oldham and towards his wife in his persistent attempts to find out the identity of Oldham's 'source'. Aware that Kemp – to whom the OGPU centre had given the code name ROLAND – was increasingly involved in the investigation into Oldham's activities, Bystrolyotov persuaded Lucy to invite Kemp over for lunch. The call to the Foreign Office from 31 Pembroke Gardens was logged by MI5 at 10.57 am on 19 July.

> Lucy: *Is that you, Kemp?*
> Kemp: *Yes.*
> Lucy: *Who do you think is over here? Joe Perelly – and he wants to see you. So can you come to lunch at 1.30 pm at my place?*
> Kemp: *Yes, surely, but what...*
> Lucy: *I am not going to tell you anything over the telephone. We will talk about it when you come. Things are desperate here. Oh, my goodness.... He [Oldham] will not be here. He's in a nursing home; he likes those sorts of places. Can you be here at 1.15 pm? Joe is ringing up to see if it is all right.*
> Kemp: *Yes, at your place, 1.15 pm.*
> Lucy: *There will not be any cocktails or anything like that.*
> Kemp: *Oh, that's all right.*[274]

This was an extraordinary risk on Bystrolyotov's part, but it was considered a risk worth taking as it was possible, albeit unlikely, that Kemp might himself be the source. Equally, there was a very real chance that Bystrolyotov was walking into a trap, so the day before he contacted Lucy to arrange the meeting with Kemp, OGPU ensured that his pistol was delivered to him. The mutual understanding was that if he was arrested he should use it on himself.

Bystrolyotov sat in Hyde Park on his 'usual bench by the lake', where he had prepared Oldham five days previously and was shocked to find that the operative who had been sent to hand over his weapon, along with his passport in the name of Alexander Gallas, was none other than his wife. Realising that this could be the last time they might see each other, Bystrolyotov later recalled, 'We said farewell to each other as if before a battle'.[275]

Bystrolyotov arrived at 31 Pembroke Gardens shortly after Kemp, who was already regaling Lucy with his concerns about Oldham's recent behaviour. To Bystrolyotov's dismay, she reciprocated, giving Kemp details about her husband's activities, including the fact that he had recently stolen a briefcase marked 'His Majesty's courier' as well as a 'red passport' for himself, items usually carried by King's Messengers on their journeys overseas. In addition, he had managed to obtain a passport for a 'scoundrel', no doubt the passport he'd secured in the name of Robert Grenville.[276]

Kemp quickly asked if she could remember anything about the man to whom it was issued but she said she could not recall anything. This was sufficient to confirm Kemp's suspicions that 'a foreign spy was somewhere near Oldham' and he announced that he had been 'entrusted to find him'. Realising that the game was virtually up, Bystrolyotov thought quickly and tried to direct Kemp's line of investigation elsewhere. He played on the growing international fears about Hitler's Germany that were being reported with increasing frequency in the press and offered to help Kemp locate the spy. He deployed his own cover story, as a representative of a German bank, to great effect.

> I know the family business situation and have some ideas about what's going on. The tracks lead to Germany where the family owns significant property. I'll risk disclosing some family secrets, although, as the trustees of a solid bank, I'm forbidden to do so. Let's not tire our lady with boring detail. May I invite you to the Ritz for lunch tomorrow, at one o'clock?[277]

It was a desperate ploy, but it worked. Kemp agreed, Bystrolyotov booked the table over the phone and the two men parted on good terms – Kemp thanked Bystrolyotov and shook his hand 'especially meaningfully'.

As soon as he had left, Kemp returned to the Foreign Office to de-brief his superiors about the conversation he'd just had with Lucy and Perelly. It would appear that Harker was in attendance, for he placed a call from the Foreign Office to MI5 instructing the General Post Office to add 31 Queen's Gate to the surveillance warrant. He informed Ottaway that Oldham 'was in the habit of going in and out and S11 should therefore be instructed to take up observation on this address'. In the light of Kemp's information, a discussion took place about what action, if any, should be taken against Oldham. Harker's notes were placed on file the same day:

> In connection with the case of Oldham, saw Mr Norton and Mr Howard Smith and discussed the legal position. Decided that I should see DPP and consult him unofficially.[278]

Howard Smith was by now the Chief Clerk while Clifford John Norton was the private secretary to the Permanent Under-Secretary of State, Sir Robert Vansittart. 'DPP' was an indication of just how seriously this had now become and referred to the Director of Public Prosecutions, Sir Edmund Tilbery Atkinson QC – a lieutenant in the Royal Naval Volunteer Reserve during World War I before switching to the Royal Air Force as a major.

Despite Atkinson's professional background – he was the legal representative for the UK during the peace negotiations and therefore in Paris with Oldham – he had been a somewhat surprising choice as Director of Public Prosecutions when he was appointed in 1930. Indeed, on being summoned to the Home Office to be offered the job, it is said that he refused because he believed that it was some sort of joke and left the room, before being summoned back to formally accept the role. You could understand why; he was not a criminal lawyer, had no previous experience of working with the department and knew none of the key staff. Most of his first two years in post were spent worrying that he might do something wrong. Some of this hesitancy was displayed during his involvement in the Oldham case.

Saw DPP who pointed out that, as regards the story of the key, two courses of action were open to us:

1. To arrest and search on a charge under the Official Secrets Act – an act preparatory to commission of offences under Section 1.
2. To interrogate and if necessary make use of the provisions of Section 6 of the Official Secrets Act 1920, bearing in mind the fact that any disclosures he may so make could not be used against him in any future prosecution.

Finally DPP unofficially gave his opinion that, in the circumstances of the case, he would deprecate a prosecution, mainly in view of the disclosures which would be made about the Foreign Office.[279]

Parker then returned to the Foreign Office to relay the news. The head of the service, Sir Robert Vansittart, was present for the next meeting. Vansittart had also attended the Paris Peace Conference and enjoyed various promotions afterwards, serving as private secretary to Lord Curzon before performing the same role for Prime Ministers Baldwin and MacDonald between 1928 and 1930. In January 1930 he was appointed to run the Foreign Office.

Subsequently saw Mr Norton, Mr Howard Smith and Sir Robert Vansittart. Sir Robert said that, before any official action was taken, he wished us to try and see whether we could discreetly ascertain what papers etc Oldham might have at the nursing home. It would appear from the statement made by Mrs Oldham to Mr Kemp that he is in possession of a document called in the FO a 'red passport', but which is actually a parchment given to any messenger of the FO carrying despatches.

There appears to be some doubt in the minds of the officials at the FO as to how – if he has obtained this document – he has done so. Mr Norton was of the opinion that his possession of this document constituted larceny, but until we know (a) whether he has

it and (b) how he got it, it is quite impossible to give any definite
opinion on this point. If he merely retained one which had been officially given to him, in the view of DPP, this would not be larceny
but merely a departmental misdemeanour.[280]

Meanwhile, as the mandarins of the Foreign Office were discussing what
to do next, Bystrolyotov made tracks for 31 Queen's Gate to alert Oldham
about what had transpired back at his house. He was still there at 5.50 pm
when Oldham placed a call to his wife. Whether it was the strain of the day's
events or the cumulative effect of Oldham's alcoholism that had ruined their
lives, Lucy snapped. Because the conversation was recorded on the phone
tap, the moment that their marriage finally ended is recorded.

> Ernest: *Is that you, Lucy?*
> Lucy: *Yes.*
> Ernest: *Ernest speaking. Can you bring me some handkerchiefs,
> socks and pyjamas?*
> Lucy: *Yes.*
> Ernest: *Joe is here. I hear Kemp has been – what for?*
> Lucy: *What is that to do with you?*
> Ernest: *I suppose you told him everything.*
> Lucy: *No, I didn't but it's about time I did. How long are you staying
> there?*
> Ernest: *Not much longer.*
> Lucy: *Well, you won't find me here. I'm finished. You've done nothing
> for me.*
> Ernest: *Oh, yes I have. I will get Joe down if you like and ask him.*
> Lucy: *I waited and you have done nothing. I have finished.
> Goodbye.*[281]

Bad news kept raining down on Oldham. With Kemp expecting a meeting
the following day and the net starting to close in, Bystrolyotov gave notice
of his intention to leave England in the morning, advising Oldham to

keep out of trouble. Sure enough, Kemp had been instructed to keep his meeting and find out as much as he could from Perelly. According to an OGPU report:

> ROLAND soon established that HANS was not at the hotel he had named and the police reported that no one with HANS's name was registered in London, which meant that he had used another name to gain entry to the country.[282]

Kemp returned to the office, but was somewhat coy about the incident and seems not to have fully debriefed his superiors. However, he had suggested that it would be more difficult than first thought to obtain access to Oldham's things at the nursing home. Harker put his initial thoughts down for Kell to review.

> As I explained to you this morning, our arrangements for having a quiet look at Oldham's things have broken down. The question arises – what action is to be taken?
>
> As you know, the man is at present under observation. I would suggest that he be kept under observation for another three or four days and, if nothing suspicious is seen – by which I mean we do not find him meeting persons outside the nursing home or receiving correspondence of a suspicious character – he should be interviewed, providing the Foreign Office have fully made up their minds that they do not propose to prosecute him.
>
> In the first instance, I would suggest that the interview should be conducted on quite friendly lines and Oldham should be asked whether he is in possession of a 'red passport' and, if so, to hand it over. He should then be asked to explain the circumstances of his visit to the Foreign Office on the evening of 13 July. Should he prove recalcitrant and refuse to reply, I think we have got quite sufficient grounds for serving him with a notice under Section 7 of the [Official Secrets] Act of 1920.[283]

Section 7 stipulated that anyone found to have attempted or made preparations to commit an offence under the Official Secrets Act would be treated
as though they had actually carried out the offence. In other words, the inves-
tigators thought that he was guilty of planning to do something wrong, but
were still not entirely sure what the exact nature of this wrongdoing might be.
Nevertheless, time was clearly running out for Oldham, with plans to bring
him in for interrogation only a case of when, not if.

> The question then for consideration is – who should conduct the
> interview? Whether it should be left to a police officer from Special
> Branch to do so, or whether it should be done by a member of this
> office who is a superintendent of police under the provisions of the
> Official Secrets Act. In any case, whoever conducts the interview
> will have to be specially authorised by an order under the signature
> of the commissioner of police.
>
> All these points will, I think, have to be finally decided after
> discussion both with the Foreign Office and the DPP.
>
> I would suggest that I should interview him, accompanied either
> by Mr Ottaway or, if it is thought better, by a member of the Foreign
> Office staff. I suggest this latter alternative as Mr Norton, when I
> last spoke to him, seemed to consider that this might be advisable.[284]

Kell agreed with Harker's suggestion that Oldham be kept under further surveillance, thus delaying the need to make a decision. A further discussion took
place on 21 July, but as before they simply ran over the same ground without
reaching any conclusions, other than the terms under which Oldham should
be questioned:

> 1. Is the interview to be conducted without invoking in any way
>   the assistance of the Official Secrets Act? That is to say, are we
>   merely to interview Oldham and try to get out of him (a) the
>   diplomatic passport if he has it and (b) some sort of explana-
>   tion of his conduct on the 13 June [sic]? DSS [Director of Secret

Service] points out that, if he declines to give us any information, our bluff is called and we can do nothing.

2. If it is proposed to proceed under Section 6 of the Official Secrets
Act 1920, it is obvious as a corollary that we should have in readiness, under Section 9 of the Act for 1911, a search warrant which,
in the event of his refusing (a) to answer and (b) to admit possession of the passport, could be sued to find out what he has got.

In these circumstances it is further a question for consideration,
if it is found necessary to use the search warrant, who is to be
employed, eg, a Special Branch police officer.

All these points will have to be considered at a joint meeting at
the Foreign Office early next week.[285]

By this stage, Oldham had hatched an elaborate plot – with Bystrolyotov's
help – to leave the country. A report prepared by Ottaway on 26 July outlined
his daily routine.

During the time he was at 31 Queen's Gate, which is a nursing
home, he was visited occasionally by his wife and a Mr Parelli [sic].
He daily visited the local public houses, drinking lots of beer and
some afternoons sat in Kensington Gardens reading and sleeping,
but he was not seen to associate with anyone.[286]

Then, on 22 July, Oldham left the nursing home and made a trip in preparation for his imminent departure.

On Saturday 22nd inst at 12.20 pm he called at the offices of the
American Express company, 6 Haymarket, where he remained five
minutes and afterwards returned to 31 Queen's Gate.[287]

This was almost certainly an attempt to secure some funds for his trip. Two
days later, on 24 July at 6.15 pm, he placed a phone call to his wife with the
help of a nursing home operator.

Ernest: *Is that you...? Ernie speaking. I am going to Vienna with Joe*
tomorrow so shall be packing tonight.
Lucy: *Ahem!*
Ernest: *Don't talk like that.*
Lucy: *Ahem!*
Ernest: *I shall be home after dinner. I thought I had better warn you,*
that's all!
Lucy: *All right! Don't worry about that.*[288]

The next morning, Oldham duly packed his belongings together and left the
nursing home. He was monitored for a while by Ottaway.

Continuous observation was kept on 31 Queen's Gate from
19th to 25th inst, on which date Oldham left the address about
10.30 am and was driven direct to his home, 31 Pembroke Gardens, by taxi cab.

He had with him a small suitcase and small attaché case and
stated that he was flying that day to Vienna.[289]

However, in an indication that he perhaps knew that he was under surveillance, or perhaps because he was naturally cautious, Oldham was able to
demonstrate the elusive qualities that had so infuriated Bystrolyotov in Paris
throughout 1930 and 1931 and managed to lose the people who were tail-
ing him. Later that day, Harker submitted a report outlining just what had
gone wrong.

Information was received at 10.00 am that Oldham had made arrangements to leave the nursing home and was proposing to go to
Vienna by air.

Immediate steps were taken to shadow him and at about
10.30 am he left the nursing home in a taxi which proceeded in the
direction of Victoria. Unfortunately, it was missed.[290]

One can sense the growing panic as Harker and Ottaway realised Oldham had disappeared. They immediately alerted the authorities in the Foreign Office.

> Various enquiries were started and at 10.45 am I was able to get in touch with the Foreign Office and inform then what had happened. Mr Norton discussed the matter with Sir Robert Vansittart and it was finally decided that, if we could find out how he was proceeding abroad, C should be informed and arrangements were to be made to warn all our controls and steps were to be taken to search him, should Oldham attempt to use the diplomatic or 'red' passport which he is alleged to possess.[291]

'C', incidentally, referred to Admiral Sir Hugh Francis Paget Sinclair who had helped to establish the Secret Intelligence Service. On his instruction, passport control officers across Europe would be watching out for Oldham.

> Spoke Major Vivian personally who informed me that this would be done as soon as we could give him the necessary information.[292]

Major Vivian – nicknamed Vee Vee – was one of Sinclair's trusted officers in SIS and a veteran of the Indian police service. His work specifically focused on the activities of Comintern. However, on this occasion, neither MI5 nor SIS were able to prevent Oldham from escaping.

> About 2.30 pm, information was received from Mr Canning to the effect that Oldham had left Croydon in an aeroplane leaving for Paris at 2.00 pm. This information was immediately telephoned to Major Vivian's secretary.[293]

Superintendent Canning was a member of Special Branch, yet another organisation involved with the hunt for Oldham – perhaps underlining the disconnected nature of British intelligence services during this period, as well as the seriousness of the situation.

Later in the afternoon information was received from Mr Canning
that Oldham had a single ticket from Croydon to Geneva and that he
was due to arrive in Cointrin [Geneva airport] at 6.45 pm, whence he
was proceeding to Geneva. Major Vivian immediately informed.[294]

With Oldham gone, there was little more that the investigating team could
do. However, in an unconnected development, steps were finally taken to secure the Foreign Office, ironically on the same day that Oldham had flown to
Geneva – a case of literally locking the stable door after the horse had bolted.

Draft letter to the stationery office stating that, as it has become
necessary to change the locks and keys of a considerable number
of presses in which highly confidential documents are kept in the
Foreign Office within the shortest possible period, the services of
a second locksmith will be required and requesting that Messrs
Chubb may be asked to supply such a man, if possible one who has
previously been employed in the Foreign Office.[295]

With her husband gone and Bystrolyotov still on the continent, Lucy was left
abandoned, with no idea what would happen to her. However, just when she
thought things could not get any worse she received a letter from Oldham's
uncle, Henry George Holloway, containing some more bad news. Without
her knowledge, her husband had been borrowing large sums of money. She
phoned Holloway at 10.00 am on 26 July to find out what was going on.

Lucy: *Can I speak to Mr Holloway? Is that Mr Holloway? This is
Mrs Oldham speaking. Your letter I received came as a great shock.
I had no idea he had been doing those sorts of things. Now, can you
come up tomorrow and have lunch with me?*
Holloway: *I think it would be best if you met me at the National
Liberal Club at 1.00 pm tomorrow and have lunch with me.*
Lucy: *Very well, but I may be a bit late as I am going to see
my solicitors.*

Holloway: *All right. I'll wait until you come.*

Lucy: *He came out of the nursing home, you know, he goes into these places periodically and now he has pushed off abroad and we don't know where he is.*

Holloway: *Don't you know where he has gone?*

Lucy: *No, we haven't any idea.*

Holloway: *Well, don't you worry about this, I expect it will be all right.*[296]

A note was made at the bottom of the page, stating that 'from another conversation it appears that Mr Holloway (Oldham's uncle) lent Oldham £500 and the latter has cleared off without repaying this.' Oldham had therefore deceived even his closest relatives.

However, he was eventually spotted by one of Vivian's agents, purely by chance, boarding a train in Geneva on 28 July bound for Paris. He had remained undetected partly because he had still not used the diplomatic passport. Yet again, the trail went cold and Oldham disappeared from view once more; he had given his pursuers the slip. Harker wrote to Wavish at the GPO on 28 July to suspend the telephone trace on Oldham's house, resigned to the fact that his quarry was abroad.

With reference to the telephone check at present in operation on Western 4571, I have come to the conclusion that this may safely be suspended for the moment, though it may be necessary to reinstate it at a later date.

The efficient operation of this check has been of the greatest assistance to us in dealing with the case, and I am very grateful for all the trouble you have taken in this matter.[297]

Although Harker tried to put a brave face on things, the reality was that Oldham was at liberty somewhere in Europe and the British secret services were still none the wiser as to what he'd been up to in the Foreign Office on 13 July.

Chapter eleven

A NOOSE AROUND HIS NECK (AUGUST– OCTOBER 1933)

In my opinion, Oldham is heading for a breakdown.

HERBERT HUNTER, MI5 SURVEILLANCE OFFICER, 30 SEPTEMBER 1933

At 5.45 pm on Friday 4 August, the phone rang in the offices of MI5; it was Superintendent Canning from Special Branch with some heartening news. Oldham had landed at Croydon aerodrome, having flown in from Basel. However, they had no idea where he went next. The previous day, Lucy had finally moved out of 31 Pembroke Gardens and taken up residence in a serviced suite of rooms at 8 Grenville Place, 82 Cromwell Gardens in South Kensington – a few doors down from where she had previously lived with Oldham. The post office informed MI5 and inquired whether the postal check should be transferred. The rather dejected response had 'in the circumstances, instructed them to suspend the check'. This decision was hurriedly reversed as soon as Oldham's reappearance was confirmed. A phone tap was installed on 5 August and Ottaway was instructed to keep watch on the property.[298]

The fact that Oldham's estranged wife remained MI5's best lead says a lot about the state of the case. In the two days following Oldham's return to the UK, the various security organisations had no idea of his whereabouts, other than to confirm he was not at his home address, the nursing home at Queen's Gate or his wife's new residence. Two further days of surveillance proved to be equally fruitless and Ottaway was told to 'withdraw observation' on 8 August.[299]

It was at this point – four days after Oldham was spotted at Croydon and then promptly lost again – that Harker decided to inform Eastwood that his former employee was back, but that he had no idea where he was. On 9 August, a meeting was convened at the Foreign Office to discuss what steps, if any, should be taken. Harker, Eastwood and Mr Lee (deputising for Norton) were in attendance and they were clearly under pressure from the very top to produce results:

> It appears that Sir Robert Vansittart is dissatisfied with the information generally which we have regarding this individual and considers that more intensive enquiries should be made both into his past and present activities.
>
> With a view to achieving this end, Mr Lee is arranging to draw all previous papers in the Foreign Office, Board of Trade and Board of Education, in which Oldham has served. In addition, Mr Kemp has been instructed to get in touch with Mrs Oldham and find out anything he can regarding Oldham's present whereabouts, where he banks and his present business activities. When this information has been collected, Mr Lee will let me know.
>
> Mr Lee expressed the view that, if possible, we should look at his banking account for the last few years. Explained to Mr Lee that this could only be done with the assistance of the DPP. Mr Lee gave me authority to say to the DPP that the Foreign Office would be glad it if were possible to have this inspection made. DSS informed.[300]

Yet with the investigation going nowhere, Eastwood found time to take a short break, delegating responsibility to his number two, Commander Cotesworth.

Aside from a request on 15 August from the Director of Public Prosecutions to Lloyds Bank to obtain a letter of introduction so that Harker could visit Oldham's branch at 6 Pall Mall, another week had passed without any real progress in locating him.

Background checks were made into Oldham's career, though concern was expressed about the difficulty involved with obtaining details of his brief time at the Board of Education so Harker, accompanied by Nigel Watson, another MI5 agent drafted onto the case, visited the bank on 16 August to gather a sense of his financial history, focusing on the period from 1927 onwards. Although no unusual patterns of deposit or withdrawal were revealed, some of the transactions alerted the authorities to the fact that Oldham had been travelling overseas on a frequent basis.

> As regards the actual sums of money passing through Oldham's account, with the possible exception of 1932 and 1933, there does not seem to be anything particularly remarkable. It is of interest to note that in 1932, on 6 May, 11 June and 19 October, cheques for £6.15.0, £9.10.0 and £17 were paid to Imperial Airways; also in 1933, on 26 May, 7 June and 21 June, cheques for £17.12.0, £15.4.0 and £15.4.0 were paid to Imperial Airways.
>
> It is also of interest to note that the account is dormant and the overdraft was paid by Mrs Oldham in June. The total sum of money paid into the account during 1933 is roughly £534. It is of interest to note that on 20 June the sum of 6,000 francs in cash was paid in.
>
> When we turn to Mrs Oldham's account, which opened in 1927, we find from 1927 to 1933 there has been a turnover of £12,244.[301]

A further visit to the bank was not ruled out while a decision was now made to search Oldham's personal possessions in the safety deposit box in the Foreign Office, rather astoundingly late, given that a month had elapsed since his break-in and two weeks had gone by without any sight of the man. Bindon had claimed in his statement on 14 July:

> Oldham says his box, of which he has the key, contains valuable
> papers. It is usual to let old members of staff come in and I do not
> know what is in the box. He actually unlocked it in my presence
> after giving me back the keys, but I couldn't see what was in it and
> he did not take anything out.[302]

In fact there was not much worthy of note – a copy of Wellsted's will, which
showed he had left 'about £22,000 to be divided between [Lucy] and her two
sons', details about their investments, correspondence about the mortgage on
their house, and a paying-in book for the Charles Street branch in Haymarket
for the Credit Lyonnais bank. It showed that Oldham had made large deposits
of £821.18.14 on 22 June and a further £279.6.7 on 7 July.[303]

However, Harker was able to update Cotesworth and Lee on 16 August
about one significant piece of news.

> The only development in the case was that Oldham had telephoned
> to a Mr Oake with whom he had previously worked at the Foreign
> Office and the latter had accordingly been instructed to ask him
> out to lunch, should he telephone again, and draw him as far as
> possible. Commander Cotesworth pointed out that possibly Oake
> owed Oldham money, as he [Oake] was generally hard up and in
> the habit of borrowing money from his friends; as far as work is
> concerned, however, he considers him reliable.[304]

This was Raymond Charles Oake, who had been appointed a temporary clerk
in 1920 but had never really risen any further. There is evidence from the
Foreign Office day books that he was increasingly used as an informal King's
Messenger, deployed on runs from Paris to Dieppe – possibly taking the bags
sent to the French capital from League of Nations council meetings held in
Geneva back to London. It may be via this connection that Oldham had struck
up an acquaintance.

Born in April 1894 and growing up in Finchley not far from Oldham's
childhood home, Oake had previously enjoyed a career in the Royal Naval

Reserve during World War I and served on HMS *President*, so may equally have been associated with Oldham's friend Billy Everett. Either way, by 1929 Oake was trusted to the extent that he was deployed on longer routes such as Bucharest and Constantinople, alongside another one of Oldham's closer associates among the King's Messengers, Charles Jesser-Davies. To contact Oake was a highly significant move by Oldham; it showed that he considered Oake to be someone he could trust.

Once more, Kemp was pressed about where Oldham might be.

> Mr Kemp, in whose room Oldham previously worked, was asked if he could throw any light as to Oldham's present address. He suggested that the solicitors, Messrs Walbrook and Hoskens, 4 St Paul's Churchyard, might know, and in our presence rang up Mr Walbrook (whom he had met with Oldham but of whom he had not formed a very good impression) and asked him if he knew Oldham's address as he (Kemp) had papers of the latter's which he wished to hand over to their owner. Mr Walbrook however could give no information on this point.
>
> Mr Kemp was seeing Mrs Oldham, who has now definitely broken with her husband, later in the day, and it was arranged that he should obtain Oldham's pouch from her and also his camera and any films which might be found lying about in the house.[305]

Kemp duly visited Lucy and obtained the pouch but was unable to procure Oldham's camera. On inspection, the pouch turned out to be empty. With the trail growing increasingly cold, attention turned to the payments made to Imperial Airways. On 19 August, Watson reviewed the traffic logs for the company and confirmed Oldham's movements between May 1932 and June 1933, revealing that he had often travelled with his wife. In consultation with the traffic manager, Mr Handover, further searches were completed on 21 August but only provided further background information. There was still no clue as to his whereabouts, although the potential extent of his activities was growing clearer. Oldham would have a lot of explaining to do.

The only other lead available was the name Joe Perelly, which had been
provided by Kemp, so the traffic indexes were searched under his name. No
reference to him could be found. MI5 decided to press for further information, so they returned to the Foreign Office once more the next day to grill
the hapless Kemp. However, even under questioning by Watson in the presence of Cotesworth, Kemp neglected to reveal the extent of his own rather
amateur investigation after Perelly had failed to show up for their meeting
scheduled for 20 July. This was when he had gone from hotel to hotel in the
vain hope of spotting the count. Instead, Kemp tried to cover his tracks and
had only the following to say:

> He thinks that Pirelli [sic], who is a Jew, is in Vienna and will report
> if he hears of him again in London. He was unable to give any infor-
> mation as to Pirelli's address whilst in London but will endeavour
> to find this out.[306]

This information was clearly gleaned from Lucy's conversation with Oldham
on 24 July, as recorded on the phone tap – she must have passed the information to Kemp at one of their meetings. Kemp also confessed to still having
failed to obtain Oldham's camera. However, he did have a rather momentous
revelation up his sleeve: Oldham had finally been spotted in London.

> [Kemp] had been informed by an official of the Sleeping Car com-
> pany, St James Street, that afternoon, that he had seen Oldham
> the previous evening [21 August] at the Unicorn public house,
> Jermyn Street.[307]

The Sleeping Car company was regularly used by King's Messengers for their
overseas journeys; doubtless Kemp had put in a quiet word with their officials
to alert him if they spotted Oldham. He would have been familiar to them on
account of his own travels to the continent. Immediately, MI5 followed up on
this crucial lead:

Further inquiries would be made as to Oldham's whereabouts and, should he be seen at the Unicorn, arrangements would be made to 'house' him.[308]

The breakthrough was not long in coming. Three days after Oldham had first been spotted in Jermyn Street, Ottaway phoned in with some good news on the morning of 25 August:

Oldham is staying at Jules hotel, Jermyn Street and that watch is being maintained on him. This address has been added to the HOW.[309]

A later report provided more details about how Oldham had been run to ground:

Observation was taken up on 24th instant in Jermyn Street where, at 6.00 pm, the above named man was seen and followed to The Chequers public house, Duke Street, where he remained in the saloon bar until 7.05 pm and, after calling at Gray's chemist nearby, entered Jules hotel, Jermyn Street. At 8.15 pm he again visited the said public house until 10.10 pm when he returned to the hotel.[310]

Estranged from his wife and with no home to go to, Oldham was drawn to an area familiar to him from his bachelor days, when he regularly visited the pubs and clubs around St James. His new residence was the Jules Restaurant Hotel, 85–86 Jermyn Street, one of a number of such establishments in the area.

So what *had* he been doing all this time? After the rather hurried departure from London on 24 July, Oldham had changed planes in Paris and flown on to Geneva. There, he travelled to Interlaken, Switzerland, to meet Bazarov and Bystrolyotov. The latter had stayed in London right to the very end to ensure Oldham's safe departure and was in 'real danger of failure with all its consequences' – there was a genuine fear that he would be caught and exposed.

The OGPU centre later praised Bystrolyotov for his 'selflessness, discipline and bravery' in circumstances that were 'exceptionally complex and dangerous'.[311]

After the habitual request to reveal his source was refused by Oldham, a change of tack was agreed. Instead of exposing himself to further risk by attempting to gain access to the cipher codes in person, Oldham was now charged with finding a successor within the Foreign Office who could do this for him. In addition, he was ordered to find out as much as possible about Britain's SIS operatives across Europe – essentially a request to compromise the entire international intelligence gathering operation, potentially putting at risk dozens of lives. It was while leaving Switzerland for Paris by train that Oldham was spotted by one such agent before his return to Basel to fly back to England on 4 August.

During this early August meeting, it was made clear to Oldham the consequences of failure; the interview was 'conducted in such a way that ARNO had formed the impression that we're on the verge of breaking off with him' and that they would financially 'cut him off completely'.[312] On his return to England, Oldham used money given to him by the Soviet agents to check into the hotel, informing Bazarov of his location on 9 August. Once he was safely settled, Oldham cautiously started to approach his network of personal contacts, including Raymond Oake.

Having lost contact with Oldham once before, MI5 were not about to let him out of their sight again. Indeed, in an attempt to find out more about his activities, a decision was taken to step up surveillance and risk 'direct contact'. In one of the most remarkable episodes of the entire affair, two MI5 operatives were despatched the following day to engage with Oldham. A detailed report on the events that transpired was filed on 28 August by one of the agents, a young man with a Scottish accent and the initials TAR.

> On instructions from Mr Harker, with whom I had been in conference early in the morning, I proceeded to Jules hotel, Jermyn Street, on Saturday 26 August and arrived by taxi at 3.00 pm.
>
> Having taken a room, No 54, on the fourth floor, I proceeded downstairs with a view to taking a look round and seeing of what

the hotel consisted. At the same time I made it my duty to impress upon the hall porter and his satellites that I knew very little about London and that I stayed in the West End very rarely and that I was only in London for the weekend and was on my way to Scotland.

I then went and took up a position in one of the sitting rooms just on the left of the front door as you come up, with a view to keeping observation on the hall in order to see whether the subject of my enquiries (Ernest Holloway Oldham) should at any time leave or enter the hotel.

Having stayed in this position for some considerable time I decided that it looked pretty peculiar for a person of my age to be seen in this hotel at such an hour (it was then about 5.00 pm) and I therefore decided to go out and get into touch with Captain Boddington – making it look to all those who were present as though I was going out for a walk.[313]

Captain Horace Frank Boddington – known to all as 'Con' – was Harker's personal assistant in B Division, with a broad remit for undertaking 'special inquiries'. Boddington had risen from a colourful background; his father somewhat euphemistically described himself on the 1901 census as a racing commission agent, more commonly known as a bookie. Eschewing a similar line of work, Boddington had found employment in 1911 as a second division clerk in the post office, before enlisting during the war to the Worcestershire Regiment as a second lieutenant, seeing active service in France. After two promotions and a mention in despatches, he was seen as a useful no-nonsense man and was given a special appointment, initially in a military capacity, at Dublin Castle. This was the heart of the British administration during the Irish war of independence, which broke out early in 1919.

Boddington joined Dublin district Special Branch, or just D Branch, which had responsibility for conducting intelligence operations on prominent Irish Republican Army figures. This was a dangerous role, as the IRA was waging a guerrilla war against British forces and the Royal Irish Constabulary (RIC). The British Army intelligence centre had created a special unit of up to 20 ex-army and active duty officers to conduct clandestine operations against the IRA, with support from MI5 officers.

Officers from D Branch would regularly meet at the Cairo café in Grafton Street, Dublin, to share intelligence and discuss plans for future raids on IRA targets, earning the nickname the Cairo Gang. Boddington was involved in a number of these operations, including a raid in Drumcondra, Dublin, in September 1920. However, the regularity of their meetings made them easy to spot and IRA counter-intelligence under the control of Michael Collins quickly identified the British men. On the morning of Sunday 21 November 1920, IRA agents assassinated 14 D Branch officers, although there were originally 35 targets; Boddington was not attacked. In retaliation, members of the feared Black and Tans – Winston Churchill's RIC reserve force of army veterans – were despatched to raid a Gaelic football match at Croke Park, where many IRA agents were suspected to be in attendance. Firing broke out, in which 14 civilians were killed; three further IRA suspects in police custody were beaten and lost their lives.

After the disaster of what was called Bloody Sunday, the British intelligence operation was severely damaged. Boddington stayed in post and by January 1921 he had become D Branch Chief of Police (Special Branch). Once the July truce had been signed, the need for intelligence operatives grew less and operatives were gradually withdrawn. Major General Boyd, the officer commanding the Dublin branch of the armed forces in Ireland, wrote in 1922 to Scotland Yard, recommending employment for Boddington and others.

On the basis of this recommendation, Boddington continued his undercover work with MI5 after his recall from Dublin. In one of his first assignments, he was able to infiltrate the Communist Party on Kell's instructions in 1923 so that the secret services could better understand what they were up to and consequently would have known at an early stage of the Zinoviev affair, in 1924 and 1925, and that the claims made by Morton about the complicity of the Communist Party were untrue. He also extensively investigated communist involvement in the navy after the 1931 Invergordon mutiny among sailors in the Atlantic fleet, focusing his inquiries on the crews stationed at Plymouth.

Over a thousand men were eventually discharged. In short, Boddington was not someone you wanted on your tail, and his presence on the case shows the seriousness with which MI5 treated Oldham's activities.

The young man identified as TAR continued his report into Oldham:

> Having got into touch with Captain Boddington and formulated a plan of campaign, I returned to the hotel and rang up the sports club where, by arrangement, I knew he would be. He came round at about 7.00 pm and we greeted each other in the hall as long-lost friends. We sat in the lounge, previously mentioned, and discussed our affairs over a whiskey and soda in loud tones, in order to make it apparent to those who might hear that we had not seen each other for at least five years.
>
> At 7.30 pm we left the hotel in order that Captain Boddington should show his country cousin a few places of interest in that area. We first of all called at the Chequers public house where we were lucky in that we saw a man whom we thought to be Oldham, wearing a dark brown suit, brown shoes, brown shirt and collar, brown tie and white horn-rimmed spectacles. Mr Hood, the proprietor of the Chequers, was also present and Captain Boddington and I made it obvious that we were out to have a good evening.
>
> Oldham left the bar, which is situated at the back of the premises, at 8.00 pm (we had not spoken to him or to the landlord). Captain Boddington and I thought it best not to follow him back to the hotel but to leave him alone for an hour or more.
>
> At 9.30 pm, Captain Boddington and I returned to the Chequers in a cheerful mood and again saw our friend Oldham sitting in the same place talking to the landlord and a Scots girl. Being in good form it did not take us very long to get into conversation with these three people, who subsequently joined us in some pretty heavy drinking. Oldham, who had previously been drinking beer when we first saw him, had switched over to plain gin.

> During the conversation in the Chequers, Captain Boddington
> mentioned that I had been advised by a friend to stay in the Jules
> hotel, whereupon Oldham pricked up his ears and said, 'Staying at
> Jules hotel? Why, I am staying there as well.'
>
> During the course of the evening I got into conversation with
> the landlord and the Scots girl and Captain Boddington was talking
> to Oldham – as far as I could make out, about crime, the law and
> the army.
>
> Oldham seemed to be intensely interested in a story which had
> been published in the *Evening Standard* of 26 August 1933.[314]

Quite what this story could be is open to question. There were no obvious
political stories published that day. The front page headline related to the sink-
ing of Lord Moyne's yacht, *Roussalka*, off the coast of Galway – all passengers
were saved, including two pet monkeys which Lord Moyne personally rescued.
However, there are a variety of other stories which might have piqued Oldham's interest, from illicit betting in a West End club to a missing Methodist
minister in Bush Hill Park, Enfield, where Oldham had grown up. Alternatively, he might simply have been interested in the football results from the first
day of the new season, with Arsenal playing out a 1–1 draw in north London
against Birmingham in the 80-degree afternoon sunshine and their neighbours
and rivals Tottenham involved in a goalless draw away to Sheffield United .[315]

> At 11.00 pm Oldham, Captain Boddington and myself left the
> Chequers and made our way to Jules hotel. On the way Oldham
> excused himself and went into a chemists (G.Gray?) in Duke
> Street, where he spent five minutes. During these five minutes
> Captain Boddington and I were able to arrange what we were go-
> ing to do for the rest of the evening.[316]

Clearly, the two agents were making decisions on the spot, taking advantage
of the circumstances as they unfolded; no doubt their course of action was
influenced by the amount of drink they had imbibed.

When Oldham rejoined us we went to Jules hotel, as Captain Boddington stated that he would like a little more to drink and that he did not believe it was possible to get drink after hours in any hotel, whereupon I decided to prove to him that it was quite possible provided one had the drink served in a room.

Oldham thoroughly agreed with this suggestion and thought it would be a good plan if we had the drink in his room, No 37, on the third floor. I got hold of the valet on his landing and ordered a little refreshment which, after a certain amount of quibbling, we decided to have in Oldham's room.

Oldham appeared to have an enormous capacity for drink and, after about half an hour, was showing signs of drunkenness, whereupon more refreshment was ordered and Captain Boddington decided it was about time that he left. Oldham and I, having bid Captain Boddington farewell, continued to make merry and after about ten minutes I found myself undressing Oldham and putting him to bed as he was in an absolutely incapable condition.

I covered him with bedclothes and decided that the time had come when I should search his belongings.[317]

This was an extraordinary risk to take – if Oldham had roused himself mid-search, then the game would have been up.

I went through the suit he had been wearing (list of contents attached), all of his drawers, the remainder of his clothes in the wardrobe and finally his two suitcases marked 'EHO'. These cases were locked but as I found his keys I did not have much difficulty.

In one of the suitcases I found a passport and various belongings, signed 'Ernest Holloway Oldham', which proved to me that this was the man for whom I was looking (list of contents of suitcases attached).

Having made a thorough search of his room I returned to my room with my notes and made out a rough copy of the particulars.[318]

Mission accomplished, but TAR wasn't finished yet.

> On the next morning, 27 August, on my way downstairs at
> 10.30 am, I called in on Oldham to see how he was. He was still in
> bed in a dilapidated condition and, on seeing me, told me to leave
> the room as he was not feeling well. I asked him if he would like to
> have a little lunch with me at about 1.00 pm, whereupon he said
> he would be delighted and would meet me in the lounge later on.
>
> I sat about in the hotel for some two hours reading the morning
> papers and then decided to go out for a walk. As luck would have it
> I ran into Mr Hunter, to whom I handed my notes of the previous
> night in order that I should not have anything on me which might
> prejudice my position should Oldham suddenly smell a rat.[319]

The aptly named Herbert Hunter was one of the staff assistants in MI5, and
was hovering around to hear first-hand how the operation had gone.

> At 1.15 pm I again went to see him [Oldham] and found him in the
> same condition. I sat in his room and chatted to him for a quarter
> of an hour and asked him various questions about himself.
>
> He said that he was staying at Jules hotel as his house was being
> redecorated and his wife was in Germany. He said that for a man
> of no occupation there was very little for him to do but drink. He
> also let slip the remark that he never touched whiskey. He also said
> that he had a very bad liver and I observed a small box of liver pills
> on the table by the side of his bed.
>
> Oldham also stated that he was a member of the Junior Carlton
> Club. This I believe to be a fabrication as I looked on the 1932 list of
> members and found that a Captain Oldham (initials different) was
> a member but not Ernest Holloway Oldham.[320]

This might have been a coincidence that another man with the same
surname was a member; given his sacking from the Foreign Office and

financial problems, it is likely that Oldham's membership had lapsed several years previously.

> I took my leave at 1.30 pm, telling him that I had a call to make and that as London was such as dull place over the weekend I had decided to travel to Scotland overnight and not on Monday morning as I had previously stated.
>
> To the best of my belief Oldham and I parted on very good terms and I do not think he is in any way suspicious of my conduct the previous night.[321]

This was an astonishingly daring raid, especially given the 'rookie' status of the operative. However, such activities were to become the hallmark of TAR; born in 1909 in Medan, Sumatra, where his Scottish father was posted as a colonial banker, Thomas Argyll Robertson would later rise to prominence during World War II. He was the brains behind the Double-Cross system of disinformation, including Operation Mincemeat, in which the body of a British 'agent' was deliberately planted on a Spanish beach with false information designed to deceive the Germans into believing that the 1943 invasion of Sicily would take place elsewhere.

TAR was a colourful character, living the high life during his training at Sandhurst – one of his contemporaries was the future actor David Niven – and, a bit like Oldham, he had developed a taste for good suits, fast cars and living far beyond his financial means. Perhaps that was how he managed to bond so successfully with Oldham on 27 August. He had been recruited by Kell only a few months previously in 1933, mainly on the recommendation of Kell's son John, who had schooled with TAR at Charterhouse. This was probably his first field mission.

In his report submitted on 28 August, TAR included a list of Oldham's possessions that he had managed to identify; one can only admire his attention to detail, especially given the amount of alcohol he too must have consumed. In Oldham's suit was a bunch of keys – one latch key, presumably to his house in Pembroke Gardens, two small suitcase keys and five other keys. One of these was quite large and TAR speculated it was a safe key and another large key might have opened a padlock. Oldham also carried around a packet of Players cigarettes, five-and-a-half pence and an unopened box of insomnia pills, clearly not necessary on the night in question. Perhaps it is the circumstances of their discovery as much as the details themselves, but Oldham's few possessions make for rather sorry reading.

Although TAR did not itemise Oldham's 'purely personal belongings' contained in the chest of drawers, he did note that they were accompanied by six small empty bottles of Booth's gin as well as a doctor's prescription, two suits, dirty clothes, a pair of grey flannel trousers, a sports coat and an overcoat. There was nothing in the writing desk.

However, the contents of the suitcases were of more interest to MI5. A number of addresses were noted from various letters and pieces of correspondence in Oldham's possession, including 'Mr JP at poste restante, bureau de poste centrale, Trouville' – assumed to be Joe Perelly – as well as a number of other overseas addresses in Vienna, Basel and Bonn. Oldham's passport showed the extent of his travels over the previous year or so, with extensive trips abroad after his dismissal from the Foreign Office. Various cheque books confirmed he was running low on cash, with a note from Lloyd's bank on 3 August that they had refused payment of £32.10.1. This was coupled with information from a book with 'a pink cover with white paper inside, with perforated lines so that various portions of the leaves could be torn out' that made it clear Oldham had arrived in the country a day earlier than the intelligence services had realised.[322]

On a more mundane note, Dr Rowan's address in Onslow Square, Kensington, was listed alongside several nursing homes, such as Old Hill House, Chiselhurst, and the Norwood Sanatorium. Lucy was accurate when she said how much he loved those places. There was also a collection of letters demanding settlement of unpaid bills, including a request for money from the Sunbeam car company regarding repairs to his vehicle. Rather endearingly, Oldham had included a note from the local vet – Hobday, Sutton, Stainton and Otterhead, of 165 Kensington Church Street – although perhaps less touchingly he still owed them £9.8.0 for 'Cairn', presumably the name of one of his dogs. His tailor, who provided his line in brown suits and monogrammed shirts, JA Baxter of 10 Hanover Street, was also included on the list. To underline the impecunious nature of Oldham's existence, a letter from Eagle Star Insurance showed that they were demanding immediate payment of £111, presumably for the £2,000 mortgage he had taken out. Given 31 Pembroke Gardens itself was security against the loan, Oldham's home was increasingly at risk of repossession.

The afternoon after TAR's departure, Oldham set out from his hotel at 4.30 pm and arrived 20 minutes later at offices of Air Union – the French airline that would become Air France later in the year – at 52 Haymarket, trailed by Ottaway. Once inside, Oldham produced a 'pink-coloured paper about the size of a railway timetable', similar to the one found by TAR during his examination of Oldham's possessions on the night of 26 August and spoke to a 'dark and stoutish man' of around 40 years of age. Once his business with the French airline was concluded, Oldham retired to a pub where he spent the rest of his evening, under Ottaway's watchful eye. Suspicious that Oldham might be making plans to leave the country once more, Watson made further inquiries with Mr Handover the next morning, who

> …had a reliable link at the Air Union and could easily get information there. I accordingly asked him to find out whether Oldham had booked a passage yesterday. He telephoned later to say that there was no indication of his having done so from the bookings for next week. I asked him about the pink book and he informed me that this was a book of vouchers which the Air Union issues. He said that I could probably get all the information I required from Mr Bamford, the English traffic manager of the Air Union, who he described as thoroughly reliable and promised to let him know that I would be calling on him. [323]

In the relatively early days of international flight and with low-tech surveillance, it was much easier for people like Oldham to slip away unnoticed, even with British passport control on high alert across Europe. Indeed, Harker ensured that SIS was put in the loop at the earliest possible opportunity, sending the list of names and addresses obtained by TAR to Vivian, in case he could shed any light on their identity. Meanwhile, Oldham continued to remain under Ottaway's observation.

> Continuous watch has since been kept until the 30th instant and it was found that Oldham spent most of his time in the hotel, but for several hours every evening visited local public houses where he was seen conversing with the proprietors and loose women frequenters. Occasionally, he returned home very drunk.[324]

On 29 August a letter addressed to Oldham was intercepted, containing a £10 note (roughly £500 in today's money); the envelope and accompanying blank sheet of paper were inspected for secret writing – none was found. A second such letter arrived on 5 September, also containing £10. Both had been sent from Paris. Given Oldham's lack of credit with the various institutions at which he banked, this was an important clue about how he was able to remain solvent – he was clearly receiving help from abroad, confirming suspicions that he had accomplices. A conference was hastily arranged for 6 September, between Harker, his deputy Captain Butler and Watson, who had handled the intercepts.

> It was decided that Superintendent Canning should be asked to make enquiries regarding the £10 note sent to Oldham. This I subsequently arranged with Superintendent Canning, who will have enquiries made through the American Express, which firm appears to have originally issued the note.[325]

Superintendent Albert Canning was in charge of Special Branch at Scotland Yard and was a key link in the investigation between the secret service and the police, whose cooperation would be required should the decision be taken to arrest Oldham. Canning's investigation into the source of the notes was inconclusive, throwing up the names CH Serridge or Serrigi to identify the person who had been paid the money on 1 August by the American Express against a traveller's cheque. Neither name was traceable.

> In view of a personal report from Mr Hunter [Herbert Hunter, the operative now in charge of surveillance] that Oldham had informed him last night (5 September 1933) that he had received a telephone call that morning from Paris on important exchange business, it was decided that Captain Booth should be asked to trace the call, if possible, and also to enquire as to the feasibility of imposing a telephone check on Jules hotel for any telephone calls coming from abroad.
>
> I subsequently spoke to Captain Booth over the telephone and he is making the necessary inquiries. For the present, Mr Hunter is keeping Oldham under periodic observation.[326]

Despite the level of surveillance in place, it seemed that a few basic errors had been made. For example, intercepts had been placed on incoming post and telegrams, but it had occurred to no-one that outgoing mail either from the hotel or the neighbouring area should be monitored. After a quick investigation into the practicalities, Watson reported back:

> Result of enquiries made of GPO as to whether there is a posting box at Jules hotel, as had there been one there cleared regularly by a postman, a scrutiny of outgoing letters might have been of considerable assistance in this case, especially with a view to ascertaining whether Oldham sent a receipt of any sort after receiving the two £10 notes from Paris, which have arrived at intervals of exactly seven days.
>
> The closest pillar-box to the hotel appears to be near St James's Church, Jermyn Street and, in view of the fact that there is a collection at hourly, and sometimes at even half-hourly intervals, it seems evident that the amount of correspondence is very considerable and that any attempt to make a scrutiny of letters posted

there would be hopeless unless Oldham was seen to post a letter at any particular time, when, providing arrangements can be made with the post office, it might be possible for a special clearance to be made.[327]

More disheartening news was to follow.

Dear Watson

Re: your telephone enquiry today concerning telephone message to Jules hotel on the 5 September. Enquiries have been made and it has been established that no telephone message from Paris (in France) was received yesterday at the hotel.

Re: the question of a 'check' on this hotel for telephone calls made from Paris. There are six lines to this hotel (Whitehall 1471) and this means that six different operators will have to be employed at the same time (one on each of the lines) for each eight hours daily. Apart from the difficulty of relieving so many of the staff for the work it is pointed out that the conversation might possibly be in French and that there is no one at the Exchange who has the necessary qualifications to translate the 'calls'.

JB Booth[328]

The inadequacies of the surveillance operation underline the difficulties that MI5 faced during this period – the rapid pace of technological change, and the sheer lack of manpower, had rendered impossible any attempts to throw a comprehensive communications blanket over Oldham in the hope of gaining an insight into his collaborators abroad. The fact that none of the potential phone operators could speak French simply compounded the problem.

Nevertheless, Watson persevered:

It was subsequently arranged that a note should be made of any continental calls going to, or coming from, Jules hotel. Captain Booth said that, if necessary, the post office could ask Paris where the calls emanated from, but we decided against doing this in view of the risk of arousing suspicion.[329]

This was a critical mistake, as it meant that all that could be collated was a frequency log rather than any meaningful leads to pass to SIS operatives abroad, who would be better placed to pick up the line of inquiry. Quite what sort of suspicion might be aroused, and by whom, is not specified. The error was emphasised by the fact that the telephone service reported two incoming calls either from Paris or via Paris to Jules Hotel on 14 September at 2.51 pm and 3.26 pm. Booth was only able to report this to Watson two weeks afterwards on 28 September, far too late to act upon the information.

It seems that the call involved further requests by Oldham for money, because on 16 September a letter containing two £5 notes was sent from Interlaken to the Jules Hotel and was intercepted on its arrival on 19 September. As far as Oldham was concerned, the money arrived in the nick of time; the following day, a letter was sent from Credit Lyonnais stating that they had to refuse payment of his cheque for £3 to Hood, the landlord of the Chequers pub, because Oldham's account was already overdrawn.

In a report dated 21 September, Hunter painted an increasingly pitiful picture of Oldham's state of affairs as his money gradually ran out.

> This man is still living at Jules hotel and there is no indication of him leaving.
>
> Most of his time, when away from the hotel, he spends at the Chequers public house, Duke Street, and he is invariably there from 6.30 pm to the closing hour at 11.00 pm, and I have, on several occasions, been in his company.
>
> While formerly, his drinks were usually spirits and the more expensive beers, he now consumes bitter and I am of the opinion he is getting short of cash. Last week, Hood, the landlord with whom he has got very friendly, cashed for him a cheque which was drawn on the Credit Lyonnais.

Last evening he was a good deal more rational than when I previously saw him. I understand that Hood gave him the hint to go slow on spirits.

Apart from breakfast, he now has no meals at Jules but gets snacks at the pub.

He appears to have no associates other than persons with whom he has become acquainted in the Chequers, among whom are certain female servants from adjoining flats, an artist named Shenaton (or similar name), whom I have never seen other than in a state of helpless intoxication, and various antique dealers in the street who use the house.

Oldham tells everyone he has to remain in Jules hotel for business reasons till about 5.00 pm and receives a number of telephone calls from the continent relating to 'international currency', regarding which he has to give quick decisions.

When in drink he becomes talkative. He has told me of journeys he made to the continent (when connected with the 'communicating' branch) with the late Earls Cozen and Grey, and, on one occasion, mentioned one Jesser-Davis, a King's Messenger, with whom he apparently was frequently working.[330]

Earl Grey, as noted earlier, was Secretary of State for Foreign Affairs between 1905 and 1916 when Oldham was first transferred to the Foreign Office; Earl Curzon acted in a similar capacity after the war from 1919 until 1924. These are bold claims but not outside the bounds of possibility, given Oldham's presence at League of Nations council meetings and associated conferences as part of the supporting team that accompanied the Foreign Secretary on such occasions.

Charles Edward Jesser-Davis is also quite interesting. Notes on him were transferred to a separate secret service file, PF 112 939, which intriguingly does not appear to have survived. Jesser-Davis enjoyed a distinguished military career, rising from lieutenant to acting captain in the Rifle Corps during the World War I, where he earned the 1914–15 Star service medal, and he was twice mentioned in despatches in 1917. On his return to civilian life,

Jesser-Davis was appointed as a temporary clerk in July 1920 before receiving his civil service certificate and subsequent appointment as King's Foreign Service Messenger in November 1921. He made frequent visits around Europe, including many of the routes that Oldham travelled. He was still in post when Oldham was appointed staff officer in 1928, so the two men would have indeed known each other well.

> He boasts of his friendship with Mr Harry Preston of Brighton, at whose hotel he frequently stayed with his wife. He often refers to his house in Kensington and explains his non-residence there to its being in the hands of the decorators and his wife being abroad with their son, who has just completed his education at Bonn university.
>
> Each night, on leaving the Chequers, he visits Grays, the chemists, of Duke Street, where Jock (a local character), the assistant, has ready for him a concoction for sleeplessness. He usually leaves Jock a bottle of beer.[331]

Indeed, Hunter expressed real concerns for Oldham's health and ended his report with the words, 'In my opinion, Oldham is heading for a breakdown'.

Two days later, there was a sudden flurry of calls from the continent. According to Watson:

> Mr Kelly (GPO) telephoned to say that a telephone message was received at Jules hotel from Paris at 2.57 pm on Saturday 23 September 1933, the conversation lasting for seven minutes. At 9.17 am today [25 September], someone at Jules hotel put through a call for Biarritz 580.
>
> GPO suggest that possibly the incoming call on Saturday originated at Biarritz, being routed through Paris, and that today's call was in answer to it.[332]

It is not known whether Oldham had anything to do with these calls. The following day, Watson was alerted to more activity.

At 10.08 am today, someone at Jules hotel telephoned to Paris, Interspecial 1420. That is the telephone number of the Banque Belge Pour l'Étranger, Rue de Bourse.[333]

Again, no connection could be made between the call and Oldham.

On Thursday 28 September, Oldham disappeared from surveillance. A report was filed by Hunter on 30 September, having made further attempts to re-establish contact with Oldham.

Last evening, I called at Chequers public house and learned that the above had not been there since Wednesday 27th inst. He had previously been in the house each evening. Attached cutting may explain his absence.[334]

The cutting was a clipped article taken from the *Star* the previous day:

A KENSINGTON MYSTERY
Unknown Man Dead in Gas-Filled Empty Kitchen
The Kensington police are trying to discover the identity of a man, aged about 35, who was found dead in a gas-filled kitchen at a house in Pembroke Gardens, Kensington.

Apart from a table, there was no furniture in the house, but in a cupboard were a number of suits of clothes, including evening dress.

The man was 5 feet 6 inches in height, well-built, clean-shaven and had dark brown hair and eyes. He was wearing a brown mixture suit and a brown striped shirt, with collar and tie to match. The shirt bore the initials 'EHO'.

It is believed that the man formerly lived at the address.

The report from Hunter continued:

I have since ascertained that the deceased referred to is Oldham and that he was in monetary difficulties. He owes money to Hood, landlord of the Chequers, to Jules, the Savoy Turkish baths and various restaurants. On the Monday prior to his death, he is said to have received a letter from Geneva, the contents of which appeared to upset him. He is stated to have been taking in large quantities a drug called feraldehide (?).[335]

This was almost certainly paraldehyde, a rather nasty remedy for alcohol withdrawal symptoms such as delirium tremens. Its side effects included hallucinations, trembling, slow heartbeat, nausea, confusion, troubled breathing and very bad breath. Prolonged use could lead to addiction, with organ damage often manifesting through a yellowing of the eyes and skin. Profuse sweating was not unknown, symptoms perhaps displayed back in July when Oldham had attempted to break into the Foreign Office for the last time.

Hunter's despatch to MI5, coupled with further newspaper clippings that appeared over the following days in the *News Chronicle* and *The Times*, as well as information from the OGPU files, provide enough information to speculate on the chain of events that led to Oldham's death.

At some point after 20 September, it seems that he was preparing to travel abroad once more to meet with Bystrolyotov. According to Bystrolyotov's biographer Draitser's interpretation of events, this was 'to deliver a list of British secret service operatives posted abroad. Whether he collected the information or not is unclear today. But he seemingly intended to take some sensitive information across the British border.'[336]

During this period, Lucy – who was apparently still in contact with her friend 'Perelly' – informed the Soviets about information she herself had received from Kemp (who was trying to find her some employment) that 'Oldham had sent a porter from the Jules Hotel to the Foreign Office with his passport and a note asking Kemp to indulge him as a friend and mark up his passport, raising it to the status of a diplomatic courier passport; the holder of such a passport was not subject to border crossing disclosures'.[337] Kemp refused and retained the document, sending a message back to Oldham via the porter that he should come and pick it up himself. If this was indeed the case, Kemp did not reveal this information to either his superiors in the

Foreign Office or MI5 – no doubt playing the amateur detective once more in the hope of claiming the glory himself for bringing Oldham to justice. This was a costly error.

Doubtless spooked by the loss of his passport and unsure about how next to proceed, it is plausible that Oldham tried to communicate his dire situation to a Soviet agent via the phone call from Biarritz via Paris on Saturday 23 September. Two days later he received the letter from Geneva. Although this was not intercepted by MI5 – another slip by the security services – nor was it found with his personal possessions either in the hotel or at 31 Pembroke Gardens, it is safe to conclude that it was sent by Bystrolyotov, as Geneva was one of his favoured operational bases. Perhaps frustrated by Oldham's continual failure to send over the material he had promised, or suspecting that the 'lost passport' was just another excuse, we can speculate that Bystrolyotov made good his earlier promise to cut Oldham off financially and indeed went further, with the threat of exposing Oldham's activities to the British authorities unless he complied with his instructions to travel to the continent – something, of course, Oldham could no longer do. This would explain the call placed to Biarritz in response to the letter from Geneva.

With his only source of income cut off, his passport seized by the Foreign Office, and faced with mounting debts at the Jules Hotel that he could not pay, Oldham gathered together his meagre possessions and returned to the only refuge he had available to him – his empty family home. There he was doubtless surrounded by memories of happier times before his wife abandoned him and his career slipped away through the neck of a bottle. Contemplating the real possibility of prosecution as a traitor should the Soviets make good their threats to expose him, Oldham sealed the kitchen, turned on the coal gas fire, lay down on the floor, and waited for his life to ebb away.

He nearly failed to carry out this final act successfully. A police sergeant, alerted by neighbours to unexpected activity in the shuttered house as well as the smell of gas, was called to investigate. On seeing Oldham lying on the floor near the gas stove, clothed in his dressing gown, the officer smashed a window and entered the property. Oldham was still showing faint signs of life so the sergeant called for medical assistance. An ambulance was summoned and Oldham was bundled into the back. He expired before he reached hospital, pronounced dead 'on the way' outside 28 Marloes Road, a few streets from his former home.

No good spy story is complete without a conspiracy theory and in Oldham's case it is provided by a cryptic comment from Bystrolyotov's memoirs. Referring to Oldham's death, he states that 'our wonderful source failed and was killed by us'.[338] There is no evidence to support the interpretation that direct action was taken to eliminate Oldham. Instead, it may simply relate to a degree of remorse or guilt felt by Bystrolyotov over the contents of the Geneva letter that triggered Oldham's decision to take his own life. No trace of foul play was noted by the British authorities, although rather bizarrely the OGPU Centre itself suspected that Oldham had been murdered – by the British.

> In order to avoid a scandal the [British] intelligence service had ARNO physically eliminated, making his death appear to be suicide[339] .

A subsequent newspaper clipping placed in Oldham's file, again from the *Star* on 2 October 1933, carried an account of the post mortem and coroner's inquest into his death.

DEAD IN EMPTY HOUSE
'Drink More Disease Than Vice', Says Coroner
The downfall of an ex-civil servant through drink and drugs was described at a Paddington inquest today on Ernest Holloway Oldham, aged 46, who was found gassed in an empty, shuttered house at Pebroke[sic]-gardens, Kensington, where he had formerly lived with his wife.

Mrs Lucy Oldham, the widow, said that her husband was dismissed from his employment through drunkenness. He had been taking drugs and drinking heavily. Two months ago he left her without means. Since then his house had been empty and she had not seen him.

A police sergeant said that he went to the house in Pebroke[sic]-gardens and entered after smashing a window, finding the man lying near a gas stove.

The man was wearing a dressing gown and he had only 5½d and a bunch of keys in his pockets.

Mr Oddie, the coroner, said that drink was probably more a disease than a vice in this case.

He recorded a verdict of suicide while of unsound mind.[340]

Oldham's age was indeed recorded as 46 years on the official death certificate, which was issued on the same day as the coroner's inquest. No doubt he looked to be heading towards his 50s, given the prolonged effects of alcohol and drugs on his body; nevertheless, in reality Oldham was still a year away from his 40th birthday.

Attending the coroner's inquest was Oldham's sister, Marjorie Holloway Barratt and her husband, George Bernard Barratt. They were forced to make the difficult decision to leave their eldest son Michael at home unattended, facing the traffic along Wolves Lane as he walked to the isolation hospital to check on his brother's state of health.

On 3 October, the surveillance operation on Oldham was terminated via a terse, two-line note from Watson. The phone intercepts on the deserted 31 Pembroke Gardens ceased.

Chapter twelve

COVER UP
(1933–1974)

Not long before he committed suicide Oldham refused to get them any more information, but the OGPU brought great pressure to bear upon him to get the full names and descriptions of his associates in order that one could be picked and tried to carry on Oldham's work for them.

NOTES MADE BY MI5 OFFICER JANE ARCHER DURING AN INTERVIEW WITH SOVIET

DEFECTOR WALTER KRIVITSKY, 1940

Oldham's MI5 file shows that once the HOW was suspended on 3 October, it was deemed pointless to continue further monitoring of overseas phone calls to the Jules Hotel, so these ceased on 4 October. A week later, Harker spoke to Norton at the Foreign Office who confirmed that no further action should be taken, and as far as MI5 was concerned the case was closed. However, within the Foreign Office the fallout had only just begun.

An internal investigation into Oldham's activities was launched, though the entire episode is now shrouded in secrecy since no files from the Communications Department were selected for permanent retention during the period 1927 to 1935. The day books of the Foreign Office, where a range of activities were recorded, are equally silent on both the original break-in, as already discussed, but equally there is no hint of any extraordinary activity throughout the summer and autumn of 1933.

The clearest indication of the seriousness with which Oldham's break-in was treated can be found from the order given on 26 July 1933 to change 'the locks and keys of a considerable number of presses in which highly confidential documents are kept in the Foreign Office within the shortest possible period.'[341] The Chief Clerk, Howard Smith, found it prudent to provide only a verbal update to the Director of Printing and Binding about the 'circumstances which render necessary the alteration of the locks'. However, it is astonishing to learn that the process was still underway in December, with no end in sight:

> I have spoken to Moore and it is clear that although good progress has been made with the changing of the locks of the FO [Foreign Office] boxes, it would be impossible to finish this work, still less to deal with the boxes of the cabinet offices, which also have to be changed, before the end of December. If Moore is left alone with this work it will mean that the old lock will remain in use much longer than is desirable. I have therefore written to Mr Todd, the director of printing and binding at the Stationery Office, asking him to agree that the second locksmith will be retained until the end of March next.[342]

A handwritten note indicated that this topic should be brought up again on 26 March 1934 – a full seven months after the original incident. Other files suggest that there were further discussions about Foreign Office security from July to October, but even the descriptions of the file content were deemed too sensitive to commit to print.

Clearly, the Foreign Office suspected that some of its confidential material had been compromised; but equally, because of the sensitive nature of some of the diplomatic correspondence and files in its possession, it did not want external bodies such as MI5 or SIS involved until it had ascertained exactly what had happened. This was why the remainder of the investigation into Oldham's activities took place behind closed doors, with the primary attention shifting to the source of his money throughout 1932 and 1933. Equally, the Hungarian Count Joseph Perelly was also a subject of great interest.

As a result, Oldham's wife – with whom he had clearly travelled abroad throughout this period – came under intense pressure to reveal what she knew, although the Foreign Office worked through the family's solicitors, Walbrook and Hosken. Kemp had previously contacted Angus Walbrook on 16 August in the presence of Harker, Cotesworth and Lee to ask about Oldham's address and shortly after Oldham's death it seems as though he was approached once again, this time with the request that he should compile a complete list of Oldham's financial transactions based on the paperwork in his possession.[343]

To cover up the fact that the real nature of the inquiry related to the potential leak of confidential Foreign Office material to an overseas power, the reason given to Walbrook was that Oldham was one of a number of employees suspected of being involved with drugs smuggling. This was a complete fabrication, but the threat of subsequent police action was sufficiently convincing to elicit the support of the solicitor. He was asked specifically to look for any connections Oldham might have had with Germany; this was probably a result of the misinformation that Bystrolyotov had fed Kemp during the meeting with Lucy on 19 July. However, the changing international situation also played a part. On 16 October, Germany announced its intentions to withdraw from the League of Nations, amid growing fears about Hitler's plans to expand his country's military capability. No doubt the Oldhams' cover story also helped add further credibility to the idea that Oldham was involved with the Germans, given that Lucy's son had indeed spent long periods of time near Bonn, as well as the recorded occasions when the couple had flown to Berlin. However, it would seem as though her familial links to Germany remained undetected and therefore not investigated.

Walbrook duly explained the situation to Lucy and asked for her assistance, but she informed him that she knew nothing about any German connection, other than the fact that Da Vinci (Bazarov) was the man who bought any material that Oldham might have procured. She considered him to be an 'evil man' who had subverted both her husband as well as her 'Hungarian count'. Walbrook clearly understood the seriousness of the situation and pressed her to reveal any details of Perelly's whereabouts since he was the link to the Germans that had dragged Oldham 'into some dirty business'.[344] It appears that the Foreign Office claimed to have evidence that Oldham's disappearance at the end of July was to take part in 'a wild binge with prostitutes' in Vienna and Berlin – a ploy intended to enrage her into a confession. However, Lucy was not fooled, and continued to claim that she knew nothing more, insistent that Perelly was of no help with the inquiries because he had merely acted as the go-between for the transactions between Oldham and Da Vinci. This was clearly disingenuous, but Lucy's role in the whole affair is somewhat shaded in mystery. If she had instigated Oldham's first approach to the Soviets in 1929, as Bystrolyotov believed, then her apparent lack of knowledge at key stages shows a remarkable ability to feign ignorance or innocence about the depth of her husband's activities and throw her inquirers off the scent. This was one such example.

However, the questions would not go away and where Walbrook failed, Kemp once again turned his hand to some investigative work. First, he visited Lucy in her new accommodation, asking after her health following the death of her husband, as any concerned family friend would. However, during the conversation he tried to subtly direct her towards the whereabouts of her friend Count Perelly, who had failed to make their meeting on 20 July. Not surprisingly, Lucy refused to cooperate, at which point Kemp lost his temper and started to threaten her, accusing her of being complicit in her husband's activities and suggesting that she too was facing arrest.

In his anger, Kemp revealed details of the investigation, including the extent of the intercepted letters and phone calls and repeated the now standard line that Oldham had been a smuggler and a spy. At this point, Lucy seems to have provided more information about Oldham's activities, but not enough to shatter the belief that Germans, rather than any other foreign powers, were involved. To the very end, she clung to her story that she had lost contact with Count Perelly and therefore could not say where he was. Once again, Lucy was lying. She had continued to write to Bystrolyotov throughout the ongoing investigation.

Whether Kemp's involvement was officially sanctioned or not is unclear. Indeed, it may well be that his questioning and threats were actually self-interest at work, as Kemp and other officials associated with Oldham, such as Raymond Oake, were interrogated by their superiors within the Foreign Office. According to Lucy, they were equally responsible for 'suggesting that she should be arrested as an accomplice'.[345]

However, the lack of concrete information made it impossible to progress the matter further and, in any case, it was decided at the very top that further digging might prove incredibly embarrassing for the Foreign Office in general and its head, Sir Robert Vanstittart, in particular. For example, there are no references made to the incident in his personal notes, perhaps unsurprisingly, given he had the most to lose from any revelations of lax security. In Kemp's humble opinion, as he revealed to Lucy once he'd calmed down somewhat, security breaches of this seriousness were extremely rare, and nothing comparable to the gravity of Oldham's activities had taken place in the last 300 years. It was exactly that sort of complacent attitude towards Foreign Office security that had allowed Oldham to carry on undetected for as long as he had.[346]

With the British sources silent, we only know how the Foreign Office handled the case thanks to Lucy's contact with Bystrolyotov. When the dust had settled, she told her friends and acquaintances in Kensington that she needed a break and then flew to Vienna where she made arrangements to meet Bystrolyotov. He first checked to see whether she was being followed, but with MI5 out of the equation, the reach of the Foreign Office was restricted to passport control and SIS and neither had been involved in the internal investigation.

Lucy's meeting with Bystrolyotov was significant for several reasons. For the Soviets, Lucy was able to provide an insider's knowledge about the state of the Foreign Office investigation, as well as confirming that by December interest in Oldham was starting to abate. However, it was clearly too risky for Bystrolyotov to return to London any time soon. He commented:

> Only in English novels does everything go smoothly for the intelligence services, all ends meet and the Tower of London mercilessly swallows those who have touched upon the secrets of the British empire. I accept that I could have ended up in the Tower, but only if Vansittart had been willing to wash his dirty linen in public and the matter had been entrusted to anyone other than ROLAND.[347]

Equally, OGPU were satisfied that Lucy had not jeopardised Bystrolyotov's whereabouts or identity, as she still believed in the Perelly fiction. It was decided that she remained a potentially useful asset, particularly if an attempt was to be made to re-establish another line of communication into the heart of British diplomacy. An offer of money was put to the 'desperate, ageing lady'.[348] Officially, the reason provided by the Soviets was that it was 'to save her and her children' – Lucy claimed that she was about to turn to prostitution because of the financial hardship she was facing, a refrain she'd used previously with Bystrolyotov. She accepted the offer 'with tears of ecstatic gratitude'.[349] In reality, it was as much to ensure she did not turn against them at a future date as for the hope of any further information about the Foreign Office.

This money was indeed important to Lucy, as Oldham's estate was finally wound up. On 30 November 1933, a letter had been sent to the Foreign Office from CF Cassella and Company Limited, inquiring after Oldham's address – doubtless another creditor chasing an unpaid bill. They specialised in making scientific instruments, particularly magnification devices and telescopes – possibly an item commissioned by Oldham to help him with his espionage activities or simply a hobby; we do not know.[350] However, claims such as this drained away the value of Oldham's meagre financial assets.

On 27 July 1934, Lucy was granted a letter of administration for his estate – no will could be found – and on 27 August, Walbrook and Hoskens submitted a notice to the *London Gazette*, published four days later, alerting anyone with an outstanding claim to make against the estate that they should put it in writing by 8 November 'by which date the assets of the said deceased will be distributed, having regard only to the claims then notified'.[351] This would not have taken long. The gross value of Oldham's estate was estimated to be £3,600 – probably the sale value of 31 Pembroke Gardens – whereas the net value of his personal estate was 'nil'.

Yet in many ways 1934 marked the beginning of the Oldham affair. The Foreign Office wished to turn their disgraced official into the forgotten spy and sweep the whole sordid episode under the carpet for many reasons – embarrassment about the break-in, ignorance about what he'd actually done and a flawed assumption about the people he was working with – but it was a

catastrophic mistake. At a diplomatic level, the Soviet Union was able to capitalise on the departure of Germany from the League of Nations and was finally
admitted on 18 September 1934, a recognition that Soviet cooperation might
be needed to counter the threat of Nazi Germany under Hitler.

In this respect, Oldham's activities in 1932 were crucial and later revelations were to show that Moscow relied upon shelves of British material and
deciphered communications, neatly filed, to help form its diplomatic stance
when dealing with the other European powers throughout the 1930s. To continue exerting a diplomatic influence, after so many years of exclusion and
isolation, required greater access to confidential information rather than less.
It is in this context that Oldham's activities need to be seen and it is with
this background that he was afforded such significance by OGPU, despite the
inherent problems associated with running him. The loss of access to the innermost secrets of the Foreign Office was a major blow to Moscow, so it is
no surprise that Bystrolyotov's attention shifted towards succession planning.

Before he died, Oldham revealed the names of several of his colleagues
whom he deemed most suitable to approach for similar activities to his own.
Two candidates were immediately identified as having the greatest potential,
one of whom was part of the British delegation to the League of Nations in
Geneva. However, this posed a problem. Bystrolyotov was still wary that British officials might be on high alert after Oldham's suicide and recognise him,
so he turned once again to his associate, Dutch artist Henri Pieck, to assist
with the recruitment.

The process seems to have begun early in 1933, when Pieck was installed
at the Hôtel Beau Rivage in Geneva. Under Bystrolyotov's guidance, Pieck attempted to cultivate friendships with British delegates working at the League of
Nations, mainly through conversations struck up at the Brasserie Universal. The
first target was a man given the codename BOY, whose real identity has never
been established. He seemed an unlikely candidate as he was 'overly prim, [and]
he treated every person who approached him during social interactions with
icy cold politeness'. [352] Indeed, he was soon abandoned for easier prey.

Next on the list was a more likely target, codenamed SHELLEY – a man
permanently short of money, mainly through his extravagant lifestyle which

had compromised his chances of marrying Enid, the step-daughter of the principal passport control officer in Geneva, Captain John Harvey (codenamed NORA and CHIEF respectively). He was also none other than Oldham's close associate in the Foreign Office – Raymond Oake, whom Oldham had contacted in August 1933 from the Jules Hotel. Pieck had already ingratiated himself with Harvey, to the point where Harvey felt comfortable telling him confidential information about senior government figures. This was a useful way to gain access to Oake via NORA. Pieck quickly came to the same conclusion as Oldham (and indeed the British authorities, judging by the notes on file), namely that Oake was a wastrel who was only one step ahead of the money lenders. Oake was a poorly paid temporary clerk, so would not have a pension to look forward to when his employment came to an end. This made him doubly vulnerable to financial temptation, and thus an important potential recruit.

Given the recent furore around Oldham's activities, it is astonishing that Oake and his associates – other unidentified colleagues within the Foreign Office given the codenames TOMMY and TED – permitted Pieck access to confidential material. One evening after dinner, Pieck followed Oake and TOMMY back to the consulate and watched on as they scrutinised the latest telegrams. Pieck had also been invited to visit them in the Foreign Office when he was next in London, where they would show him Room 22 and then go for a drink in the nearby pub – something that actually transpired on Christmas Day 1933. Pieck observed Oake open a combination lock safe and examine the contents. On discovering that Oake had already spent his December wage packet on drink, Pieck immediately volunteered to lend him sufficient money to cover some cheques Oake had issued, thus creating the foundations for financial dependency.[353]

Pieck exerted greater influence over Oake throughout 1934, inviting him to spend a week with Pieck and his wife in Geneva in March – where he offered to help alleviate some of his monetary worries. Posing as an intermediary for a Dutch bank interested in the British perspective on the economic climate, Pieck wondered if Oake would like to earn a little extra money by obtaining information for him to pass on, including some political material. Oake agreed.

Although his first deliveries in April were of little use and he was unwilling to provide original materials to Pieck for copying, by the summer he was 'processing serious secret correspondence'. This did not last; by July he was getting cold feet and in August refused to provide any further packages, claiming that 'I don't want to go to prison just before the wedding'.[354] Yet with his financial situation still rocky and the wedding on the horizon, Oake agreed to reconsider. He tentatively mentioned to his future father-in-law that he was acting part-time for an intermediary representing a bank, which Harvey thought was a good idea. Yet still Oake failed to bring anything of use to Pieck, partly because he was unable to gain access to relevant material. Some of the difficulties Oake faced in obtaining information can be discerned in a report that Bystrolyotov sent back to Moscow via Theodor Mally in October 1934:

> SHELLEY's potential remains unknown. He sits in a room with 20 other officials, at a table at which sit four others. Only a small part of the correspondence passes through his hands which he cannot copy on the spot. He must look for material in other rooms, in which he has no official business. Whether this is a consequence of measures taken after the ARNO case is not known. SHELLEY carefully conceals all details regarding his work so it is extremely difficult to give him guidance. Maybe the fear he expressed in July was of his having been caught somewhere he was not supposed to be.[355]

By December, with Mally despatching Pieck to London to threaten Oake and Bystrolyotov waiting in the wings should help be required, it became apparent that nothing would persuade Oake to continue – his fear of discovery was too great and the potential use of blackmail was discounted in case it jeopardised the next target, a man called John Herbert King. He had been introduced to Pieck by Oake in October 1934, and was another temporary clerk in the Communications Department. According to a report by Bystrolyotov:

> In Geneva, COOPER [Pieck] had become acquainted with a cipher clerk named King. He is about 50 years old, an Irishman who

lived in Germany for about ten years and speaks German perfect-
ly. A lively and inquisitive person, not stupid but well-educated.
He draws a sharp distinction between himself with his cultured
ways and the 'pompous fools' of Englishmen. He likes music and
is knowledgeable, and is keen on the theatre. He is very eccentric
and likes magic.

King is in dire need of money because he has to support himself on a small salary, as well as his grown-up son, a student, and
his wife. In spite of his length of service he is not given promotion because of his Irish background and he likes to have a drink at
someone else's expense... He would borrow money and being an
Irishman does not like Englishmen and makes friends very easily
with foreigners.[356]

Once again, the classic combination of festering resentment, poor career
prospects, a need for money and a liking for alcohol were present; King was
given the codename MAG and was cautiously approached by Pieck in early
1935, once it became clear that Oake would not cooperate. Pieck used his
growing social network in London and Dutch business credentials to impress
King and deployed the same cover story – that he was an intermediary for a
large bank that needed regular political information. King duly obliged for a
set fee, starting with the weekly Foreign Office summaries, though as with
Oake he was reluctant to hand over original material. One factor in his caution was the recent furore surrounding Oldham and the whispered stories
that continued to swirl around Whitehall that MI5 and SIS agents were now
monitoring activities. Therefore, after his first lunch with Pieck, King decided
to seek advice from Harvey, which Bystrolyotov only discovered in July 1935:

MAG said that after his first lunch with COOPER he had returned
to CHIEF and had reported that a foreigner had entertained him
and that Geneva was full of suspicious characters. He had sought
his advice and CHIEF had replied that Pieck was a personal friend
and deserved complete trust. This, according to MAG, had enabled

him to develop his friendship with COOPER, but when the latter
offered him work with the bank he had suspected that he might be
CHIEF's agent.[357]

This is a revealing insight into the climate of suspicion that had been created
amongst Foreign Office junior staff, completely undone by Harvey's acceptance of Pieck's status. As a result, King gained the confidence to obtain some
crucial intelligence for Pieck's 'banker' – the first delivery contained an account of the Foreign Secretary Sir John Simon's meeting with Adolf Hitler,
including demands made by the German leader to change the terms of the
Treaty of Versailles. Simon's impression was that war might be imminent if a
unified stand could not be achieved in the face of German aggression.

King was able to provide further information about the innermost workings of the Foreign Office ciphering system, furnishing Bystrolyotov with insight into the way his informers accessed this confidential material and the
risks they had to run:

> [MAG] first turned his attention to the book in which the most
> important incoming telegrams were registered after they had
> been deciphered and after a summary had been prepared for se-
> nior Foreign Office personnel. However, what had seemed prac-
> tical in theory turned out to be impossible to implement. MAG
> worked in the cipher room with SHELLEY and TED, but on the
> afternoon shift they operated in pairs, one writing the decrypted
> text onto a flimsy in pencil while the other read the telegram.
> The flimsy was then passed on to the next room where the King's
> Messengers, who were ranked more senior than the cipher clerks,
> awaited their assignments. They were responsible for typing the
> telegrams, destroying the original flimsies, and entering summa-
> ries into a log known as the day register. The incoming telegrams
> were then passed for internal distribution to the office messen-
> gers, who were usually retired warrant officers, while the outgoing
> telegrams were circulated to the senior staff for approval before

being sent abroad. MAG handled the day register every day, entering new telegrams, but on the occasion he attempted to read some of the other pages he was noticed by one of the couriers who challenged him. Alarmed by this experience, MAG decided that he could not use the day register and instead concentrated on the Foreign Office daily bulletins, which hitherto had been supplied by ARNO. According to SHELLEY, ARNO and MAG, these files are kept in the couriers' room and MAG had no official access to them, as he discovered when he tried to look at one, and was spotted by a courier who warned him not to take 'his book', indicating that each was the responsibility of an individual courier. They were in constant use by the couriers, who kept them permanently in their sight making access impossible, so MAG opted for old copies of the daily bulletins which were scheduled for destruction.[358]

This was where Oldham's status had enabled him to obtain so much material without arousing any suspicion. As staff officer, he was the highest-ranking official beside the head and deputy head, who were involved with other tasks. Oldham would have been justified in keeping an eye on all aspects of the ciphering and despatch operation.

The document shredder, which in ARNO's time had stood in the basement, is now in a ground floor corridor, not far from MAG's room. However, when he chose his moment to steal the bulletins from the machine, which was guarded, he was asked why he was in that particular corridor and who he was looking for. MAG had no excuse and therefore had abandoned the attempt. In these circumstances MAG was left with the telegrams which he handled legitimately.[359]

The descriptions provided by the men – along with eyewitness confirmation from Pieck – shone a light into the heart of the Foreign Office, although it was clear that everyone was more suspicious of unexpected behaviour following the Oldham incident. It also underlined just how important Oldham had become to the Soviets, given the challenges they faced with finding a suitable replacement. Yet King proved adept at finding ways around the inconvenient scrutiny of colleagues and by May 1935 was handing over highly sensitive material that he had often personally deciphered, to prove his use to Pieck's banker.

Control of King passed from Bystrolyotov to Theodor Mally in September 1935, with Pieck still acting as the main point of contact whilst Mally set up an operational base near the Foreign Office in a flat at Buckingham Gate – this was the location where King would deliver material to be photographed. It was originally intended that Aleksander Orlov (OGPU agent and *rezident* in London) would be used for the delivery of the films to be taken to London, but he was involved with his colleague Arnold Deutsch (another Soviet agent) on other business; instead, responsibility was granted to Walter Krivitsky (codename GROLL, a Soviet intelligence officer). He was rather a poor choice, since he spoke no English, was inexperienced in photography and was soon withdrawn. By the end of 1935, Pieck was also unable to travel to London due to personal circumstances, so Mally had to run King himself.

During this period it is possible to glean a bit more insight about the way Oldham's activities had been viewed by his colleagues, as his name cropped up on several occasions. King made the first reference shortly after he started delivering material to Pieck, noting that he now knew Oldham had been providing material to the 'banker' before he had, although King thought Oldham was 'a fool who took documents openly and ruined himself'.[360] Clearly, Oldham's removal of material had been known about by junior colleagues and it is rather astonishing that no-one higher up had acted to stop him, emphasising once again the naivety and misplaced trust of the time. Equally, King and Oake probably helped mask the real significance of Oldham's treachery, given their own belief that they were merely helping a banker rather than passing valuable secrets to the Soviets. A second reference was made in August 1936, when King revealed to Mally the various theories that had circulated amongst the Foreign Office staff to explain Oldham's death. The most popular was that Oldham had been in the employ of the French and that the story of his suicide masked the fact that British intelligence services had killed him, placing his body in a gas-filled room to make it look like he had taken his own life.[361]

Overall, King was credited by the Soviets for providing an invaluable insight into British diplomacy in the late 1930s. The information was often used to generate tension and disharmony between Britain and Germany, via leaks to the German embassy in London, to further Soviet interests. Indeed, it is possible that the Molotov–Ribbentrop Pact made on the eve of World War II was the culmination of a process that had started with Oldham's leaks which had enabled the Soviets to manipulate the international political situation to their advantage.

King was only the latest in a line of moles within the Foreign Office that began with Oldham, but 1934 saw another key development in Soviet intelligence operations in England – ideological recruitment from the higher echelons of society, a technique that was adopted in response to some of the challenges that Oldham had posed from 1929 onwards. Operatives like Oldham, Oake and King were important sources of information, but the very factors that made them easy to recruit – financial motivation, disenchantment with their jobs, a weakness for alcohol – equally made them liabilities, as the traumatic experience of handling Oldham had demonstrated.

An alternative, potentially longer-term strategy was adopted in response to the Oldham case, namely to recruit communist sympathisers to the Soviet cause from universities such as Oxford and Cambridge, where graduates were more likely to secure higher positions within the British establishment. Thus the Cambridge spy ring was developed after Oldham's death by Arnold Deutsch, through his recruitment of Kim Philby, Anthony Burgess and Donald Maclean in 1934, joined by Anthony Blunt and probably John Cairncross (the alleged 'Fifth Man').

However, Stalin's great purge of the Communist Party and Soviet government saw the network of Great Illegals dismantled overnight. Deutsch and Mally – who had been transferred from handling King to the Cambridge ring in 1937 – were suddenly recalled, the latter executed in 1938 while Deutsch appears to have died in the Soviet Union in the early 1940s. Agents such as Ignace Reiss, who had first recruited Pieck, were eliminated abroad and, following the murder of Reiss, Pieck stopped meeting King and quietly dropped out of sight.

The alternative to arrest, show trial and execution or imprisonment in a gulag was defection. Aleksander Orlov, who had returned to Russia in 1935, fled to Canada before he could be arrested in 1938. He was followed the next year by Walter Krivitsky, who ended up in the USA, fearing for his life. In August 1939 he spoke to journalist Isaac Don Levine, who published an article in the *Saturday Evening Post* that claimed (among other things) that two Soviet agents were working deep within the British government. Levine passed information to the British Ambassador in Washington, Lord Lothian, that a man named 'King, in the Foreign Office Communications Department' was selling state secrets to Moscow. He also mentioned a second source in the Political Committee of the Cabinet Office, unnamed. MI5 was informed and King was placed on three-week long sick leave until he was arrested under the Official Secrets Act and asked to explain various irregularities, including unaccounted bank notes in his safe deposit box. On 25 September, he was interviewed by Vivian, by this date a colonel and Head of counter-espionage in SIS. Guy Liddell in MI5 noted in his diary on 27 September:

> The case of King is developing in an interesting way. The notes in his safe deposit have been traced to Pieck, a Dutchman and Soviet agent and also to the Moscow Narodny bank. Another man in the code section of the FO [Foreign Office] is also involved. His name is Major Grange [actually Quarry]. He has been suspended pending interrogation. Another individual named Oake is being interrogated. It seems doubtful that he is very closely involved.[362]

Although he initially denied the accusations that he had sold secrets to the Soviets, three days later King confessed, giving the motives for his actions:

> I am not a permanent civil servant and am not entitled to a pension. I felt that by this means I could obtain some money to provide for when I retired without in any way endangering the security of

the state. I handed to Pieck, from time to time, copies of telegrams coming in from embassies – for example, reports of conversations between Hitler and Sir Neville Henderson or between Kemal Ataturk and the ambassador in Turkey or some such persons. There were sometimes eight or nine pages of roneoed matter [duplicated from a stencil] – sometimes three or four – never more than ten. They were never of any great political importance. The telegrams were always decoded copies and never in cipher. They were spare copies that were available in the room.[363]

King was tried in secret at the Old Bailey on 18 October 1939, found guilty and sentenced to ten years' imprisonment, of which he served less than seven years before his release in July 1946. Details of the case were kept from the press at the time and even the MI5 witnesses were driven to court in curtained cars to protect their identity. Shortly afterwards, Vivian provided a summary of the case in a report entitled 'Leakage from the communications department, Foreign Office' and came to some startling conclusions and drastic recommendations.

First, Vivian claimed that SIS had been given notice of Pieck's activities two years previously, through the revelations of an unnamed agent, 'X', who had wished to regain the trust and employ of the British government by providing them with information.

The full story was therefore in the possession of the SIS nearly two years ago and, though in no consecutive form, could have been acted upon then had it been credited. It was, however, treated with coldness and even derision, largely as a result of the prejudice against X himself.[364]

Once again, the chance to swoop on an alleged breach of Foreign Office security had not been acted upon – to great cost. However, one of the reasons that SIS ignored the testimony of X was that Pieck had given the name of his Foreign Office insider as Sir Robert Vansittart, rather than King:

> For the purpose undoubtedly of discrediting X's story in the un-
> likely event of his passing it to the British authorities... It is a trib-
> ute to Pieck's intelligence that this is precisely the effect it had.[365]

With King safely in prison, Vivian outlined the actions taken against other officials named during the investigation.

> RC Oake of the communications department was interrogated
> at the Foreign Office before King was examined. He made a
> fairly good impression, but we were left with a feeling that he
> was withholding facts regarding monetary relations with Pieck,
> with whom he had undoubtedly been on terms of close intimacy
> until 1935. Oake was again interrogated on 26 September when,
> under pressure, he reluctantly admitted that he had owed Pieck
> a sum of £60, which debt Pieck had cancelled at the time of his
> (Oake's) wedding in 1935.[366]

Oake was interviewed twice more, and although the conclusion was reached
that it was unlikely that he had actually sold Foreign Office secrets:

> Oake must have had knowledge or at least definite suspicion of
> the real nature of Pieck's activities and we do not doubt that, in
> receiving monetary and other presents from Pieck, Oake knew
> that he was receiving payments for services rendered... He was
> suspended from duty on 25 September and should not, it is con-
> sidered, be reinstated. There is no question of a prosecution as the
> evidence is deficient.[367]

Another official was sacked as a result of the inquiry – Major Francis John
Quarry (as opposed to Grange, as per Liddell's diary entry mentioned above),
who had only worked at the Communications Department since January
1938 and made a voluntary statement on 25 September when the affair first
came to light. In Vivian's opinion:

> It is considered that Quarry is unlikely to have had any crimi-
> nal connections with Foreign Office leakages...On the other
> hand, he is of an unsavoury type which we consider should not
> be engaged in a key position, such as that of a cipher officer; he
> has been closely associated with members of a criminal conspir-
> acy... He has been suspended and we do not feel he should be
> permitted to return to duty.[368]

A range of other names associated with Pieck were investigated, later referred
to as the 'cipher boys'.

> In the course of inquiries it was ascertained that J Russell,
> R Kinnaird, Captain HBW Maling and CB Harvey, all of the
> Communications Department, had known Pieck. They were
> therefore interrogated in the course of 26 and 27 September.[369]

Russell was the closest to following Oake and Quarry out of the door and it
was left to the discretion of the Under-Secretary of State to determine whether he stayed. However, as Vivian noted at the end of his report, a decision was
taken to remove all staff in the Communications Department to other posts,
and replace them with new men:

> So far as the Communications Department of the Foreign Office is
> concerned, the Under-Secretary of State's action in making a clean
> sweep of the existing staff of this Department will at least have se-
> cured that Department from any dangers latent in its personnel of
> which we have not become aware through this investigation. Our
> uncertainty as regards other Departments of the Foreign Office
> and other government offices, owing to the indications we have
> had of recent leakages, remains unrelieved.[370]

Agent X's testimony also enhanced the credibility of Krivitsky's earlier
statement, which until this point had been open to question. There was also

the concern that further leaks had occurred since 1937 to the Italians and Germans, as well as the unidentified 'second source' higher up in government – 'an ugly, unsolved puzzle' in the words of Vivian.[371] Inquiries were made to see if more information could be obtained from the former Soviet agent in person.

Eventually, Krivitsky agreed to visit the UK in January 1940, travelling under the pseudonym 'Walter Thomas'. Arrangements were made for him to be interviewed by Vivian, Harker (on the verge of taking over from Kell as Head of MI5) and Jane Sissmore, now Mrs Archer following her marriage the previous autumn. Archer conducted an extensive series of interviews, compiling an 85-page report that became the bedrock of British understanding of the Soviet intelligence network. She expected to be told about the activities of King, but throughout the evening of 23 January and throughout the following morning, Archer was startled by revelations about an earlier Soviet mole, none other than Ernest Oldham.

Full transcripts of Krivitsky's testimony were noted at the time and then written up over the next few weeks and added to Oldham's file, in line with standard practice to cross-reference information on named individuals. For the first time, the full extent of Oldham's treachery was revealed to the British security services, although it is not clear whether the significance was realised at the time. Krivitsky's account was somewhat confused, mixing up dates and important details while switching from vagueness to precision within moments. For example, he claimed not to know Bystrolyotov's real identity but then described in great detail his earlier career. He also stated that Orlov was originally assigned to Oldham. The final report compiled by Archer is worth noting in full, as it shows just how much information the security services had at their disposal by February 1940.

> At some date which Kritivsky cannot remember but believes was about 1930 or 1931, a man called Oldham, employed in the cipher department of the British Foreign Office, called at the Soviet embassy in Paris offering to sell British diplomatic ciphers and other secret material to which he had access.

At that time Valovitch, Deputy Chief of the Operod [Operations Department] of the GUGB [Headquarters Staff of the OGPU] was in Paris working at the embassy under the name of Yanovitch. Yanovitch at first refused to see Oldham believing him to be an agent provocateur. A month later Oldham called again, bringing specimens of material to which he had access. On this, though still suspicious of Oldham, Yanovitch arranged with him for further supplies of Foreign Office material in return for substantial money payments. He gave Oldham the 'service' name of ARNO.

For some time Oldham was allowed no contact with OGPU agents in London and was obliged to take his material to Paris himself, although Yanovitch realised the importance of his information. As soon as the OGPU were satisfied that Oldham was not a British double-cross agent it was arranged that a man should be sent to London specially to handle this material and obviate the risk and delays caused by frequent journeys to Paris. Oldham was of a highly nervous disposition and a heavy drinker. Yanovitch accordingly decided that the agent despatched to London to handle his material should have the close supervision of Oldham as his sole responsibility.

Oldham's OGPU guardian arrived in London on a Greek passport. Krivitsky cannot remember his name but recollects certain details of his earlier career. He was at one time an intelligence officer in General Wrangel's army. As a Soviet secret agent he did important work in Bulgaria in 1920 when a White Russian force was in process of formation there. During the Stamboullist period he managed to steal three ships lying at Varna and despatch them to Odessa, thereby causing considerable trouble as the ships happened to be French owned.[372]

There is a note made at this point to explain that Stamboullist referred to Aleksandr Stamboliski, who was prime minister of Bulgaria from 28 March 1920 until he was assassinated on 8 September 1923.

During the period of this man's role as 'guardian', Oldham was dismissed from the Foreign Office for drink. Completely in the hands of the OGPU and in dire straits for money, he continued to obtain Foreign Office material by making use of his previous position there. Krivitsky described how immense was his own astonishment when he heard that in spite of his dismissal Oldham was still allowed free access to the Foreign Office to visit his friends. During one of these visits Oldham took an impression of one of the important keys and thereafter was able to bring away material from time to time. The key in question was made from the impression by the Fourth Department and that is how Krivitsky first came to hear the story.[373]

The 'Fourth Department' was responsible for military intelligence and was run by General Yan Berzin. He too fell victim to Stalin's purge and was shot in the cellars of the OGPU headquarters on Lubyanka Square, Moscow, on 28 July 1938.

About this time Oldham's 'guardian' was relieved by a second OGPU agent also the holder of a Greek passport. This man's service name was 'HANS'. He was here as a representative of the Amsterdam firm of GADA, which firm was specially created by the OGPU to give him the necessary business cover. The surname adopted by 'HANS' is believed to have been Galleni or Galeni. Galleni was a cultured and good-looking man. On one occasion, while travelling from London to the continent, he was in the same carriage with a British King's Messenger, who actually asked him to look after his bags while he left the carriage. Galleni did not try to take the opportunity of tampering with the bags as he could not believe that a diplomatic courier would make such a request to a stranger in good faith![374]

Further evidence, if any was needed, of the careless attitude to security demonstrated by members of the Communications Department. It is interesting that Krivitsky mixed up Pieck and Bystrolyotov, though Oldham did travel to Amsterdam on occasion and may have been involved with developing the cover that was used to great effect with Oake and King.

> Galleni had a very difficult time. Oldham had become a confirmed drunkard and drug addict. He was so nervous that only by threats of exposure and the cutting-off of financial supplies could he be persuaded to continue his visits to the Foreign Office. Galleni was constantly at his side. He took him abroad for a holiday and in London stayed with him either in hotels or in his own home. His nerves were in such a condition that on one occasion he created a scene in a cinema because Galleni momentarily forgot to rise for 'God Save the King'. About this time also Galleni was considerably worried as he had some reason to think that a British Secret Service agent had got into touch with Oldham who had somehow aroused suspicion.[375]

This last claim was marked in the file and a question mark added. Though it is certainly true that Oldham had aroused plenty of suspicion, claims made by Donald McCormick, aka Richard Deacon, in his book *With My Little Eye*, that 'it was [Guy] Liddell who used to meet the mysterious Foreign Office cipher clerk, EH Oldham, in a west London public house and who seems to have managed to cover up the involvement of Oldham with the Soviet intelligence service' can be dismissed on the grounds that there is no supporting evidence.[376]

As it appeared that Oldham would shortly break down completely, Galleni concentrated his efforts in trying to obtain from him sufficient details of the private lives of his colleagues to guide the OGPU in their attempts to obtain a future source for the same material. Oldham at first refused to supply the requisite information but after considerable pressure had been brought to bear on him and his wife, he gave Galleni five or six names. One of these names was that of JH King, also employed in the Foreign Office Cipher Department.[377]

A direct link between King and Oldham was thus established.

> Shortly afterwards Oldham committed suicide and Galleni left the
> country. Later, during November and December 1936, Galleni is
> known to have been living at a hotel in the Rue Cambon, Paris.
> There are only one or two hotels in the Rue Cambon, which is a
> very short street.[378]

The fallout from the King case and Krivitsky's revelations was meant to
lead to the wholesale removal of existing members of the Communications
Department to other jobs, to be replaced by new untainted staff. It seems this
was not entirely followed to the letter. According to Antrobus, writing a few
months later in 1940:

> Shortly after the outbreak of war, the Communications
> Department as I knew it came to an end. Its typists and duplica-
> tor operators remained but most of the male members of its staff
> became King's Messengers pure and simple, without the ciphering
> and coding duties... the new King's Messengerships were natu-
> rally offered to those who had long been cipher officers and an en-
> tirely new staff had to be engaged for the coding and ciphering.[379]

At least security was tightened up considerably:

> If you want to get into the Foreign Office today you will have to
> run the gauntlet of a small army of policemen, doorkeepers and
> chuckers-out; in fact you will not get in at all unless you make it
> clear that you have a good reason for doing so and when you are in,
> you will be shadowed everywhere by a polite and courtly gentle-
> man of unmistakable muscular development.[380]

Yet despite the thoroughness of Archer's interview and report, chances were
still missed to identify the 'second source', or indeed clues that might have

revealed the identities of Maclean and Philby, who were obliquely referred to by Krivitsky. Furthermore, MI5 failed to seize upon some of the suggestions thrown up by Krivitsky's testimony around Oldham, possibly because it was seen as a cold case rather the cornerstone of the 'cipher boys' spy ring. In his original interviews, Krivitsky had provided two pieces of information that seemed to directly implicate Lucy in Oldham's activities:

> She was aware of the USSR people who worked with Oldham, but did not know the names of the British who supplied him with information.
>
> If Mrs Oldham is still alive, she will know a great deal about the Greek. He thinks that if we fail to trace her, we could still find it out because the Greek stayed at a hotel in the Rue Cambon between November and December 1936.[381]

No attempts to trace her whereabouts were made at the time. The only additions to Oldham's file came in 1946 and 1947, when a decision was taken to tie up one loose end that had puzzled the British since 1929 – the claims made by Bessedovsky that British ciphers had been offered to the Soviets in Paris by Mr Scott. An opportunity presented itself with the defection of Leon Helfand to the USA in July 1940 whilst working at the Soviet embassy in Rome. A file had been kept on him by MI5 since the late 1920s and his defection generated some interest within British SIS, as a leak from the British embassy in Rome had long been suspected. Interestingly, one of the men involved in reopening inquiries was none other than Kim Philby, who pressed for a further interview with Helfand. Almost as an afterthought, a set of questions relating to the identity of Mr Scott was requested on 14 December 1946 by MI5 officer Michael Serpell:

> In addition we would like Helfand to be interrogated about the Englishman who, according to Bessedovsky, was interviewed by Helfand at the Soviet embassy in Paris [with a reference to SIS correspondence dated 6 December 1929] and suggest that the questions might take the following form: 'We understand that Helfand

was in Paris from 19 March 1926 to 28 January 1930. Did he, during that time, interview an Englishman at the Soviet embassy who offered to sell a British cipher? If so, what was the name of this Englishman and can Helfand give us a description of him? Show Helfand photographs of Ernest Holloway Oldham and William Arthur Scott. Does Helfand recognise either of these photographs as being the Englishman in question?'[382]

When interviewed by SIS on 28 February 1947, Helfand provided a fairly inaccurate version of events, failed to name the man who approached him and could not recognise either photograph. Nevertheless, two months later, a note was placed on Oldham's file that linked Bessedovsky's account to Krivitsky's, and in October Serpell forwarded another report from Oldham's file to Roger Hollis, the future Head of MI5 after 1956 and at the time involved with Counter-Subversion activities. However, there the matter was left for a further three years, until Henri Pieck surfaced after World War II and agreed to be interviewed by MI5 in the spring of 1950. It is clear that the main area of interest was finding out more information about King, though the Oldham case was mentioned in the same context in a briefing note prepared on 6 April 1950:

> It was evident that he had a fair knowledge of the King case which he said he had picked up from gossip. It was agreed that he need not be told about Oldham and that our policy in regard to the information he should be given must be determined by the information which Pieck gives us.[383]

It is clear that the nature of the inquiry was highly sensitive, and confirmed that deliberate steps had been taken to cover up the Foreign Office leaks in the 1930s.

> Moreover, as government policy in the King case had been to keep the whole thing quiet, no gratuitous information should be given to [REDACTED] in this connection.[384]

The interview with Pieck took place between 12 and 16 April and proved very revealing, as he named several key people that he tried to snare as well as those with whom he had some success:

> Before leaving for Geneva, Pieck was instructed to make contact first with Mr O'Donnell of the British consulate and it was intended that through him he should meet other employees of the Foreign Office. He therefore took an apartment above that of Mr O'Donnell and he still remembers trying to provide himself with an excuse for meeting O'Donnell by dropping a pen from his window which he hoped would land somewhere inside O'Donnell's property. Unfortunately the pen landed in the street.[385]

Pieck was more successful mingling with British folk at the clubs in Geneva, such as The Bavarian and the International Club where associates such as Alec Russell, interpreter for the League of Nations, and Challoner James, correspondent for the *Daily Mail*, facilitated his introduction to British officials. One of the officials was clearly still well connected in high circles, as his name was redacted from Pieck's interview. Pieck also provided more detail about Harvey and Oake, confirming that Oake had undertaken some work on his behalf, as well as the indiscretion of Harvey that made the whole operation possible.

> It was through Harvey and his daughter Enid that Pieck got to know Raymond Oake and other Foreign Office employees. Pieck remembers with amusement how one day Harvey forgot his keys and allowed him to fetch them from the office. At that time Pieck thought his reliability was being tested so [he did not make] use of this opportunity.
>
> Pieck's first candidate for recruitment was Raymond Oake [who] lived considerably above his income. Pieck was continually [lending him] money and did not rate him very highly. After leaving Geneva [he visited] Oake in England. He went to stay with

him in Herne Bay and Oake visited him in Holland. Pieck told Oake the same story he told King about the possibility of his earning money through a banker at The Hague in exchange for confidential information from the Foreign Office. Oake, however, did not respond... Pieck met Oake for the last time at his wedding in London. Oake, Pieck admits, was 'a very bad mistake'.[386]

However, Pieck was able to provide more information on 'Hans', whom the intelligence services had gradually connected to Joe Perelly and Galleni. Given his artistic talents, he sketched him as well.

> Description: height, about 6 feet 1 inch; black hair; dark eyes, wore spectacles; childish face; always appeared to be smiling; Soviet national; appeared to come from the Caucasus or Kirghizstan [sic], as he was slightly Asiatic in appearance; had engineering experience; spoke English with an American accent. Hans knew America and England very well and had a good knowledge of English life and customs.
>
> Hans first met Pieck in 1933 in Amsterdam and remained as his controller until early in 1936. He relinquished control of Pieck after JH King.
>
> Hans had a very good knowledge of the British Foreign Office for Pieck considers he was briefed very well while he was running JH King.[387]

Given the additional information that Pieck was able to provide and finally recalling Krivitsky's advice from 1940, Oldham's case file was reviewed once more in the hunt for Hans/Perelly/Galleni. A note in Oldham's file, made on 26 May 1950 by Ann Glass, records her recollections of a meeting she'd had two days previously with Oldham's former friend and associate Thomas Kemp, who had somehow managed to not only remain in post at the Foreign Office, despite his role in the Oldham scandal and the purge of the Communications Department in 1939, but indeed rise further through the ranks. In 1940, George Antrobus painted a glowing picture of Thomas Kemp's role in organising the work of the King's Messengers:

> The man who has had the charge of these things for many years is an encyclopaedia of unique knowledge... he is in touch with all the travel agencies, railway companies, and steamship lines to every part of the world. His name is Mr Thomas Kemp and he is, I think, the calmest and most self-possessed person I have ever met.[388]

At the time of Glass's interview, Kemp been granted a certificate for the Executive Class of the civil service two years previously, having been appointed a Higher Executive Officer on 1 April 1946. Rather undermining Antrobus's testimony, Kemp was only able to shed a little light on a possible way that Oldham was able to smuggle information out of the Foreign Office, even when he was on site.

> It was difficult to sort out the scraps of information which Mr Kemp was able to recall, but in referring to the generally lax state of things existing at that time in regard to King's Messengers, he said that Oldham had, without authority, made out several courier's passes.[389]

This enabled him to despatch material to a chosen destination, but still required someone to take them. Clearly no-one was working with Oldham so he needed an unwitting accomplice. Once again, Kemp put forward a possible candidate:

> Mr Kemp also told me that a colleague of Oldham's in the cipher department was a certain Commander Acland, who had a crippled son who was wounded in the 1914 – 1918 war. This man was anxious to get a job in the Foreign Office but was not successful; Oldham used quite frequently to give him the bag to take to Rome and it was Mr Kemp's impression that Oldham was

using young Acland as an unconscious courier and it was also Mr
Kemp's impression that Rome was in some way connected with
Oldham's espionage activities.[390]

When pressed for more detail about Joe Perelly, Kemp's 'encyclopaedic'
memory grew somewhat hazy.

> Kemp of course remembered the Oldhams very well but he did
> not at first recall anything about Joe Pirelli [sic]. However, he later
> said that he did remember such a man having been mentioned by
> Oldham and Mrs Oldham, but was not sure whether he himself
> had met him. In view of this he was not, of course, able to give me
> a description of Pirelli [sic].[391]
>
> I showed Mr Kemp the drawing made by Pieck of HANS and
> he looked at it for some time, saying that the face did seem familiar
> to him.[392]

Kemp was hiding behind the fact that 17 years had elapsed since the Oldham
suicide had been covered up and probably did not want his role in proceedings
dragged up again in case they damaged his new seniority. Indeed, given his role
in tracking Joe, it was stretching credulity to breaking point to suggest that he
was not sure whether he had met him – something picked up by Glass later
in her report. It may simply have been embarrassment, to be confronted with
the image of a man who had made him look foolish and almost brought his
career to an abrupt halt.

> It will be seen from 21a of Oldham's file, extract at lv of Pirelli's
> file, that Mr Kemp did in fact meet Joe Pirelli in 1933, but since he
> does not remember him the only hope of discovering whether he
> may be identical with Pieck's HANS is to try and find Mrs Oldham
> through her sons, the Wellsteds.
>
> While gossiping about Oldham, Mr Kemp said that Mrs
> Oldham would certainly remember Pirelli and suggested that we

should be able to find her through her sons by her first marriage, Thomas and Raymond Wellsted. Mr Kemp has not heard of her since the beginning of the war, when she went to join her son Raymond who was in the army and stationed in Belfast.[393]

This line of investigation would instigate the final tragic act in the Oldham saga as attention turned to the whereabouts of his widow in the hope that she might be able to reveal more information about Pirelli/Hans. Records show that Lucy had taken a series of furnished lodgings in west London with her son, James Raymond Wellsted, in the 1930s before indeed joining him in Belfast during the war. They reappeared in Hammersmith in 1945 and 1946 before dropping out of official records. However, within a month of Ann Glass's note, Lucy had been found – floating in the Thames, her body dragged out of the water at Richmond Pier at 5.55 am on 27 June 1950.

An MI5 agent, WJ Skardon, was hastily despatched to find out more from the coroner's officer for Richmond, PC William Bridges, who was attached to the nearby Kingston police station. Skardon filed a report on 4 July based on his discussion, which raised almost as many questions as it answered:

> Certain difficulties have arisen in this case since the only person who could identify the body, Bohdan Tymieniecki, a Pole and the landlord at 24 Drayton Street [Ealing, where Lucy had been living in furnished apartments] was able to do so only to a limited extent. He said that the clothing was the clothing of Mrs Oldham and the earrings on the body were hers, but he thought that the face was fuller than that of his lodger. The autopsy shows that the body was in the water for about half an hour and there would be no change in such a short time, although it is agreed that the effect of refrigeration does have the effect of producing a somewhat bloated condition.[394]

At the time of her death, Lucy had been living with James Wellsted, but according to the report he

...vanished from the same address at the same time, or within a few minutes, of his mother on the morning of 26 June.[395]

James was eventually apprehended and charged on 10 July with obtaining £3 by fraud, while various other creditors came forward demanding money. He was put on probation for two years, with the chairman of the magistrates stating that his was a 'tragic case'. At the coroner's inquest into Lucy's death, a verdict of suicide was returned with worries about her financial situation given as the main reason for drowning herself in the Thames.

> There seems to be a sufficient reason for mental depression in the case of Mrs Oldham, due to the fact that her banking account with the Westminster Bank, Ealing branch, is overdrawn. Correspondence found at her lodgings by the coroner's officer also shows that Coutts' Bank, Park Lane branch, have closed Wellsted's account and asked him to return unused cheques. Further letters indicate that Wellsted is in debt and has uttered a number of worthless cheques locally during recent months.[396]

Yet there are inconsistencies that do not quite add up. Both mother and son were unaccounted for during a period up to 24 hours and at least from 2.30 pm the previous afternoon (witness statements disagree on the exact time of their last sighting) before Lucy's body was recovered from the river the following morning. Where were they during this time? Why had Lucy ended up in Richmond and decided to end her life by drowning at 5.30 am? It is unlikely that we will ever know the answer. It is tempting to speculate that she was alerted about the reopening of the investigation into her husband's activities, and that it was primarily focused on her. Given Kemp's former connection with the Oldham family it is not unreasonable to assume that he let her know what was happening. It may have been this knowledge that drove her to suicide.

With Lucy dead, there seemed little point in pursuing the inquiry further. In any case, far more damaging revelations were to follow with the flight of Burgess and Maclean to Moscow in 1951, holding a press conference on

11 February to announce their defection to the USSR. Five years later, the King affair became public knowledge when Levine published a book about the case in America. The Foreign Office at first denied the story and then, embarrassingly, was forced to admit the leaks once they realised a Member of Parliament was planning to raise a question in the House of Commons. Intriguingly, Thomas Kemp chose this year to retire from the Foreign Office, enjoying a full pension until his death in Sussex in 1978.

One last effort was made to contact Lucy's older son, Thomas Wellsted, at the height of the Cold War in 1974, part of the Fluency Committee's attempt to flush out any further Soviet operatives within government after the defection of Philby in 1963. However, Wellsted could provide no further information about Oldham or Perelly, other than a photograph taken in the garden of the Bell Inn at Hurley around 1926. Thereafter, Oldham's file was left to gather dust.

What the British forces did not know was that the hunt for Bystrolyotov had been in vain. Oldham's handler had also been caught up in Stalin's purge and, following his return to Moscow in 1935, witnessed at first-hand the end of the Great Illegals and the dismemberment of the entire espionage machinery. Abram Slutsky died in mysterious circumstances on 17 February 1938; Mally was imprisoned on 7 March 1938 and executed six months later; Bazarov was arrested on 3 July 1938 and Bystrolyotov was rounded up on 18 September. He was sent to the prison camps, and was not released until 1954. Bystrolyotov died in 1975, but not before revealing some of the secrets of his work as a Soviet agent to Emil Draitser in an interview in 1973, just before the final entries were made on Oldham's file. Bystrolyotov had outwitted the British to the last.

*****

When writing about shadowy figures such as Ernest Holloway Oldham, it is tempting to claim a retrospective significance when the contemporary reality was something different. This is usually a result of the historian's curse of hindsight, when mistakes can be spotted and consequences more easily discerned over a longer period of time. The men and women of the Foreign Office, MI5, SIS and Special Branch were not afforded such perspective, nor did they have anything like the surveillance technology of today. Card indexes, phone taps and a network of contacts were their tools, so success depended primarily on their wits, instinct and hard work.

Nevertheless, the case of Oldham and the 'cipher boys' should rightly rank alongside the Cambridge spy ring as one of the greatest breaches of British security in history. The decision to hold an internal investigation within the Foreign Office conducted by amateurs such as Kemp, rather than hand the entire matter over to the professionals, meant that the full extent of Oldham's activities were left undetected for a decade. It was preferable to cover up the entire episode and protect the reputation of senior civil servants rather than pursue the unpalatable concept that highly confidential material had been sold to overseas agencies. However, other parties were equally culpable.

The operation from 14 July onwards was compromised by mistakes – in particular the decision not to intercept phone calls from the continent when Oldham was holed up in the Jules Hotel which might have led SIS to Bystrolyotov, or indeed the hesitancy to bring Oldham in for questioning for fear of the revelations that might ensue. Perhaps most damaging of all, no investigation was ever conducted into his travels abroad either before or after his dismissal from the Foreign Office, especially given his position at the League of Nations or pivotal role at the heart of Room 22. Indeed, the reluctance to believe a trusted official within the Foreign Office had betrayed state secrets can be traced all the way back to 1929 when Bessedovsky jumped over the wall of the Soviet embassy in Paris talking about 'Mr Scott'; the wrong man was under suspicion until 1947. Even after Oldham's death, MI5 and SIS had the name Perelly with which to work but failed to pursue this line of inquiry and it seems that no attempt was made by Vivian or his associates to link the King inquiry to that of Oldham until 1950.

It is this catalogue of cumulative failure that allowed Oldham to become the forgotten spy, a legendary figure and a cautionary tale within the Foreign Office amongst junior staff. Yet no widespread changes were made within Whitehall until after the King case, when Oake and Quarry were dismissed and the entire Communications Department staff were replaced with the exception of Kemp, who not only kept his job but also earned advancement, perhaps on the tacit understanding that he would maintain his silence over the events of 1933. Even then, the entire affair was deliberately covered up until 1951. In contrast, when the Soviet sources are examined, it is clear that great importance was placed on Oldham's activities, and he was seen as a key informant during a difficult period for Soviet intelligence. He was the man who had given access to the heart of the British diplomatic machinery.

The flow of information, patchy at first but invaluable during the pivotal Lausanne Conference, demonstrated to the Soviets the necessity of having men on the inside. Thus Oldham became the first in a line of moles within the Foreign Office who provided sensitive intelligence, while the parallel policy of cultivating ideological recruits from universities, who would take up prominent positions within the establishment, was launched in the wake of Oldham's death. It is no coincidence that OGPU mourned the loss of one of their key assets. It is only the British who have not accepted Oldham's status as the progenitor spy who, if not the man who started Cold War espionage, certainly helped shape its terms of reference.

Yet it is easy to overlook the person amidst the hyperbole. One of the reasons that this book concentrates on Oldham's entire career, rather than just events after 1929, is that it hopefully gives greater perspective to the forces that shaped his life. In many ways, he is a tragic and complex figure, a product of his time as the world struggled to come to terms with cataclysmic events and Britain moved from the Victorian era to a new, fast-paced age of technology and rapid change. On one hand he was a war hero, fighting for King and country only to return home a changed and damaged man, stepping back into civilian life in a government department that had failed to stop the carnage in the first place and then asked to help shape the peace that defined the world in which he lived. On the other hand, he was weak and greedy, prepared to betray the same King and country for financial gain to support the lifestyle to which he had become accustomed and literally addicted.

It is easy to write Oldham off as another hopeless alcoholic, but clearly he was an intelligent and skillful man who had transcended his station in life – the ability to hold OGPU at bay after first contact for nearly two years, followed by the equal ability to give British intelligence the slip for a month at the end of his life, shows that he could have been a formidable asset to British intelligence had he been given the chance in 1918. Indeed, it is tempting to speculate that, had he been brought in for questioning by MI5 and SIS in the summer of 1933, Oldham would have been devastatingly useful as a double agent. The role of Lucy is equally hard to fathom – was she a fully complicit Lady Macbeth figure who suggested that Oldham should sell secrets to foreign powers to prop up her lavish lifestyle, or yet another victim of events as her life spiralled increasingly out of control? In the murky world of espionage, nothing is clear-cut and there are no definite answers.

It should be no surprise to learn that one person at least had a strong view on the matter and it seems fitting that the last word should go to one of Oldham's contemporaries and our companion throughout, the proud King's Messenger George Antrobus. His feelings of hurt and bitterness and his sense of betrayal are contained in a passage that he wrote in 1940 with Oldham clearly in mind. It still has the power to sting today. Initially, Antrobus's polemic was sparked by indignation towards people who brought the name of the messengers into disrepute, but it soon became far more specific:

> King's Messengers suffer more severely from pretenders to their own title. It is bad enough to find that some bumptious, overbearing, Englishman-abroad, whipper-snapper with a temporary red passport has been calling himself a King's Messenger and making the name stink in the nostrils of porters, ticket collectors, and customs officers – all of whom are the Greyhound's [King's Messenger's] best friends and with whom he takes great pains to keep on the friendliest of footings. It is far worse when a downright knave takes his name in vain.
>
> This has happened more than once, but the most serious and embarrassing instance of it concerned a man – I can hardly call him a gentleman – who was himself a Foreign Office official. He was a clever little upstart, a permanent civil servant, with a face like a

rat and a conscience utterly devoid of scruples. He took advantage
of his position to make himself an agent for smuggling articles of
value in the bags and when a consignment of particular importance
turned up he provided himself with a red passport and took the bag
in person. He had of course a confederate in the embassy at a big
European capital and his delinquencies were not discovered until
after his death.

It turned out that he had married a wealthy woman whose assets
he had succeeded in transferring to himself. He lived in impressive
style, with a fine house in London; a big car, and a smart chauffeur;
he arrayed himself, if not in purple, at least in fine linen and fared
sumptuously. So sumptuously indeed did he fare that he contracted
delirium tremens, absented himself from office and rounded off
an interesting career by committing suicide. I am afraid, with all
our humanity, we never succeeded in producing anything in the
least like this permanent civil servant; I comfort myself with the
thought that he was not typical of his order.[397]

Given the way that the King affair was covered up, it is astonishing that
Antrobus was permitted to publish this passage – another sign of lax Foreign
Office security, perhaps? However, it is interesting that Oldham attracted Antrobus's withering and vitriolic verdict rather than King. Given some of the
earlier passages in Antrobus's book about the plight of the temporary clerks,
he perhaps had sympathy for the actions of the cipher boys, given his own
future without the financial security of a pension.

Maybe Oldham deserved Antrobus's epitaph, but then people can be weak
or greedy, make terrible mistakes for which there seems no chance of retri-
bution and pay the ultimate penalty; the repercussions of their actions often
resonate many years down the line in the most unexpected ways. However,
consider the words of one of Ernest's nephews, Anthony Stanforth, who has
been instrumental in piecing together many of the family connections described above:

We wonder how much Ernest's parents knew, and whether they protected Michael and my mother from the details. My mother only ever spoke well of her brother. She clearly idolised him, and said his death was from 'never having properly recovered from being blown up in the Great War.' No mention of marriage, suicide, or worse. But that was another age, when shameful secrets were kept hidden, even within the family.[398]

For better or for worse, Ernest's tale is now told in full. This book is partly written for those who have been unwittingly affected by events outside their control. It is a lesson that history is woven from many different perspectives with unforeseen repercussions, not just for the principal players, but for the families that often stand in the shadows and suffer equal or greater collateral damage and loss.

ACKNOWLEDGEMENTS

This book has been one of the most difficult, challenging and enjoyable that I've ever written and it would not have been possible without the help and support of some very special people.

Firstly, a big thank you to Elly and Heather at Heather Holden Brown Agency for securing the commission with Blink Publishing and Clare, Karen and Joel for their belief in the book and professionalism in turning it from concept into reality. Your support and brilliant work is really appreciated and it is quite literally true that this book could not have been written without you.

One of the biggest debts of gratitude must go to my research collaborators on this project, Ned Kershaw, Susan and Anthony Stanforth, and Michael and Eileen Barratt. I've been picking away at Oldham's story ever since Susan and Anthony had flagged up the fact that his MI5 file had been released to the National Archives in 2002. Susan was the first person within my family who reviewed the file and realised the significance of the story and followed up with research in relevant secondary literature. Michael was already regularly sending over snippets of information from the USA about the Oldhams and Holloways, gleaned from his store of family knowledge and ceaseless research online – since this is a book about revelations and secrets, it is fair to state I am *not* the main genealogist in my family! The resolution of his childhood story of adventure from 1933 was thus solved by accident and I was provided with a convenient 'badge of honour' for my subsequent work on *Who Do You Think You Are?* Sadly, Michael passed away in October 2015, but he was able to hear the story of his uncle told in full for the first time.

In particular, I must thank Anthony and Susan for painstakingly reviewing the text for errors; if any remain, they are of my making. Yet unknown to us, Ned had already conducted some amazingly detailed research into Oldham's life, fascinated by the fact that this extraordinary story had been overlooked completely in the histories of the period – attention perhaps naturally gravitating towards the Cambridge spy ring and subsequent Cold War espionage. I say unknown, but Ned first made contact with me in 2006 after my connection to Oldham had been featured in the *Telegraph*; we swapped emails and then drifted out of touch. However, out of the blue, Ned resumed correspondence again in January 2014 just before I was due to give a talk about Oldham at the National Archives the following month; with extraordinary kindness, he agreed to share his thoughts, research notes and chronology during the preparation of this current work. Without his collaboration, this book would not have progressed in the direction that it has taken, as quickly as it has.

I would also like to thank some other people who have contributed to this book – mainly for their willingness to look things up at short notice! Michael Meadowcroft, honorary archivist at the National Liberal Club for investigating Henry George Holloway; Juliette Desplat for wading through the Mitrokhin archive at Churchill College and assisting with Russian pronunciation; Nigel West, who also came to the February talk at the National Archives and shared his views on the subject; John Simkin for his advice, and general contribution to the Spartacus Network, a great online education tool for anyone who's not viewed it already and Genevieve Bovee, who must be tired of post-midnight emails asking for 'just another quick look-up that's urgent', but nevertheless always delivers the goods. Finally, I am indebted to Emil Draitser for answering my final panicked questions and sharing his recollections of meeting Bystrolyotov in person. His book, *Stalin's Romeo Spy*, remains the standout work if you want to fully understand the danger, drama and difficulties that a spy in the 1920s and 1930s faced.

However, as usual, I leave the biggest vote of thanks until last, which goes to my family. I am often asked how I find the time and headspace to write, living in a house surrounded by four small children and a new baby. It's easy – they are a daily reminder of what's important in life, a sense of perspective that was clearly missing from Oldham's existence. So this book is partly for Elizabeth, Charlotte, Chloe, Alice and new arrival Matilda (Lucy was never seriously considered as a possible name, all things considered).' I must also profusely thank my mother, who encouraged me to 'write stories' since I was at school and now helps with the children. However, the final and unending debt of gratitude remains with my wife Lydia, who is a constant support, tower of strength and source of inspiration; she is surely on the path to sainthood for coping with the children while I lock myself away to write. The line always goes up.

BIBLIOGRAPHY

There are several key publications that lie behind this one. The first is Emil Draitser's account of Oldham's handler, Dimitri Bystrolyotov, based on an interview that took place in 1973 just before the Soviet agent's death. This is supported by Nigel West and Olgev Tsarev's account of Oldham's activities during this period. Both works draw heavily on Bystrolyotov's files in the KGB archives, from which many quotes are taken.

Equally, the accounts of life in the Foreign Office by Tilley and Gaselee, and Wheeler-Holohan are important; but the marvellously irreverent and idiosyncratic memoirs of George Antrobus help to paint a vivid picture of Oldham's working environment during the period covered. Tragically, Antrobus was killed in World War II when his home suffered a direct hit during a German bombing raid; he never saw his work in print.

Most of the key works are listed in the endnotes, including articles and books used for short quotes. The following is a core expanded reading list that has been used to research Oldham's life and times.

C. Andrew, *The Defence of the Realm* (Penguin, 2009)

C. Andrew and V. Mitrokhin, *The Mitrokhin Archive* (Penguin, 1999)

G. Antrobus, *King's Messenger 1918–1940* (Herbert Jenkins, 1941)

G. Bessedovsky, *Revelations of a Soviet Diplomat* (Williams & Norgate, 1931)

E. Deacon, *With My Little Eye* (Frederick Miller, 1982)

Prince Lichnowsky, *My Mission to London, 1912–1914* (George H. Doran, 1918)

E. Draitser, *Stalin's Romeo Spy* (Duckworth Overlook, 2011)

W. Duffy, *A Time for Spies* (Vanderbilt UP, 1999)

Viscount Grey, *Twenty-Five Years 1892–1916* (Frederick A. Stokes, 1925)

K. Jeffrey, *MI6: The History of the Secret Intelligence Service* (Bloomsbury, 2010)

A. Mallinson, *1914: Fight the Good Fight Britain, the Army and the Coming of the First World War* (Bantam, 2013)

H. Nicholson, *Peacemaking 1919* (Houghton Mifflin, 1933)

J. Tilley and S. Gaselee, *The Foreign Office* (Putnam, 1933)

R. C. Tucker, *Stalin in Power: The Revolution from Above, 1928–1941*, (Norton & Company, 1992)

S. Twigge, E. Hampshire and G. Macklin, *British Intelligence* (The National Archives, 2008)

N. West and O. Tsarev, *The Crown Jewels* (Harper Collins, 1998)

V. Wheeler-Holohan, *The History of the King's Messengers* (Grayson and Grayson, 1935)

P. Wright, *Spycatcher* (Viking Penguin, 1987)

Primary sources

There are precious few family archives for Ernest Oldham. In fact, the first time many of his relatives even knew what he looked like was when his MI5 file was released, containing the two snapshots included in this book. When his parents died on the Isle of Wight, the house was cleared by the family but no material relating to Oldham was found to have survived. Ironically, given Oldham's putative posting in the Diplomatic Service, his parents' house was called 'Rio'. Piecing together many of the family details has involved standard genealogical sources, many of which are available online from websites such as www.ancestry.co.uk, www.findmypast.co.uk and www.freebmd.org.uk –

civil registration certificates, census returns, passenger lists, electoral lists and street directories.

The key primary sources for Oldham's story can be found at The National Archives, Kew, hidden amongst the records of the Foreign Office. As stated in the text, most of the registered files produced by the Communications Department have been destroyed during the crucial period of Oldham's activity. Instead, the four sequences of day books were explored (TNA series FO 1103) – over 100 files with infrequent glimpses of Oldham's work or, towards the end, his absences. Equally, the main series of registered correspondence of the Foreign Office proved surprisingly fruitful, with additional references to Oldham's summons to jury service, and the mysterious receipt of a package from Spain in the early 1920s, located but not included in the main story. A summary of his career can be found in the annual *Foreign Office Lists*.

If anything, the intelligence records provide far more detail, given the files that were kept by MI5 on Soviet agents including Oldham. Most of these are also at The National Archives in series KV 2, with background information about MI5 in KV 4. Much material remains unreleased, as Andrew's authorised account of MI5 makes clear; and virtually nothing has appeared in the public domain from the Secret Intelligence Service (MI6).

Oldham's military history was compiled from his service record, supported by extracts from the unit war diaries. These are also held at The National Archives, along with many more resources for tracing the movements of combatants during the terrible war that tore apart so many lives.

From the Soviet side, the KGB files were inaccessible – hence the reliance on the works cited above. However, much material was deposited in the Churchill Archives, Cambridge, by Soviet defector Vasili Mitrokhin who had painstakingly made copies of intelligence reports that passed through his hands. Even now, Russian interest in the Mitrokhin archive continues, with two 'journalists' taking extensive pictures of the material in the Churchill College archives during the autumn of 2014; rather ironically, given Oldham's sartorial preference, both were dressed in brown suits.

ENDNOTES

1   Author's personal email correspondence
      with Michael Barratt
2   Ibid
3   Jenny Keating, History in Education
      Project, Institute of Historical Research,
      University of London (December,
      2010) p.1
4   From oral family history gathered together
      by Michael Barratt
5   Keating, p.3
6   TNA ref. CSC 10/3635
7   J Tilley & S Gaselee, *The Foreign Office*
      (London, 1933) p.154
8   Ibid pp.167–168
9   Ibid p.168
10   G Antrobus, *King's Messenger 1918–1940
      Memoirs of a Silver Greyhound* (London,
      1941) pp.115–116
11   V Wheeler-Holohan, *The History of the
      King's Messengers* (London, 1935) pp.viii–ix
12   Antrobus p.94

13   Ibid p.19
14   Ibid p.200
15   Ibid p.202
16   Tilley, Gaselee p.172
17   Ibid pp.172–173
18   *Correspondence respecting the European Crisis*
      (HMSO, 1914) no.5 p.9
19   Ibid, no.10 p.12
20   Prince Lichnowsky, *My Mission to London,
      1912–1914* (New York, 1918) p.34
21   Viscount Grey, *Twenty-Five Years, 1892–
      1916* (New York, 1925) p.20
22   Tilley, Gaselee p.174
23   A Mallinson, *1914: Fight the Good Fight
      Britain, the Army and the Coming of the First
      World War* (London, 2013) p.6
24   *The Times*, 5 August 1914
25   Ibid
26   Lord Derby's speech to the men of
      Liverpool, 28 August 1914
27   Wheeler-Holohan p.106

28   Ibid p.112
29   Tilley, Gaselee pp.180–181
30   Ibid p.181
31   TNA ref. WO 339/112210
32   Tilley, Gaselee p.173
33   Ibid p.181
34   Wheeler-Holohan p.115
35   Tilley, Gaselee p.182
36   Ibid p.195
37   TNA ref. WO 339/112210
38   Ibid for these and other details of
     Oldham's training and military service
39   Ibid
40   Ibid
41   Dr A Morton, *Sandhurst and the First World
     War: the Royal Military College 1902–1918*
     (Sandhurst Occasional Paper No. 17,
     2014) p.17
42   For Oldham's movements in the 5th
     Battalion see TNA ref. WO 95/1902
43   Ibid
44   For Oldham's movements in the 1st
     Battalion see TNA ref. WO 95/1609
45   Ibid
46   Ibid
47   Ibid
48   Ibid
49   Ibid
50   Ibid
51   TNA ref. WO 339/112210
52   TNA ref. WO 158/962
53   WO 95/1609
54   Ibid
55   Ibid
56   Ibid
57   Ibid
58   Ibid
59   For details of Oldham's injury and
     subsequent treatment, see TNA ref. WO
     339/112210
60   TNA ref. FO 371/3220
61   Ibid
62   Ibid

63   Ibid
64   Ibid
65   TNA ref. FO 371/3221
66   Antrobus pp.24–25
67   Tilley, Gaselee p.200
68   M L Dockrill and Zara Steiner 'The
     Foreign Office at the Paris Peace
     Conference in 1919' (International
     History Review, 1980) p.56
69   H Nicholson, *Peacemaking 1919* (York,
     1964) p.242
70   Ibid p.229
71   Dockerill, Steiner p.62
72   Ibid p.64
73   Nicolson pp.122–123
74   Dockerill, Steiner p.67
75   Ibid p.66
76   Ibid p.60
77   Ibid p.68
78   Nicolson, p.314
79   TNA ref. FO 371/3220
80   Nicolson p.262
81   *The Times*, 11 March 1919
82   Ibid
83   Ibid
84   Ibid p.70
85   Nicolson p.335
86   Ibid p.368
87   Ibid p.371
88   TNA ref. FO 369/1462
89   Ibid
90   TNA ref. FO 366/788
91   Ibid
92   Ibid
93   Tilley, Gaselee p.298
94   Antrobus p.46
95   Ibid p.45
96   Ibid
97   Ibid p.97
98   Ibid p.98
99   Ibid
100 Ibid p.150
101 Ibid pp.99–100

102 Ibid p.100

103 Ibid pp.100–101

104 Ibid p.101

105 Ibid p.102

106 Ibid pp.103–104

107 Ibid p.49

108 TNA ref. FO 1103/8

109 Antrobus pp.64–65

110 Ibid p.66

111 Ibid p.65

112 Wheeler-Holohan p.256

113 Antrobus pp.65-66

114 Wheeler-Holohan p.125

115 Antrobus p.67

116 Ibid

117 Ibid

118 TNA ref. FO 1103/17

119 Antrobus pp.67–68

120 TNA ref. FO 1103/4

121 TNA ref. FO 1103/19

122 TNA ref. FO 1103/30

123 Wheeler-Holohan p.106

124 R. C. Tucker, *Stalin in Power: The Revolution from Above, 1928–1941* (London, 1992) p.34

125 Minutes of the Second Congress of the Communist International

126 For an overview see S Twigge, E Hampshire and G Macklin, *British Intelligence* (London, 2008)

127 For more information on SIS (MI6) see K. Jeffrey, *MI6: The History of the Secret Intelligence Service* (London, 2010) p.83

128 For a detailed history of MI5 see C Andrew, *The Defence of the Realm* (London, 2009)

129 Dockerill, Steiner p.83

130 Grigori Zinoviev, 'Declaration of Zinoviev on the Alleged "Red Plot", *The Communist Review*, vol. 5, no. 8 (Dec. 1924) pp.365–366

131 TNA ref. FO 366/812

132 Ibid

133 Antrobus p.62

134 Ibid pp.62–63

135 TNA ref. FO 1103/50

136 D Sinclair, *Two Georges: The Making of the Modern Monarchy* (London, 1988), p.105

137 TNA ref. FO 366/838

138 Ibid

139 Ibid

140 TNA ref. FO 1103/56

141 TNA ref. FO 1103/61

142 Minutes of the Fifteenth Congress of the Communist Party of the Soviet Union (Bolshevik)

143 *Launceston Examiner*, 27 April 1898

144 *Launceston Daily Telegraph*, 28 February 1902

145 *Emu Bay Times*, 19 March 1902

146 As recounted in B. Bryson, *One Summer America 1927* (London, 2013) p.84

147 *The Times*, 2 February 1907

148 TNA ref. KV 2/808

149 Information drawn from Wellsted's will, proved in London in 1919

150 Information from Post Office directories and electoral lists

151 TNA ref. KV 2/808

152 *Derby Mercury*, 9 February 1898

153 *London Gazette* entries

154 Information from Post Office directories and electoral lists

155 TNA ref. FO 1103/29 and FO 1103/30

156 *Chelmsford Chronicle*, 19 June 1931

157 TNA ref. FO 371/14050

158 Ibid

159 G. Bessedovsky, *Revelations of a Soviet Diplomat* (London, 1931), p.243

160 Ibid pp.243–244

161 Ibid p.244

162 Ibid p.245

163 Ibid

164 Ibid p.246

165 Ibid pp.247–248

166 Ibid p.248

167 TNA ref. KV 2/2670
168 TNA ref. FO 1103/92
169 *Daily Telegraph*, 25 October 1929
170 *Townsville Daily Courier*, 29 October 1929
171 *Canberra Times*, 29 October 1929
172 *Daily Herald*, 29 October 1929
173 TNA ref. FO 1103/92
174 TNA ref. KV 3/12
175 TNA ref. KV 2/2398
176 Our knowledge of Dimitri Bystrolyotov
     is provided by Emil Draitser's biography,
     Stalin's Romeo Spy (London, 2011) based
     on an interview conducted with the
     author in 1973. The following passages are
     predominantly based on the Soviet files
     cited in this book, along with contributions
     from N West and O Tsarev, *The Crown Jewels*
     (London, 1998)
177 Draitser p.110
178 Ibid
179 TNA ref. KV 2/2681
180 Draitser p.110
181 TNA ref. KV 2/2681
182 Draitser, pp.110–111
183 See Draitser pp.113–114
184 West p.63
185 See Draitser pp.111–112
186 For details of the operation see Draitser
     pp.113-120
187 See Draitser pp.125–126
188 Draitser p.126
189 For details of the confrontation, see
     Draitser pp.126–127
190 Antrobus p.86
191 Draitser, p.128
192 TNA ref. KV 2/808
193 Ibid
194 TNA ref. FO 366/811
195 Oxford Dictionary of National Biography
196 Bessedovsky p.247
197 *Chelmsford Chronicle*, 19 June 1931
198 Antrobus p.184
199 Ibid p.185

200 Ibid
201 TNA ref. FO 1103/100
202 Ibid
203 Draitser p.128
204 As contained in Draitser's account,
     pp.128–129
205 Draitser pp.129, 132 and 145
206 *Survey of a Quarter of a Century of the
     Treatment of Alcoholism and Other Drug Habits*
     (London, 1932)
207 Draitser p.129
208 West p.68
209 Draitser p.130
210 Ibid
211 TNA ref. FO 1103/100
212 Ibid
213 Ibid
214 TNA ref. FO 1103/101
215 TNA ref. KV 2/808
216 TNA ref. FO 610/295
217 TNA ref. FO 1103/106
218 Ibid
219 Draitser p.131
220 TNA ref. KV 2/804
221 West pp.68–69
222 TNA ref. KV 2/808
223 For these two quotes, see Draitser
     pp.133–134
224 TNA ref. FO 371/15929
225 Ibid
226 TNA ref. FO 371/15930
227 Ibid
228 TNA ref. FO 371/15931
229 Cited in West p.69
230 Cited ibid p.70
231 Draitser p.136
232 TNA ref. FO 1103/106
233 Ibid
234 Draitser p.136
235 Ibid p.135
236 Cited in West p.70
237 Draitser p.137
238 Ibid p.135

239 Ibid
240 Cited in West pp.71–72
241 Antrobus p.189
242 TNA ref. KV 2/808
243 Ibid
244 Ibid
245 Ibid
246 Cited in West p.74
247 Movements from KV 2/808
248 Draitser p.144
249 Ibid pp.144–145
250 Cited in C Andrew and V Mitrokhin *The Mitrokhin Archive* (London, 1999) p.63
251 Antrobus pp.189-190
252 Cited in West p.74
253 TNA ref. KV 2/808
254 Cited in West p.74
255 Draitser p.146
256 TNA ref. KV 2/808
257 Ibid
258 Ibid
259 Ibid
260 Ibid
261 Ibid
262 Ibid
263 Ibid
264 Ibid
265 Ibid
266 Ibid
267 Ibid
268 Cited in Draitser pp.148–149
269 H Romanis, *The Compleat Surgeon the Autobiography of the Surgeon WHC Romanis* (Suffolk, 2013) p.119
270 TNA ref. KV 2/808
271 Ibid
272 Ibid
273 Ibid
274 Ibid
275 Cited in Draitser p.149
276 Draitser p.150
277 Cited in Draitser, ibid
278 TNA ref. KV 2/808

279 Ibid
280 Ibid
281 Ibid
282 Cited in West pp.74–75
283 TNA ref. KV 2/808
284 Ibid
285 Ibid
286 Ibid
287 Ibid
288 Ibid
289 Ibid
290 Ibid
291 Ibid
292 Ibid
293 Ibid
294 Ibid
295 TNA ref. FO 1103/112
296 TNA ref. KV 2/808
297 Ibid
298 Ibid
299 Ibid
300 Ibid
301 Ibid
302 Ibid
303 Ibid
304 Ibid
305 Ibid
306 Ibid
307 Ibid
308 Ibid
309 Ibid
310 Ibid
311 Cited in Draitser p.153
312 Ibid p.159
313 TNA ref. KV 2/808
314 Ibid
315 *Evening Standard*, 26 August 1933
316 TNA ref. KV 2/808
317 Ibid
318 Ibid
319 Ibid
320 Ibid
321 Ibid

322 Ibid (where all these contents are itemised)
323 Ibid
324 Ibid
325 Ibid
326 Ibid
327 Ibid
328 Ibid
329 Ibid
330 Ibid
331 Ibid
332 Ibid
333 Ibid
334 Ibid
335 Ibid
336 Draitser pp.157–158
337 Ibid p.157
338 Ibid p.159
339 Cited in Andrew p.64
340 TNA ref. KV 2/808
341 TNA ref. FO 1103/112
342 TNA ref. FO 366/918
343 The following information is derived from Bystrolyotov's correspondence with Lucy, recounted in Draitser pp.160–162
344 Cited in Draitser p.160
345 Cited in West p.75
346 Ibid
347 Ibid
348 Cited in Draitser p.161
349 Ibid
350 TNA ref. FO 1103/113
351 *London Gazette*, 31 August 1934
352 Draitser p.163
353 Much of this information is contained in Pieck's files collated by MI5 TNA ref. KV 2/812-814
354 Cited in West p.79
355 Cited in West pp.79–80
356 Ibid p.81
357 Ibid p.87
358 Ibid p.85
359 Ibid pp.85–86
360 Ibid pp.87–88
361 Ibid p.88
362 TNA ref. KV 4/185
363 TNA ref. KV 2/816
364 Ibid
365 Ibid
366 Ibid
367 Ibid
368 Ibid
369 Ibid
370 Ibid
371 Ibid
372 TNA ref. KV 2/804
373 Ibid
374 Ibid
375 Ibid, also KV 2/808 where the statement is questioned
376 R Deacon, *With My Little Eye* (London, 1982), pp.226–227
377 TNA ref. KV 2/804
378 Ibid
379 Antrobus pp.226–227
380 Ibid p.189
381 TNA ref. KV 2/804
382 TNA ref. KV 2/2681
383 TNA ref. KV 2/814
384 Ibid
385 Ibid
386 Ibid
387 Ibid
388 Antrobus p.103
389 TNA ref. KV 2/808
390 Ibid
391 Ibid
392 Ibid
393 Ibid
394 Ibid
395 Ibid
396 Ibid
397 Antrobus pp.188–189
398 Family email correspondence

INDEX

The Forgotten Spy